Sensational Piety

Bloomsbury Studies in Material Religion

Series editors:
Birgit Meyer, David Morgan, S. Brent Plate, Crispin Paine,
Amy Whitehead and Katja Rakow

Bloomsbury Studies in Material Religion is the first book series dedicated exclusively to studies in material religion. Within the field of lived religion, the series is concerned with the material things with which people do religion, and how these things – objects, buildings, landscapes – relate to people, their bodies, clothes, food, actions, thoughts and emotions. The series engages and advances theories in 'sensuous' and 'experiential' religion, as well as informing museum practices and influencing wider cultural understandings with relation to religious objects and performances. Books in the series are at the cutting edge of debates as well as developments in fields including religious studies, anthropology, museum studies, art history and material culture studies.

Buddhism and Waste
Edited by Trine Brox and Elizabeth Williams-Oerberg

Christianity and Belonging in Shimla, North India
Jonathan Miles-Watson

Christianity and the Limits of Materiality
Edited by Minna Opas and Anna Haapalainen

Figurations and Sensations of the Unseen in Judaism, Christianity and Islam
Edited by Birgit Meyer and Terje Stordalen

Food, Festival and Religion
Francesca Ciancimino Howell

Islam through Objects
Edited by Anna Bigelow

Material Devotion in a South Indian Poetic World
Leah Elizabeth Comeau

Museums of World Religions
Charles D. Orzech

Qur'anic Matters
Natalia K. Suit

The Religious Heritage Complex
Edited by Cyril Isnart and Nathalie Cerezales

Sensational Piety

Practices of Mediation in Islamic and Pentecostal Movements in Abuja, Nigeria

Murtala Ibrahim

BLOOMSBURY ACADEMIC
LONDON • NEW YORK • OXFORD • NEW DELHI • SYDNEY

BLOOMSBURY ACADEMIC
Bloomsbury Publishing Plc
50 Bedford Square, London, WC1B 3DP, UK
1385 Broadway, New York, NY 10018, USA
29 Earlsfort Terrace, Dublin 2, Ireland

BLOOMSBURY, BLOOMSBURY ACADEMIC and the Diana logo are
trademarks of Bloomsbury Publishing Plc

First published in Great Britain 2023
This paperback edition published 2024

Copyright © Murtala Ibrahim, 2023, 2024

Murtala Ibrahim has asserted his right under the Copyright, Designs and
Patents Act, 1988, to be identified as Author of this work.

For legal purposes the Acknowledgements on p. xii constitute an
extension of this copyright page.

Cover image © Murtala Ibrahim

Bloomsbury Publishing Plc does not have any control over, or responsibility for, any
third-party websites referred to or in this book. All internet addresses given in this
book were correct at the time of going to press. The author and publisher regret any
inconvenience caused if addresses have changed or sites have ceased to exist, but
can accept no responsibility for any such changes.

A catalogue record for this book is available from the British Library.

Library of Congress Control Number: 2022933168

ISBN: HB: 978-1-3502-8230-8
PB: 978-1-3502-8234-6
ePDF: 978-1-3502-8231-5
eBook: 978-1-3502-8232-2

Series: Bloomsbury Studies in Material Religion

Typeset by Newgen KnowledgeWorks Pvt. Ltd., Chennai, India

To find out more about our authors and books visit www.bloomsbury.com
and sign up for our newsletters.

This book is dedicated to my late parents
Ibrahim Rabiu and Zakeeya Ibrahim

Contents

Figures

Preface

Nigeria is a religiously highly diverse country, and Muslims and Christians have been living side by side for a long time. Religious pluralism in Nigeria has undergone multiple challenges with long-standing mutual suspicion, mistrust and conflicts. While many scholars focus on inter-religious contestations and conflicts, this book moves the debate to another level. It proposes that another dynamic is unfolding between Christians and Muslims that is characterized by conviviality, interfaith joint action programmes, mutual influences and even borrowing of each other's religious forms. As research so far has tended to focus on the peculiarity of each religious tradition, the issue of bringing Christians and Muslims within a single research framework barely arose. This book offers new directions in comparative anthropological research on the intertwinement of Christian and Muslim religious practices in Africa. Focusing on two religious organizations, Christ Embassy and NASFAT, in Abuja, the capital of Nigeria, the book offers a detailed comparative analysis of the religious forms mobilized in prayer, preaching and engagement with new media. The comparative approach reveals that, notwithstanding the seemingly opposed world views and divergences between Muslims and Christians in the urban environment, they all face similar challenges and apply similar techniques for meeting the challenges posed by the precarious Nigerian urban environment. It is through practices – especially those conducted in (semi-)public settings – that people from different religious persuasions define, encroach on and feel the weight of the presence of each other.

This book is born out of a PhD thesis which was supervised by Professor Birgit Meyer. The thesis was a sub-project under a broader project framed as 'Habitats and Habitus: Politics and Aesthetics of Religious World-Making' funded by Alexander von Humboldt Foundation from 2012 to 2017. The project was situated at the Leibniz-Zentrum Moderner Orient (ZMO) Berlin. The materials contained in this book have been collected from more than a year of fieldwork between 2013 and 2014 in the Nigerian federal capital of Abuja. Conducting ethnographic studies on two different religions that exist in an environment defined by an endemic ethno-religious conflict and tensile social relationship is a real challenge. For instance, Christian interlocutors are suspicious of and question the intentionality of a Muslim researcher if the research subject involved their religious beliefs and practices and vice versa. Coming from a Muslim background I encountered this problem and had to spent an enormous time for diplomacy and negotiation to overcome it. However, due to my Muslim background I did not encounter resistance in NASFAT despite the differences in the approach to Islam between Hausa and Yoruba Muslims.

The comparison aspect of Habitats and Habitus project captured my interest because I hailed from Jos North, a city roughly divided between Muslims and Christians and famous as one of the epicentres of conflicts between the two religions. Coming from a Muslim background and living in a Muslim neighbourhood, while for long periods working among Christians, my life traversed between the two groups. As a result I became a keen observer of how Muslims and Christians perceive each other, the social fault lines that separate and how they negotiate and attempt to manage their differences. While traversing the two lifeworld that on the surface exist in parallel universes with an extreme chasm between them, I became fascinated with subtle strings that connect, entangle and bind the two groups together. To my surprise, even during the bloody religious conflicts that occurred between 2001 and 2011 Muslims and Christians were using similar arguments to justify their claims and circulate exactly identical conspiracy theories to castigate each other. These indicate the existing hidden current that connects the two groups which is responsible for producing such similarities despite the existence of social tension and conflicts. This current could be located in a complex social dynamic that results from sharing the same habitat and everyday interactions. The Habitat and Habitus project gave me a good opportunity to explore and compare religious practices between Pentecostal Christians and Muslims, which I explicate in this monograph.

After the introduction, Chapter 1 examines the issue of coexistence, plurality, mutual observation and focus on each other's practices in the city of Abuja. In Chapters 2 and 3, the thesis introduces Christ Embassy and NASFAT and shows how both stand in critique to mainline Christianity and Islam. The chapters also demonstrate how the two groups resemble each other in form (though not so much in content) as well as the transformative of ways of being Christian/ Muslim in the two groups. The subsequent chapters (Chapters 4, 5 and 6) focus on practices of prayer, preaching and engaging with the new media technology as points for comparison. These chapters reveal similarities and differences in these practices and mutual borrowing, in a context in which Pentecostals set the tone for a new emergent religiosity that is more individualistic and emotional in nature. The thesis explores dynamics of inter-religious borrowing in a context of coexistence, albeit under unequal conditions since NASFAT borrows more from Pentecostals than vice versa.

Acknowledgements

I would like to express my special appreciation and thanks to my principal supervisor Professor Birgit Meyer and co-supervisor Professor Hansjörg Dilger. You have been tremendous mentors for me. I would like to thank you for encouraging my research and for allowing me to grow in my academic career. Your advice, insightful comments and encouragement, and also the hard questions about the thesis as well as on my career have been priceless. Without your precious support, it would not have been possible to conduct this research. Moreover, I want to express my gratitude to Duke University Press and Brill Academic Publishers for granting me permission to reuse materials I published with them. These materials which constitute part of Chapter 1 and Chapter 6 of this monograph appear in an edited volume titled 'Spirit and Sentiment: Affective Trajectories in African Urban Landscape' and Journal of Religion Africa, 47(1), respectively.

Special thanks to many people in NASFAT and Christ Embassy. I am immensely indebted to the National Chairman Board of Trustee of NASFAT Alhaji Lateef Wale Olasupo, who gave me a warm welcome to participate in NASFAT activities and remained supportive throughout my fieldwork period in Abuja. I would like to express my special gratitude to the national deputy secretary of NASFAT Mustapha Bello and the imam of Abuja central branch Ali Agan as well as the branch chairman S. Q. Giwa whose support was invaluable to my work. I will not forget the constant assistance of Hassan Abdulkareem who was always ready to answer my questions about the activities of NASFAT. In Christ Embassy my special gratitude goes to Pastor Kolapo Segun and Pastor Arams Bulus who paved the way for me into Christ Embassy. My appreciation of Pastor Remi Adekunle cannot be overemphasized; I am grateful for his patience in answering my questions about the church and its teachings. I also thank Paul Tseka and Sarah Ladoja for their help with regard to my research. I would also like to express my appreciation to my friends in Berlin Dauda Abubakar, Rahina Muazu Hannah Nieber, Peter Lambertz, Anandita Bajpai, Stephan Binder, Adela Taleb and Abdoulaye Sounaye as well as Daan Beekers and Pooyan Tamimi Arab in Utrecht for their warm friendship, precious advice and fruitful exchange of ideas. Special thanks to my wife Fatima Khamis and son Adeel Ibrahim for their unending love and patience throughout the period of revising this monograph.

Introduction

Murtala: What is your perception about Muslims?

Chidi: Hey! Muslims love to perform their daily prayers. Whether in the market or during office hours, Muslims suspend their routine activities and pray. Even during long journey travelling such as from Abuja to Kano, Muslims stop and pray beside the road. The calls to prayer from mosques are ubiquitous and fill the atmosphere in Muslim areas. I think this is the reason why a long time ago Muslims were referred to in Hausa language as *Masallata* or prayer people. I admire their devotion to God, but sometimes I became upset and irritated if they blocked the road during Friday prayer or a driver stopped for prayer during long journey travelling or if their loudspeakers are too loud.

Murtala: What other things do you know about Muslims apart from prayer?

Chidi: They want to reach God through Muhammad; I think they see Muhammad as their Messiah.

Murtala: What is your perception about Pentecostals?

Usman: While growing up in the 1980s, I had many Christian friends and what I know about Christianity is that Christians believe God is three in one and Jesus is the son of God. Presently a new form of Christianity appeared which is called Pentecostal. Everything about Pentecostals is loud: loud preaching, loud prayers and loud music. They put me under serious stress when I was residing at Court Road in Karu, close to a big Pentecostal church. When I relocated to Nyanya, I felt relief. When I watch Pentecostals' television programmes, seeing them become excited and falling to the ground, I feel disturbed. In fact, they are too emotional in their worship.

These conversations are part of my interviews in Abuja with Chidi, a thirty-three-year-old male Christian and a member of Christ Embassy, and Usman, a forty-year-old male Muslim who is a member of Nasrul-Lahi-li-Fatih (NASFAT), concerning their perceptions of each other's religion. These remarks suggest that on many occasions, it is through religious practices that Muslims and Christians define one another, encroach on the life of one another and admire each other. The remarks spotlight a general feature which I encountered over and over again through my research: that Muslims and Christians have much awareness about each other's religious practices, such as prayers or media use, but do not necessarily have a deeper understanding of each other's theology or world view. Religious practices, especially those conducted in (semi-)public settings, make people from different religious persuasions feel the weight of the presence of the religious 'other'. Even though Muslims and Christians meet each other and interact daily in public spaces and neighbourhoods, it is the encounter with each other's religious practices that brings to the fore the reality of their co-presence. This book takes practices as a starting point for comparing and exploring the relation between Muslims and Christians, and Islam and Christianity. It is important to note that embodied religious practice falls within the domain of material turn in the study of religion, which I will elaborate in one of the sections below.

The two religious groups selected for the purpose of this book are Christ Embassy and NASFAT. Christ Embassy and NASFAT are major players among the myriad religious groups flourishing in the Nigerian capital city. Three important practices of mediation in the two groups have been chosen – prayers, preaching and technologically mediated religious practices – for comparative analysis. The aim of the comparative approach taken in this book is to reveal a complex inter-religious dynamic that goes beyond the predominant focus on conflicts in many academic works (Frederiks 2010).

Since this book aims at a comparative study of Muslim and Christian groups, NASFAT has been selected because it has systematically responded to the challenges of Pentecostalism more than any other Muslim organization. Peel (2015: 187) writes, 'NASFAT ... is probably the most effective response to the born-again phenomenon, from which it has consciously adopted many practices and strategies.' As a result, NASFAT is a suitable candidate for comparison with Pentecostal churches. Given that it is Pentecostal Christianity in general that poses a serious challenge to Muslim communities through the domination of the Nigerian public sphere, most of the major Pentecostal churches in the country, such as Redeemed Christian Church of God (RCCG) and Mountain of Fire and Miracle (MFM) Ministries, could be compared with NASFAT with almost an equal result. This is so because most of the Pentecostal churches in the country share similar world views, theologies and practices, notwithstanding their differences. Moreover, it is the basic practices of Pentecostalism, such as its highly emotional mode of religiosity and emphasis on prayers, that appeal to many urbanites, including Muslims, particularly in the south-west and the central region.

Among the many possible Pentecostal churches to study, Christ Embassy has been selected because it is one of the major Pentecostal churches which has not been studied by academic scholars despite its extensive outreach and influence on Nigerian society. As will be shown in the body of the book, many practices in Christ Embassy – both religious and extra-ritual activities – have their comparable counterparts in NASFAT. Moreover, both Christ Embassy and NASFAT project themselves as modern, progressive urban religious movements that attempt to address the aspirations of the young upwardly mobile professional class in the Nigerian urban environment. The two groups have been selected for comparison in order to highlight an inter-religious dynamic of relations between Muslims and Christians based on mutual influences afforded by a shared habitat.

Religious coexistence and comparative approach

Religious coexistence in Nigeria has undergone multiple challenges over the years as a result of the Nigerian government's inability to manage religious diversity effectively. This challenge has been accentuated in the aftermath of returning to civilian rule in May 1999 after decades of military dictatorship in the country. The long-standing mutual suspicion and mistrust between Muslims and Christians degenerated into ethno-religious riots that devastated different parts of northern Nigeria. The recurrent religious conflicts undermine peaceful coexistence and hamper amicable Christian–Muslim relations in the country. Problematic Christian–Muslim relations are not limited to Nigeria alone but occur in different parts of Africa. Martha Frederiks (2010) examines in detail the evolving Christian–Muslim relations in Africa and maintains that presently the relationship between the two groups has deteriorated as a result of the surfacing of fundamentalist religiosity that is characterized with exclusivist and antagonistic tendencies. Frederiks affirms that the wave of terrorist attacks in different parts of the world also contributes in straining Muslims' relations with Christians, where Islam is viewed as a violent religion that threatens world peace.

Other developments which further increased polarization between the two
religious groups are Christians' concerns about a perceived Islamic resurgence,
which manifests in polemical preaching that targets Christians and demands
the implementation of *shari'ah* in some parts of Africa. Islamic resurgence
coincided with the rise of Pentecostalism, which has a negative attitude towards
the religious 'other'. These developments 'reflect the ambiguity that is part of the
21st century reality of interfaith relationships in sub-Saharan Africa' (Frederik
2010: 271). Hassan Mwakimako (2010) noted similar developments in Kenya
which undermine Christian–Muslim relations. Mwakimako maintains that
Muslim–Christian relations in Kenya are riddled with distrust and antagonism
as a result of Muslims' demand for the establishment of Islamic courts and
terrorist bombing in the country.

Muslims' encroachment into the political arena led by the reformist
Islamists attracted serious opposition from Christians, especially Pentecostals.
Controversial issues such as the demand for the creation of *shari'ah* Supreme
Court; the admission of Nigeria into the Organization for Islamic Cooperation
(OIC) by General Ibrahim Babangida; the introduction of criminal aspect of
shari'ah by twelve northern states; and recently the introduction of Islamic
Banking by the Central Bank Governor Sunusi Lamido Sunusi each time create
serious tension that threatens the unity of the country. These kinds of events
heighten competition and rivalry, demand and counter-demand between
Muslims and Christians that on many occasions result in deadly conflicts. The
introduction of Islamic Banking by the Central Bank created a bitter altercation
between the former president of the Christian Association of Nigeria (CAN)
Pastor Ayo Oritsejafor who happens to be Pentecostal and the Muslim elites
in the north. Oritsejafor accused Islamists of a hidden agenda to Islamize
Nigeria, stressing that Christians will never agree. However, it is important to
not be overwhelmed by the negative picture of relations between Christians
and Muslims painted above. There is another dynamic going on despite the
tensions and distrust between the two religious groups. This other dynamic
is characterized by conviviality, interfaith joint action programmes, mutual
influences and even borrowing the forms of each other's religious practices.

However, notwithstanding this positive dynamics, anthropologists rarely
conduct a comparative study with the aim to produce a single anthropology of
Islam and Christianity. As anthropology tends to focus more on the peculiarity
of each religious tradition, the issue of bringing two distinct traditions within a
single research enterprise barely arose. In the discipline of comparative religion,
by contrast, the focus is on bringing together different religious traditions

in a comparative framework. In this field, however, there is little interest in ethnographic study, as it focuses more on the systematic comparison of the doctrines and creeds of world religions and aims at deeper understanding of the fundamental philosophical concerns of religion such as ethics, metaphysics, and the nature and form of salvation. However, ethnographic-based comparative framework reveals interesting similarities, contrasts, overlaps and dynamics of lived religion that shape and reshape religious coexistence (Beekers 2020).

Nigeria is a religiously highly diverse nation and Muslims and Christians have been living side by side for a long period of time. John Onaiyekan (1992: 48) quoted Archbishop Teissier of Algiers describing Nigeria as 'the greatest Islamo-Christian nation in the world'. What he means here is that there is no other nation where so many Christians and Muslims live side by side. Many ethnic groups in the country include both Muslims and Christians (albeit in different proportions). It is common in some parts of the country to find both Muslims and Christians in the same family; in some cases even brothers and sisters may practise different religions (Nolte and Jones 2015). Muslims and Christians are living as neighbours, friends, business partners, colleagues in offices, school mates and spouses in inter-religious marriages as well as in many other forms of social interactions. These interactions bring the two parties very close to each other, either in harmonious or tense relationships. Benjamin Soares (2006: 3) asserts that 'it is a mistake to treat Muslims and Christians as monolithic communities that interact as block. … [T]he boundaries between Muslims and Christians have not always been rigid, fixed or unchanging.' The fluid boundaries that exist between the two groups engendered mutual exchange of some practices between members of the two religions. A Christian preacher in northern Nigeria can preach wearing a Muslim cleric's dress and using many Arabic words, or start his talks with '*In the name of Allah the beneficent the merciful*', which is a typical Muslim expression. In some parts of the country, especially in the south-west and north-central, people easily migrate from one religion to another or visit other religious services. For instance, a Muslim youth may convert to Christianity with minimal opposition in his family and vice versa.[2] Considering this mutual sharing it would be lopsided to focus only on the conflicts that keep occurring between Muslims and Christians in some places. Muslims and Christians in Africa have a multifaceted relationship that transcends the simple coexistence-conflict model advocated by many scholars (Frederiks 2010: 263). This means that there is much more in encounters between Christians and Muslims in Nigeria than only conflict. Even though there are many separate works in both historical and anthropological literature on Islam and Christianity, there are few research works on the encounter or relationship between the two religions.

So far, few scholars employ comparative framework. For instance, Larkin and Meyer (2006) presented a study on thriving Pentecostal and Islamic reform movements in West Africa with a particular focus on Nigeria and Ghana. They concede that the two movements are drastically different from one another in many ways. Despite their differences, the movements share many things in common as in the case of their opposition to certain cultural traditions which they perceive as dangerous to the 'true faith'. They also bitterly oppose what they take to be occult practices such as witchcraft, sorcery and divination. In addition, they criticize established religions in their environments, such as Catholicism and Sufism, as having deviated from the 'true path'. Marleen de Witte (2008: 10) also highlights the need for a comparative approach. She suggests that scholars should equally take into account the ways in which Pentecostal and charismatic ideas and forms have their repercussions outside Pentecostalism, on non-Pentecostal and non-Christian religions such as neo-traditional movement. Peter van der Veer (2016) tasks anthropologists to adopt a comparative approach as a prime way to understanding human societies. In the words of van der Veer (2016: 11), 'Anthropology is highly equipped to engage problems of translation and of bridging different semantic universes.' According to van der Veer, this unique quality of anthropology stands in stark contrast with mainstream social sciences whose quantitative techniques often result in over-generalization and promote Western cultural presuppositions and Eurocentrism.

Hansjörg Dilger (2014) also places Muslims and Christians under a single framework of study in urban and peri-urban Dar es Salaam as he explores and compares making and remaking of urban space through health care interventions by Muslim revivalist movements and Pentecostalism in the city. Dilger (2014: 64) argues that 'the comparison of revivalist neo-Pentecostal and Muslim organisations may show how these various, mutually reinforcing struggles for social and political visibility are embedded in longstanding histories of religious diversity and competition in urban settings'. The mutual influences in the religious sphere have been visually demonstrated by Janson and Akinleye (2015) in their photo essay on the Lagos–Ibadan expressway, which they dubbed the spiritual superhighway. The authors show how NASFAT, which is a new Muslim religious organization, copied the spatial practices of the Pentecostal church MFM Ministries through establishing its own prayer camp on the expressway which stretches to 1,000 acres of land and accommodates up to 500,000 worshippers. According to the authors, NASFAT borrows Pentecostal terminologies such as 'crusade' and 'night vigil' to refer, respectively, to its Sunday prayer meeting and all-night prayers (which attract tens of thousands of people, including Christians). The study of Janson and Akinleye resonates well with the findings of Dilger (2014) in Dar es Salaam, where Muslim revivalists and neo-Pentecostal churches compete to inscribe their presence in the cityscape through health care intervention.

In chapter nine of his book, *A Century of Interplay Between Islam and Christianity*, John Peel (2015) traces the development of Christian–Muslim encounters among the Yoruba (and Nigeria in general) and the changing mutual influences between the two religious groups. Peel maintains that there is soft, or non-aggressive, competition between Muslims and Christians within the ambient culture of the Yoruba. Peel notes that among the Pentecostal-influenced Muslim groups, the most formidable one and also the most successful is NASFAT. Peel further suggests that even though NASFAT is rooted in Islamic orthodoxy, it has also adopted managerial language that is also appropriated by Pentecostalism. Moreover, Peel (2015: 189) finds remarkable similarities between NASFAT and the RCCG, particularly in their extra-ritual activities which involve provision of welfare and development services to their members, and in this respect, 'NASFAT follows a trail that RCCG has blazed.'

Moreover, Peel (2015) disagrees with Meyer and Larkin on the issue of similarities between Pentecostalism and Islamic reformists. Peel suggests that Islamic reformists have a trenchant political agenda that aims at *shari'ah* implementation contrary to Pentecostalism, which is an apolitical movement that thrives outside a state. According to Peel (2015: 195), prosperity and politics which underscore the orientation between the two movements 'can be seen as contrasting ways in which believers are prompted to realize themselves and so to shape their worlds'. However, in my view Peel's (2015) argument that Islamic reformists such as *Salafi* downplay the importance of health overlooks the fact that currently *Salafi* reinstate the centrality of well-being through propagating prophetic medicine and other Islamic forms of healing claimed to be based on the *sunnah* of the Prophet.[3] *Salafi* also dabble in exorcism (*ruqiyya*) and fighting demonic afflictions with Qur'anic verses. In addition, even though *Salafi ulama* (religious leaders or scholars) do not preach prosperity in the same way as Pentecostals, their lifestyle is far from frugal living, as affirmed by Peel. The relationship between the *Salafi* ulama and the politicians affords them opportunities for a lavish and flamboyant living. When NASFAT is taken into consideration, the similarities with Pentecostalism become even more conspicuous. This is because NASFAT categorically promotes prosperity and well-being and does not show interest in changing political order through the implementation of *shariah*. For these reasons, when practices and form become the focal point for comparison, as advocated by Meyer and Larkin, many points of convergence between Muslim and Christian groups begin to emerge. It is in line with this point of view that this thesis adopted a comparative approach based on religious practices, form and lived religion.

This book aims to contribute to and expand on this novel trend of conducting comparative anthropological research on Christians and Muslims in Africa. The book attempts to expand on the comparative approach developed by leading scholars. It will do so by selecting and comparing a set of important practices, such as different genres of prayers, preaching and engaging with new media in Christ Embassy and NASFAT, in an ethnographic manner. I do not intend to compare religious beliefs, doctrines, creeds or world views of Christ Embassy and NASFAT per se. Instead, I focus on lived religion, aptly defined by Beekers (2020: 103) 'as the contextualized ways in which people experience, express, and enact religion in their everyday lives'. I will also focus on practices of the two movements that occur regularly and spill over into the public space. This is because lived religion is more dynamic and tends to be more exposed to external influences than doctrines and creeds. In the same vein, the book will not compare or analyse the contents of the sacred texts of the two groups, but instead will focus on textual practices such as recitation, reading or listening to the Holy Scriptures.

Material and aesthetic approach

Furthermore, the analysis in this book is conducted within the analytical lens of the material turn in the study of religion. The material turn in general began as a response to the 'discursive turn' prompted by post-structuralism's crises of representation, and it essentially examines the roles that objects play in human action as well as their signification. The turn to materiality is further accentuated by the humanities' inclination towards hierarchical binaries that privilege culture over nature, minds over bodies, and words over things. The material turn in the humanities and social sciences points to the recentring of material things and phenomena – objects, practices, spaces, bodies, sensations, affects and so on – in academic scholarship (Hazard 2013). Matter appears as an ontologically and epistemologically inescapable subject of academic research within the paradigm of materiality (Kuusela 2016). Scholars of the material turn reiterate how humans and inanimate material things act upon each other. They also spotlight how things have the potency and capacity not only to hinder the will of humans but also to behave as forces with trajectories, propensities or predispositions of their own (Woodward 2007; Bennett 2010). This means material objects can signify; they can incorporate, facilitate, assist and carry meanings. Moreover, material turn pays attention to the symbiotic interplay between humans and inanimate things, which indicates action and experience with materialities. In this vein, materiality could also be regarded as *taking part* in the interaction (Kuusela 2016).

Scholars of religion join the trend of the material turn and appeal to discard long-standing biases that denigrate the role of material things, the body and emotions in the study of religion. For instance, Birgit Meyer and Dick Houtman (2012) argue that the denigration of materiality originated from the one-sided Protestant emphasis on belief that influenced modern study of religion. Meyer and Houtman call for correcting this bias that privileges mentalistic elements and beliefs over matter and bodily performance. They urge scholars to explore the concrete manifestation of religion by looking at objects like relics, amulets, dress codes and feelings and sensory experiences like seeing, hearing, smelling, as well as bodily performances in specific gestures and rituals. Despite variation in approach, methodology and detail in the material turn in the study of religion, there is a relative convergence in 'rejection of the interiority, ideality, and emphasis on transcendence that long held sway in considerations of religion, in favor of exteriority, materiality, and immanence' (Jones 2016: 1). In agreement with many scholars such as Birgit Meyer (2012), David Morgan (2010) and Webb Keane (2008), Manuel Vásquez (2011) also argues in favour of a material turn in the study of religion. He criticizes the lopsided attention to a mentalistic dimension of religion such as dogmas and creeds at the expense of embodied practices. He encourages refocusing towards the body: mobile, disciplined, biologically constrained and enabled, vulnerable, beautiful: the point being not an atomized body but rather a body-in-the-world.

The material turn in the study of religion is conceived and tackled from multiple angles by different scholars in the field. Hazard (2013) dissects these approaches and outlines them into four categories: things as symbols, material disciplines, phenomenology and new materialism. According to Hazard, scholars in the first category approach material things and practices in the domain of religion as symbols for deeper meanings and ideas. In a nutshell, material things and practices are signifiers that embody immaterial entities such as values, beliefs and true essence. The duty of a scholar is to decode and interpret these symbols which are embodied in the objects. Scholars who subscribe to the view of material discipline (e.g. Talal Asad and Saba Mahmood) argue that material things and practices are not mere expressions of prior ideas or beliefs and do not obediently signify meanings. Rather, these scholars propose that material things and practices serve as applicators of power in ways that discipline human subjectivity. Phenomenology takes human experience and consciousness as its central focus of analysis. One of the foremost scholars in this category is David Morgan, who conceives of the human body as the locus of consciousness and experience as well as the subjective interface with the exterior material world. The fourth category is the new materialism, which receives little attention from scholars of religion. Scholars in this emerging field argue that 'material things possess a remarkable range of capacities that exceed the purview of human sense or knowing', and that 'the materiality of material things themselves must be carefully considered, rather than merely interpreted for their implications on human concerns' (Hazard 2013: 64).

In my view, all the four categories listed above could be useful in analysing different material manifestations of religion, despite their seeming contradiction with each other. Due to the multiplicity and complexity of religious expressions, each of the four categories could fit different strands of religious expression. It is for this reason that I approach the materials in this book through the multiple paradigms of material turn described by Hazard. For instance, I look at the prayer performances of Christ Embassy and NASFAT through the lens of embodiment, wherein the human corporeal body becomes the central focus of analysis. I also examine the preaching practices of my case study within the framework of material discipline, which aims at creating a certain type of religious subject. Finally, a phenomenological approach has been applied to my interlocutors' engagement with the new technology, particularly digital religious sounds, texts and images.

Since this book operationalizes the notion of mediation and sensational forms, it is important to examine how scholars of religion conceptualize the terms. Birgit Meyer conceived religion as 'a practice of mediation through which a distance between the immanent and what lies 'beyond' it is posited and held to be bridged, albeit temporarily' (2012). She asserts that it is appropriate to locate religion in a set of practices through which a sense of the divine is generated and experienced by believers. This implies that religious practitioners employ material forms and the human body in its attempt to mediate or reach out beyond the ordinary. Meyer employs the term 'media' to refer to something that serves as transmitter across gaps or limits. Any material object can be made to serve as religious media, ranging from figurines, paintings, the human body, text, images, incantations, pictures, language and icons (2012). She argues that anything can be 'configured to function as religious media as long as it has been authorized and authenticated in a longstanding religious tradition' (2012: 26). In this vein, practices of mediation use media to transcend limitations and reveal what is normally beyond human perception. Practices of mediation draw divine power and make it accessible to human feeling and cognition. In this context, a variety of religious practices and rituals could function as practices of mediation as long as they are capable of providing access to the extra-empirical reality.

Meyer introduces the notion of 'sensational form', which she describes as a 'configuration of religious media, acts, imaginations, and bodily sensations in the context of religious tradition or group' (2012: 26). These configurations might be in the form of routine performances or formats that are authorized and authenticated, thereby invoking personal and group identity and generating experiences of divine presence. Sensational forms shape and restructure religious mediation through performances that engage the human body and senses. Sensational forms, Meyer argues, are formal procedures that are followed in a religious setting and usually deploy the use of material media for the purpose of contacting or negotiating the invisible. Sensational forms can be described as techniques of the body that hone the human senses through routine practices in order to produce certain kinds of feeling or generate intense emotions. This book will situate the notion of mediation, sensational form and lived religion as the focal point of comparative analysis between Christ Embassy and NASFAT. The book will juxtapose a variety of practices in Christ Embassy and NASFAT and observe convergences, parallels and connections concerning mediation, sensational forms and lived religion that may hitherto go unnoticed in non-comparative account (Beekers 2020).

Pentecostalism and Islamic movements

Since Christ Embassy is a major Pentecostal church in Nigeria, it is essential to look into the development of Pentecostalism in order to contextualize the church within the broader framework of the Pentecostal spectrum. Understanding the development of Pentecostalism in Nigeria will shed light on the rise of Christ Embassy. In addition, in contrast to Izala and the *Salafi*, NASFAT cannot be defined as Islamic reformist; however, it is one of the prominent Islamic groups flourishing alongside the reformists. In this section, Pentecostalism and Islam in

Africa as well as NASFAT are placed within the major literature on Christianity and Islam in Africa. However, since scholars do not pay adequate attention to Christ Embassy, I relate the church to some scholarly works on Pentecostalism in Nigeria (and Africa).

From the mid-twentieth century there has been an explosion of growth in Pentecostal movements throughout the world. The Pew Forum Report states that 'in direct and indirect ways, Pentecostal beliefs and practices are remaking the face of world Christianity' (2006: 1). Many scholars agree that Pentecostalism is the most rapidly growing religion of the present era. Anderson, Michael and Andre (2010: 2) assert that 'in the past thirty years Pentecostal membership grew by about 700 per cent, which represent about a quarter of the world's Christian population and two-thirds of all Protestants'. The origin of Pentecostalism has been usually traced to the so-called Azusa Street revival in Los Angeles in 1906. Pentecostal churches effectively utilize some aspects of globalization such as information and communication technologies (ICTs), which include satellite television and the internet, ease of travelling, migrant communities and modern marketing strategies to extend their outreach around the globe. This process facilitates the rise of mega-churches that have branches in different parts of the world with members who cut across ethnic, national and racial boundaries. Meyer (2010a: 113) highlights the fact that even the names of these mega-churches, which on many occasions contain words such as 'international' or 'global', are an indication of their engagement with globalization.

The exponential growth of Pentecostalism happens largely in the Global South. The worldwide growth towards over 523 million Pentecostals happens outside the geographical area of the West in areas such as Africa, Latin America and Asia (Adogame 2011). Kwabena Asamoah-Gyadu (2004: 10) quotes Hastings, saying that 'for a time when chapel buildings in many parts of Western Europe are being converted into pubs, clubs, restaurants, warehouses, cinemas, museums, residential facilities, these same secular facilities are being refurbished for the use of churches in sub-Saharan Africa'. The Pentecostal movement is increasingly affirming the shifting of the gravity centre of Christianity to the south, with Africa having a fair share of global Pentecostal outreach.

The nature of the present Pentecostalism makes it difficult for scholars to agree on one universally accepted definition or even accepted classification. However, Asamoah-Gyadu (2004: 12) defines it as 'Christian groups which emphasise salvation in Christ as a transformative experience wrought by the Holy Spirit and in which pneumatic phenomena including "speaking in tongues", prophecies, visions, healing and miracles … are sought, accepted, valued, and consciously encouraged.' From this definition it would be right to say that emphasis on the experience of the Holy Spirit and pneumatic gifts is the unifying factor among different Pentecostal strands across the world. A broad definition as proposed by Asamoah-Gyadu is necessary due to the varieties of Pentecostal expressions and lack of central authority among the Pentecostal churches. In addition, behind the label Pentecostalism we find a striking multiplicity of movements, and it is a highly fluid and fickle phenomenon. A certain organizational diversity is part of Pentecostals' capacity to adapt to local demands and show their ability in marketing strategies and entrepreneurial capacity. The term 'Pentecostalism' embraces what many scholars describe as classical Pentecostals, neo-Pentecostals, charismatic, neo-charismatic and denominational Pentecostals (Adogame 2011).

In Nigeria Pentecostalism achieved an outstanding expansion since the 1970s, and it is one of the most rapidly growing religious movements in the country. Pentecostal churches are established on a daily basis and they are acquiring and converting hitherto unthinkable places such as cinemas, night clubs and stores into churches everywhere in the country. Radio and television broadcasting is saturated with Pentecostal programmes and advertisements. Nigeria has been the site of Pentecostalism's greatest explosion on the African continent, and the movement's extraordinary growth shows no signs of slowing. A marginal current within Nigerian Christianity in the early 1970s, by the turn of the millennium Pentecostal or Born-Again Christianity had become its overwhelmingly dominant form, counting tens of millions of adherents, and powerfully influencing Christian practice and doctrine across all denominations (Marshall 2009: 2).

There is no doubt that this explosion has challenged traditional and mainline churches such as the Roman Catholic Church and Anglican Church in the country. Some of the traditional churches have begun to adopt Pentecostal practices in order to retain their members who are continually drifting away to Pentecostal churches. By the mid-twentieth century elements of Pentecostal experiences, such as baptism by the Holy Spirit, speaking in tongues and laying of hands, began to penetrate into the practices of historic churches including the Roman Catholic Church, which resulted in the birth of the Catholic Charismatic Renewal (Lado 2009). The influence of Nigerian Pentecostal Christianity extends to different parts of the world. These churches have numerous foreign branches and their pastors travel around the globe for healing crusades, conferences and other activities. So, Nigerian Pentecostalism contributes significantly in the ever-expanding globalization of this form of Christianity.

However, Kalu (2008) highlights a caveat that the actual size of Pentecostalism in Nigeria is difficult to ascertain. This is due to the fragility and transiency of the movements that make them susceptible to schism and splintering over doctrine, theological rifts, moral lapses, personality clashes, competing ambition and financial crises. The continuity of a group may depend on the capacity to maintain a moral code that disciplines the body, speech and sexuality of both leaders and followers. Kalu argues that within the atmosphere of rapid growth, there is a tendency for the observers to lose sight of the fact that many Pentecostal groups disappear as quickly as they appear, decimated by schism, power struggles or funding constraints. So, it is important to not mistake the constant appearance of new Pentecostal groups as a sign of absolute growth. Furthermore, Kalu asserts that the Pentecostal movement is not immune to the fate of routinization of charisma; therefore, some Pentecostal groups age quickly and their charisma becomes routinized as the institutions become bureaucratized.

Scholars divided historical development of Pentecostalism in Nigeria into three phases. The first phase could be dated from the 1930s and was characterized by interactions between indigenous Pentecostal forms called the Aladura churches and foreign denominational Pentecostal churches from the United States (e.g. the Faith Tabernacle) and Britain (e.g. the Apostolic Church). Many practices of Aladura churches have striking resonance with the foreign Pentecostal movements as in the case of fervent prayers, spirit possession and public evangelism. Aladura churches' encounter with foreign Pentecostals yielded mutual interactions that entailed the development of Pentecostal expressions that emphasized experience of the Holy Spirit and speaking in tongues, effective prayer, visionary guidance and a less formalized African style of music and worship (Adebaye 2006).

The second phase of churches (1970s and 1980s) emphasized holiness and the experience of the Holy Spirit, expressed through speaking in tongues, conversion or being born-again, spiritual warfare and evangelical fervour. This period saw the rise of interdenominational campus fellowships and a strong emphasis on biblical inerrancy. The leaders of the Pentecostal movements in this period formed a new elite of graduates whose identification with the movement seemed to have enhanced its social rating. Most of the Pentecostal churches that emerged in this period express disapproval to the Aladura groups for accommodating elements of traditional African religions into the Christian religion (Adebaye 2004).

The third wave of the Pentecostal explosion in Nigeria began in the 1990s and the churches in this spectrum are dubbed by some scholars as neo-Pentecostal movements. The churches in these new movements emphasize, among other things, financial breakthrough, material success, healing and the gift of prophecy (Folarin 2010). However, Adebaye (2004: 137) explains that, whether classical or neo-Pentecostalism, a common thread that runs through Pentecostal Christianity is the experience of a new life articulated in personal narratives of conversion, and the transition from an 'old' life to a 'new' one. The emphasis is on the prosperity gospel and faith. Some churches also emphasize deliverance and healing. Examples of neo-Pentecostal churches are Mountain of Fire and Miracles (1989), Sword of the Spirit Ministries (1989), Fountain of Life Church (1992), House on the Rock (1994), Daystar Christian Centre (1995) and Christ Embassy. These churches are led by young, upwardly mobile, educated professionals who appropriated modern marketing techniques in their evangelism. With its emphasis on prosperity, health and wealth, Christ Embassy is one of the neo-Pentecostal groups.

There has been a debate among scholars concerning what accounts for the emergence and rapid expansion of Pentecostalism in the country. For instance, Matthews Ojo (2006) points out the important role played by the Inter-Varsity Christian Student Union movement in the emergence of Pentecostalism in Nigeria. He also regards the socio-economic forces as factors behind the rise of the movement and operationalizes the concept of economic theory of religion to describe the success of Pentecostalism in Nigeria. He affirms that Pentecostal Christianity in Nigeria has succeeded as a result of a neoliberal and free market for religion, which fosters competition, innovation and creativity among religious entrepreneurs. Another factor which may account for the expansion of Pentecostalism is the lopsided emphasis on material success, which proves to be very attractive to the vast impoverished population.

Paul Gifford (2004) also offers an economic model as the cardinal factor behind the success of Pentecostalism in Africa. He opines that while many historical churches such as Presbyterian, Anglican, Catholic and Methodist emphasize salvation in the afterlife, Pentecostal churches favour wealth and success in the here and now. Asamoah-Gyadu (2004) agrees with Ojo and Gifford on the connection between prosperity gospel and spiritual empowerment and the precariousness of life in a world of poverty and political instability. He sees the emphasis on success, healing, blessing and prosperity as a new and Christian expression of the role of African religion as strategies for survival. The author states that the Pentecostals succeeded because they address issues that were neglected or downplayed by the established mission churches. These issues may be the relation between salvation and material well-being; the problems of evil spirits, curses and magic; and the relation between the present generation and the ancestors. By contrast, Kalu (2008) takes a different trajectory and argues that Pentecostalism and charismatic movements have an indigenous African basis despite the contrary assertion by some scholars. Writing from the insider point of view, church historian Kalu rejects the idea that the origin of Pentecostalism lies in socio-economic transformations and that the explanation of the success of born-again movements is grounded in experiences of social insecurity. Kalu's book basically offers a critique of Western scholars' explanations of the African Pentecostal explosion. He rejects the emphasis placed on the role of outside forces in the development of African Pentecostalism. If we are to judge some Pentecostals such as Christ Embassy by their own words, certainly privileging the economic aspect of life cannot be overemphasized. However, an economic model cannot fully explain the Pentecostal phenomenon, because the experiential dimension of their religiosity, as explored in this book, is a crucial part of their identity.

The domination of the public sphere by Pentecostals elicits major reactions in Nigeria, which in the case of NASFAT results in negotiated borrowing of Pentecostal practices. This trend is very visible in Nigeria where many non-Pentecostal churches such as Roman Catholics and Anglicans have seen their members drifting away to the new Pentecostal churches. As a result, the old historical churches decided to accommodate some Pentecostal practices in order to retain their membership. So, NASFAT is certainly not alone in utilizing the successful Pentecostal forms and methods as a strategy for retaining membership. Other Muslim organizations that copy NASFAT are springing up in both Abuja and Lagos. Pentecostal churches have become a dominant force in shaping a new religiosity in the sense that other mission churches (and even some Muslim groups) are following their trend, particularly their modes of worship and engagement with the media.

The traditional religious landscape among the Muslims of Nigeria was characterized by Sufi movements such as Tijjaniyya and Qadiriyya. In the northern part of the country, the 1960s and 1970s saw the appearance of many new religious movements and organizations. The most notable among them is Jama'atu Nasril Islam (JNI), which is a Muslim umbrella organization, under the leadership of the Sultan of Sokoto, Alhaji Sa'ad Abubakar III, and founded by former premier of northern Nigeria Sir Ahmadu Bello with the aim of unifying Muslims and serving the cause of Islam. Tijāniyya is currently the predominant Sufi brotherhood in northern Nigeria, though it was not a significant force in the region until the appearance of the charismatic Shaykh Ibrahim Nyass (1900–1975) and the revivalist *faida* (flood) movement that he initiated, which continues to reverberate across West Africa today. The advent of the *faida* movement is believed to have been foretold by the founder of the Tijāniyya brotherhood, Shaykh Ahmad Tijani (1737–1815), and it refers to the flooding of divine knowledge, as well as spiritual and material blessings, into the world. Shaykh Nyass claimed to be the embodiment and harbinger of *faida* (Brigaglia 2014). In 1937, upon meeting Shaykh Nyass during a pilgrimage to Makkah, the emir of Kano, Nigeria, Alhaji Abdullahi Bayero (d. 1953), gave him his oath of allegiance and declared himself a disciple of the Shaykh. As a result, other prominent Tijāniyya leaders in northern Nigeria also offered their allegiance to Shaykh Nyass and took up the mission of propagating the *faida* movement through teachings, writings and linkages with the trader networks across the country (Brigaglia 2014).

Izala, in short, is the first radical Islamic reform movement in northern Nigeria. The movement was founded by Sheikh Isma'ila Idris in 1978 with the sole agenda of purifying Islam from innovations, un-Islamic cultural practices and what he described as deviant Sufi practices. The movement also denounces some folk Islamic practices such as using amulets, drinking washed scriptural verses written on slate, exorcism and sorcery. According to Loimeier (1997), the renowned Sheikh Abubakar Gumi had prepared the ground for the emergence of Izala. He was one of the first scholars to oppose Sufi practices in northern Nigeria. He utilized both print and electronic media such as newspaper and radio to propagate his anti-Sufi and anti-innovation teachings from the 1960s until his death in early 1992 (see also Larkin 2008, in *Aesthetic Formations*). Since its formation Izala has experienced rapid growth. By now it is one of the largest religious organizations in the country, with millions of members throughout Nigeria and neighbouring countries. The organization has established thousands of schools with hundreds of thousands of students throughout Nigeria and other West African countries. Unlike some radical groups who distance themselves from the government, Izala leadership is close to the government and politicians and actively encourages Muslims to cooperate with political authorities. In their effort to increase their chances of winning elections, politicians solicit the support of Izala through gifts and donations. The recent movement that appears on the scene and is close to Izala is *Salafism*, whose ideology has been propagated by Nigerian students who studied in Saudi Arabia. The ideology of the *Salafi* is based on the notion of restoring the pristine form of Islam as it was practised by the Prophet and his companions. The development of Islamic reformism in the north has turned Islam into a powerful political ideology and a vehicle for political identity. As a result, many Muslim religious leaders assumed soft political power through commanding their millions of followers to vote or not vote for a certain candidate and political party (Loimeier 1997).

Responding to the Islamic reformists' political overture, Pentecostalism which initially was highly apolitical is becoming a highly politicized movement in the country. The interest of Pentecostals in politics is not only a reaction towards Muslims' demands but also expresses a desire to sanitize the Nigerian polity that they see as being permeated by massive corruption and bad governance through religious revivals. Pentecostals are calling for born-again Christians to join politics because according to them, godly people should not fold their arms while watching morally bankrupt people ruin the country. In the same vein a famous Pentecostal pastor, Chris Okotie, formed his own political party, the 'Fresh Party', and contested for the presidential elections in both 2003 and 2007 under its banner.

In the south among Yoruba Muslims, Islamic organizations and movements have a long history.[4] The most famous ones are Ansar-Ud-Deen Society, Ansarul Islam Society, Nawaruddeen Society, Akhbaruddeen Society and Ahmadiyya movement. Most of these organizations were established in the early decades of the twentieth century and arose partly in reaction to the activities and challenges of Christian missionaries. They established schools in order to avoid the proselytizing of Muslim children in missionary schools. Apart from these older Islamic societies there are prayer groups (such as *As-Salatu* group) which devote a substantial part of their time to special group prayers in order to receive blessings from God. The prayers take place on designated days either in the mosque or in the house of a particular member. Some notable examples of these groups are Lagos Central Mosque *As-Salatu*, Nurudeen Asalatu and *Asalatu Agbaye* group, among others (Adetona 2012: 103).

NASFAT does not fall under the category of Islamic reform movements such as Izala or *Salafi* groups because it does not have a clear-cut theological reform agenda. Moreover, NASFAT cannot be described as one strand among the older Yoruba Muslim organizations as it is responding to unique contemporary challenges and consciously attempts to differentiate itself from them. Rather NASFAT is part of the prayer groups, but it added some elements in order to respond to the challenges of Pentecostalism. The founders, according to Soares (2006), intended NASFAT to be both non-sectarian and non-political, but over time the movement focused on questions of piety and ethics and became deeply engrossed in social and economic activities. Soares (2006) argues that NASFAT's involvement in business activities, which it has sought to link explicitly with Islam, has been rather distinctive, helping to define it as an Islamic social movement that challenges some conventional terms and categories of analysis of Islam.

Ethnographic research methodology has been employed in this study; semi-structured interviews and participant observation were adopted as primary tools of data collection. Moreover, document analysis was employed because there are many written materials such as books written by the leaders of the two groups that include transcripts of sermons, constitutions and hymn books. General information about the two groups (such as origin and development, founders, teachings, world views, organizational structures, nature of membership, relationship with political power and social welfare) has been acquired through interviewing leaders from each movement and literature written by scholars and leaders of the two groups.

Numerous interviews have been conducted among members of the two groups and stratified random sampling has been adopted. The interlocutors have been categorized based on age and gender. Furthermore, I engaged in balanced participant observation (which implies partial participation in group activities) during weekly attendance of services. The weekly services included are NASFAT's Sunday Asalatu, Friday prayers, monthly night vigils, special prayer classes, seminars and conferences. For Christ Embassy, the weekly visits covered were Sunday worship, Monday and Wednesday evening fellowship, monthly night vigils, crusades, Night of Bliss and other special activities. In participating in these activities I collected a significant amount of data concerning the three foci of the research: prayers, preaching and engagement with new media technologies. In addition, I engaged some members in informal conversations about their experiences in the organizations.

The fieldwork was conducted in eleven months in Nigeria's capital, Abuja. Abuja was chosen as a location for the research because Christ Embassy and NASFAT have considerable number of memberships in the city and materials related to the research are available. Due to the middle-class nature of the city, there are many influential members in the city. In addition, most of the national activities of the two movements in the north take place in Abuja. Moreover, regarding confidentiality of my interview subjects, I had an agreement with them to ensure their anonymity. Thus, all the names of the interlocutors mentioned in the body of the work are pseudonyms except the names of the founders and leaders of the two groups.

Organization of the book

The book is organized into six chapters. After the introduction, Chapter 1 examines how dynamic religious presence shapes the Abuja cityscape, particularly how the public sphere of the city becomes a stage that mediates various kinds of religious expressions, from physical structures, to sounds and images. Similarly, the chapter looks into how Abuja as a federal capital with a concentration of wealth and influential people shapes religious activities and relationships between political elites, religious leaders and lay followers. This trilateral relationship converts and instrumentalizes religious participation and networking in the city into a means of building social capital. The chapter demonstrates that although Christianity and Islam belong to different religious traditions, they produce similar patterns of responses to myriads of urban challenges. It also highlights the fact that cohabiting in the same environment and exposure to the same external social forces acting on society foster mutual influences and similar practices among Muslims and Christians.

This chapter offers a thematic study of Christ Embassy by exploring themes such as the origin and development of the church, organizational structure, membership, perception of others, cell activities, fundraising, worship services and the spiritual rhythm of time. The chapter also investigates the church's miraculous healing activities and places them within the purview of symbolic healing advocated by some anthropologists. The chapter demonstrates how Christ Embassy, a successful Pentecostal church, distinguishes itself from others by taking a unique approach to the prosperity gospel that emphasizes the power of the human mind as a tool for transforming external circumstances. The chapter suggests that the success and global outreach of Christ Embassy could also be partly explained by how the church is run as an efficient business enterprise with motivational regimes that optimize the productivity of the members who are part of the bureaucracy of the church.

Chapter 3 analyses various themes related to NASFAT. The chapter traces a brief history of the organization, organizational structure, fundraising and youth activities. The chapter argues that the pre-eminence of NASFAT among variety of Islamic expressions hinges on its ability of consciously negotiated borrowing of the forms of Pentecostal practices such as Sunday worship service and prayer ceremonials. NASFAT provides sensational religious practices and socio-economic services that respond to the emotional and social needs of young urban Muslims. Where applicable, the chapter will examine the influences of

Pentecostals in some practices of NASFAT as well as similarities and differences in some activities between NASFAT and Christ Embassy.

Chapter 4 compares the practices of prayer in Christ Embassy and NASFAT. Three genres of prayers have been compared in the chapter: prayers of adoration, prayers of aesthetic speech and prayers of instrumentality. The chapter argues that prayers of adoration and prayers of aesthetic speech in Christ Embassy and NASFAT facilitate the process of mediation by orchestrating bodily experiences of affect, which members recognize as a 'divine touch' or 'the presence of God'. It also argues that the instrumental prayers in the two groups attempt to establish communication with the divine and achieve the desired goals through the performative power and semiotic systems ascribed to the language of the prayers. The concepts of semiotic ideologies (Keane), sensational forms (Meyer) and speech act theory (Austin 1962) have been used to analyse the three genres of prayers.

Chapter 5 compares preaching practices in Christ Embassy and NASFAT. It explores different aspects of preaching, such as themes, styles, religious authority and the ethics of listening to preaching. The chapter argues that preaching in Christ Embassy and NASFAT is a practice of mediation that is enhanced by several factors, such as eloquence, the authority of the preachers, as well as preaching paraphernalia such as dress, background music and preaching assistants. These factors establish preaching as an aesthetic style due to the preachers' ability to mobilize human senses and thereby make preaching performances a highly emotional experience. The chapter approaches preaching in Christ Embassy and NASFAT as a form of governmentality that manifests as a potent technology of the self that aims to produce and shape religious subjects, generate spiritual experiences and respond to the needs of urbanites.

Chapter 6 explores and compares digital religion in Christ and NASFAT. The chapter shows how mobile phone technology has been appropriated by members of Christ Embassy and NASFAT and transformed into a potent religious medium that facilitates a link with the divine. The chapter demonstrates that mobile phone technology in Christ Embassy and NASFAT is used as a religious medium that facilitates religious mediation through hosting varieties of religious resources, such as sermons, Qur'anic recitation, religious music, text, online religious performances and images, among members of NASFAT and Christ Embassy. As a result of the multilayered applications of the mobile phone in the religious sphere, the leadership of both groups authenticated its use and accommodated it in their religious performances. Authenticating the use of mobile phones in a religious setting defined the role of new media as an integral part of religious practice.

1

Religious diversity in the dream city

Introduction

Cities are human settlements in environments characterized by high population density, complex social institutions and massive human-built structures. Cities normally have complex systems for transportation, housing, utilities and the concentration of development that greatly facilitates interaction between people and businesses, benefiting both parties in the process (James 2013). Religion, as one of the important social institutions, shaped life in the city and vice versa. Recently, urbanization has exploded in Nigeria and cities provide a laboratory for different forms of social experimentations and innovations. Religion plays a substantial role in this regard, with contributions that range from offering creative means of handling urban challenges to being a catalyst in social contestations that sometimes aggravate social fault lines and result in tension and conflicts.[1]

Many scholars who investigate the interconnection of relationships between religion and Nigerian cityscapes focus on explosive Pentecostal activities in southern Nigerian cities, particularly Lagos. For instance, Osinulu (2013) draws a connection between the spatial practices in Lagos and the existence of the spectacular Pentecostal prayer campuses along the Lagos–Ibadan Express Way. Taking the Canaanland of Winners Chapel as a case study, he demonstrates how the site is organized into miraculous infrastructure as well as the place of access to divine power and performance of mastery over the forces shaping African societies. In her research in the city of Lagos, Ruth Marshall (2015) explores ways in which the Pentecostal engagement with spiritual practices engenders new social and ethico-political topographies and novel ways of thinking about community and citizenship in the city. Butticci (2010) studies the impact of the visual and material world of Pentecostalism in urban spaces that led to the transformation and re-articulation of Lagos into a city of 'spiritual warfare' and how Nigerian Diasporas transfer these sensorial regimes to Italy. Despite the importance of Abuja as federal capital coupled with its dynamic religious activities and diversity, so far this city has received little attention from scholars.

This chapter examines how religions shape the Abuja cityscape and soundscape, and how the public sphere of the city becomes a stage that mediates various kinds of religious expressions from buildings, to sounds and images. The chapter also explores the complex religious diversity of the city and how state and various religious actors struggle to manage the diversity in order to preserve peace and avoid the destructive ethno-religious riots that devastated some neighbouring cities. Moreover, the chapter also looks into how Abuja as a federal capital shapes religious activities and the relationship between political elites and religious leaders. Before going further into these issues, the chapter briefly sketches the historical background of the city. Finally, the chapter argues that religious diversity in northern Nigeria may not necessarily result in conflict but can give rise to an interesting social interaction that involves cooperation in order to achieve a common goal.

In addition, religious diversity in Abuja points to the existence of people from different religious and sociocultural backgrounds sharing the same living space in the city. This situation engenders mutual influences that have both similarities and differences in religious practices among Muslim and Christian communities. The chapter attempts to shed light on the environment within which Christ Embassy and NASFAT thrive and the social forces that shaped their world views and practices.

Abuja: The federal capital territory

Abuja, the federal capital territory (FCT), is the capital of Nigeria and is located in the centre of the country. It is a planned city, built mainly in the 1980s, that officially became Nigeria's capital on 12 December 1991. The city of Abuja has a population of 3,652,000, making it the fourth most populous cities in Nigeria (Macrotrends 2022). Abuja has witnessed a massive influx of people. This growth has led to the emergence of many satellite towns, which include Zuba, Gwagwalada, Kuje, Bwari, Kubwa, Nyanya and Abaji. The unofficial metropolitan area of Abuja has a population of well over 3 million and comprises the fourth largest urban area in Nigeria (PLAC 2006). According to Nnamdi Elleh (2001), the development of a master plan for the FCT was awarded to the International Planning Associates (IPA), a consortium of three American firms: Planning

Research Corporation; Wallace McHarg, Roberts and Todd; and Archisystems, a division of the Hughes Organisation. The FCT has borders on the north with Kaduna state, on the south-east with Nasarawa state, on the south-west by Kogi state and on the west with Niger state.

Abuja was chosen as the new capital of Nigeria when it was apparent that overcrowded population pressure in Lagos demanded relocation to a more convenient environment. On 4 February 1976, a decree was signed establishing the FCT of Abuja and setting up the Federal Capital Development Authority (FCDA), the organization charged with the task of developing the new capital. The geographical location of Abuja is considered as a neutral ground both ethnically and religiously by many Nigerians. Abuja city and its surrounding territories have been experiencing immense population growth for long periods of time. One of my interlocutors pointed to me a sprawling neighbourhood in Karu, a district close to the city centre, that is bustling with people and activities, telling me that seven years ago the settlement did not exist; it was just a vast farmland. There has been a prolific development of squatter settlements and shanty towns within the city limits. Abuja has six area councils in the FCT, each subdivided into wards headed by local councils. The minister of the FCT is the overall leader and is appointed by the president. Abuja hosts the headquarters of the Economic Community of West African States (ECOWAS). The city also has the regional headquarters of the United Nations (UN) and the Organization of Petroleum Exporting Countries (OPEC).

The first people to arrive in Abuja when the construction of the city commenced in the early 1980s were employees of the FCDA. Large-scale migrations occurred after 1992 when the federal government relocated to the city. As the federal ministries began to relocate from Lagos to the new capital, their employees moved to the city and its satellite towns. Now the majority of the inhabitants are working either with the government or other private institutions such as financial firms and hotels. Professionals such as doctors and lawyers and different of types of business people also migrated to the city. Petty trading by migrant residents dominates the streets and markets of the satellite towns. Young boys compete in trying to sell all sorts of goods amidst the tedious traffic jams in the nearby satellite towns. Moreover, the unequal distribution of wealth is conspicuous in the city, and many residents complain about the situation. Abuja is home to Nigeria's so-called big men, and people usually attribute the wealth of these people to corrupt practices and alliance with the politicians.

Abuja as the city of dreams

In this section, I intend to provide a portrait of the city of Abuja through the lens of Walter Benjamin's notion of the city as phantasmagoria. In his groundbreaking, albeit unfinished, magnum opus, the Arcade project, Benjamin invokes the phenomenon of phantasmagoria to describe the nineteenth-century labyrinthine arcade of Paris, with its elegant shops and fashionable consumer goods. Phantasmagoria was a popular eighteenth- and nineteenth-century form of theatre entertainment that used techniques such as magic lanterns and shadow puppetry to create optical illusions. Benjamin saw 'Paris as the home of the phantasmagoric: the so-called dreaming collectivity and the architectural forms it spawned, commodity fetishism and fashion, and the concept of "progress"' (Gilloch 2002: 104–5). Benjamin conceived of the city as both the setting for and the product of the fantasies of the collective unconscious, anchored in the edifice of utopian wish-images: frozen representations or objectifications of genuine wants and aspirations that remain unfulfilled or thwarted (Gilloch 2002). I regard the Abuja cityscape of shopping malls and gated communities as well as flamboyant infrastructural projects as a collage of collective phantasmagoric dreams and the locus of the desires and wishes of and for modernity.

Abuja is a microcosm of Nigeria in the sense that ethno-religiously diverse groups coexist in the city.[2] Both Christianity and Islam have a strong visibility in Abuja's cityscape. Since the mid-1990s, Abuja has grown exponentially, with new buildings rising and gradually changing the landscape into a mega metropolis. Construction cranes have become part of the structure of the city. The roads have been widened, and in some places ten lanes have been laid to accommodate the ever-growing amount of traffic. Several flyovers have been built to ameliorate the traffic congestion.

The passing luxury cars further adorn the new rising structures of steel and glass. The buildings of government ministries and other institutions pervade the city centre. Some of the buildings in the city are intended to showcase the prestige and power of the state. One such building is that of the Ministry of Defence, which was designed in the form of a gigantic naval ship. Bekker and Therborn (2012: 1) write that 'the nation-state projects its power through the urban landscape and spatial layout of the capital city. This power is manifested in the capital's architecture, in its public monuments and the names of its streets and public spaces.' In many countries of the world, particularly in the Global South, 'capital cities are supposed to make statements. They often represent the best face of their countries, in both symbolic and concrete terms.' This is precisely the case with Abuja, where the presence of the state manifests itself in the spatial configuration of the city (Adebanwi 2011: 2).

Residents and visitors to Abuja are often stunned by the radically new city plan, with its aesthetically designed architecture. This experience invokes dream-like, phantasmagoric imageries of the city that induce specific affective sensations. Phantasmagoria suggests that many surface appearances of the city give it a dream-like or ghost-like quality (Pile 2005). Pile further asserts that 'Cities were different moreover, because they were constantly throwing people into contact with new experiences, new situations and new people' (2005: 17). One of my Christian interlocutors, who worked with a satellite installation company in the city, expressed his view thus:

> I have lived in Abuja for seven years now, but still I am not able to shake off the powerful appeal I feel toward the aesthetic landscape of the city. The city still shouts back at me. There is a strong appealing force the city has, which I would call Abujaness. This can be likened to a beautiful seductive lady who uses make-up with expensive cosmetics and charming beauty to seduce people. If you are rich and powerful you can date this lady, if you are poor, you can only dream of having her. (Interview, 2 March 2014)

This statement mirrors the imagination of many Nigerians, which is that for them Abuja is only a pleasant and glittering dream: the city is 'real' only for the rich and powerful. The statement also highlights a profound form of spatial exclusion and alienation that defines the city of Abuja. Those with low incomes, both among government employees and the self-employed, are pushed to the settlements far outside the city and forced to suffer a gruelling daily commute ritual into the city due to the exasperating traffic jams. This daily ritual in and out of the city, which gives people a taste of something they cannot possess, generates both desire and anger among the excluded lower classes. One interlocutor stated, 'Every time I travel to Abuja, my impression is that I am in a movie. Finding myself in the midst of strange buildings and vehicles, and even some white people passing by, I feel lost in this non-real movie like scenery' (interview, 27 March 2014). Another interlocutor stated, 'Having grown up in a small impoverished city in Plateau State, I felt disoriented in Abuja. The city looks out of place to me, it is not authentic; it is too artificial to me. Even the lifestyle of the people is artificial' (interview, 25 March 2014).

By dissociating Abuja from authenticity and realness, or likening it to a movie scenery, it has come to be labelled as a city of dreams, its unique structures

Figure 1.1 Central Bank of Nigeria, Abuja. Source: Author.

prompting wishful thinking and enthralling imagination. As a city built from scratch and still in the process of development, Abuja constantly mesmerizes its inhabitants with new structures and new spatial layouts, hence evoking desires and aspirations. Abuja is an expression of the dreams of the future initiated as part of the modernization project conceived by the nation's ruling elites. To many people, living in Abuja implies stepping into a dream of the future that is difficult to realize for the country's population as a whole.

This imaginary world of Abuja as a dream city is captured, enhanced and disseminated by the northern home video movie and music industries. The centres of the northern film and music industries are Kano and in a small scale also Jos and Kaduna. But these centres lack modern and fanciful infrastructures that abound in Abuja. As a result the majority of the film and music producers begin to shoot their movies in Abuja even though they are mostly based in Kano.

The obvious reasons to shoot in Abuja and focus on the imposing structures of the city such as the flyovers, multistorey glass and steel buildings, elegant interior decorations of sitting rooms and exquisite gardens are to entice the imagination and taste of the audience for the modern lifestyle and its refined material culture. This is precisely what Birgit Meyer (2015a: 84) observes in Ghanaian video films as she argues that 'these movies may best be regarded as both mirrors of and windows unto a popular imaginary of urban modernity, with its particular material culture, lifestyle, and notions of personhood and belonging'. Similar to Ghanaian movies, northern Nigerian film and music video clips also mediate the city of Abuja and expand its popular imaginary world into a modern, neoliberal utopian city of dreams. As Meyer notes, the films become mirrors and windows through which people access the vision of the city as it is reconfigured and represented on the screen through editing, selected shots and other techniques of film craft.

Shopping malls: The landscape of desire

Shopping malls are a recent arrival in the Nigerian cityscape. Until recently, they could only be found in Lagos, and they only began to appear in the urban landscape of Abuja in the last decade. Nowadays, there are several major shopping malls in Abuja, including Ceddi Plaza, Dunes Centre, Silverbird Entertainment Centre, The Capital Hub, Jabi Lake Mall, Grand Towers Abuja Mall and Grand Square. One of the most famous of these is Ceddi Plaza, a shopping mall located within the Abuja Central Business District. It contains about fifty-five specialty shops, offices and service providers, including a champagne lounge, movie theatres, a photo studio, clubs, restaurants and bookstores. Another important shopping centre in Abuja is Jabi Lake Mall, built on the shores of Jabi Lake, Abuja's largest body of water. Jabi Lake Mall has attracted international retailers such as the South African supermarket chain Shoprite and the popular appliances store Game. The mall has significantly boosted business in the local supply chain and offers goods presently unavailable elsewhere in Nigeria.

Similar to their counterparts around the globe, Abuja malls feature gigantic vaulted spaces that suggest a sacred liturgical or secular-civic function. The malls also allow in natural daylight, which supports softscapes – made up of interiorized palms and shrubs – that are reminiscent of a tropical vacation setting. They also feature enclosed streetscapes that refer to an idealized social space free of the inconvenience of weather and the dangers and pollution of the automobile (Goss 1993: 24). To invoke Benjamin, shopping malls in Abuja constitute an important dream world of the city, as well as profound affective spaces, the loci of enchanted commodities that orchestrate desire, and are symbols of spectacle in capitalist modernity. The combination of affect, enchantment, desire and spectacle conflates to create the phantasmagoria of shopping malls and of the city as a whole.

The architecture of shopping malls, the configuration of design, lighting, event management, logistics, music and sometimes live musical performances are all specially designed and arranged to generate an affective response from visitors. These affective responses are invoked through the enormous diversity of available cues, in the form of a profusion of images and other signs, the wide spectrum of available technologies and the more general archive of events. This spatial configuration of variety, glittering and attractive, is an intentional form of landscape engineering that gradually pulls itself into existence, producing affect, emotion and new forms of power (Thrift 2008: 203). The affect and emotion that transform Abuja's shopping malls into affective spaces also play a role in attracting consumers and keep them coming back.

Unlike in high-income countries, shopping malls in Nigeria, and in Abuja in particular, are only affordable for the upper classes. The spatial organization, atmosphere and ambience of the malls contrast with the messy, noisy and chaotic traditional marketplaces on the outskirts of the city where most of the lower classes do their shopping. Many people from the affluent class express a sense of liberation from the psychologically intense haggling that takes place in these informal marketspaces. Haggling in the informal sector in Nigeria is a skill that allows lower class shoppers to buy commodities at the best price. Most of the lower class members of Nigerian society, particularly women, develop sharp interpersonal skills that enable them to effectively navigate and negotiate the informal market environment; this, combined with extensive knowledge of the market vendors, allows them to get the best deal. Since most rich people do not have the necessary haggling skills, shopping malls liberate them to buy low-quality products at many times the original price. Unlike the limited regulations of the traditional marketplaces on the outskirts of the city, Abuja's shopping malls are contrived and highly regulated spaces.

Apart from the affective architecture, expensive fancy and foreign commodities add to the magic of the malls and further transform them into a phantasmagoric dream world. As one of my interlocutors put it,

> The first time my boyfriend took me to the Jabi Lake Mall I felt as if I was catapulted into a magical wonderland. I came face to face with beautiful designer clothing, shoes, necklaces, wristwatches, which I felt strong desire to possess but unfortunately neither I nor my boyfriend have the money to buy. I came back happy and excited for seeing new things and unhappy because I do not have the means to possess them.

The feeling experienced by this interlocutor indicates how the configuration of space and fancy commodities generates affect in the shopping mall, which is certainly enhanced by what Karl Marx describes as commodity fetishism. Marx's notion of commodity fetishism explains how in a capitalist system, commodities are perceived as acquiring inherent surplus value that gives them the semblance of a mystical appearance, described in terms of theological niceties and metaphysical subtleties (1990: 65).

Shopping malls in Abuja also function as places to showcase high social status. People who cannot afford the expensive commodities displayed in the malls nevertheless visit them in order to be seen and to create the impression of high social status. In this regard, shopping malls have become performative grounds where people of a lower class can act as high class. It is for this reason that Abuja malls have become the ultimate sites for dating, where some young men take their girlfriends and overstretch their pockets in order to impress them and elevate their own status. Despite the fact that most of the commodities and services in the malls are beyond the reach of the lower classes, Abuja's shopping malls are promoted as public spaces with a neoliberal vision of consumption, in which credit card citizenship allows everyone to buy an identity and to vicariously experience a preferred and desired lifestyle, nominally without any principles of exclusion based on accumulated wealth or cultural capital (Zukin 1990: 41). These aspirations and promises notwithstanding, Abuja's malls remain a strongly confined or purified social space beyond financial capacity of the downtrodden and indigent members of society.

Despite the fact that people of lower class status visit shopping malls in order to experience or taste the lifestyle of the higher class, the experience is qualitatively different. The difference lies in the financial capacity of the affluent class and the elites to purchase expensive consumer commodities in the malls. The power to procure fancy consumer goods in the malls becomes an important marker of high-class status and is therefore a means for the social production of difference. There is a colloquial term in the Hausa language for mimicking higher status through shopping malls: *chara* which translates to pretentiousness in English. It is clear that the capacity to buy expensive commodities exposes the limitations of *chara* and differentiates this mimicry from the real thing.

Both visiting malls and buying expensive commodities have become signs that mark social class identity. People do not only shop in the malls but also observe what others buy and what they wear. The urban politics of shopping malls plays out through the shoppers' mutual gazes, their internal conversations and their subjective impressions of others, through which they categorize each other along the social hierarchy of class and wealth. Shopping malls are signs that signify the new lifestyle of the spectacular neoliberal urbanism unfolding in Abuja and phantasmagoric dream world that defined the city.

Gated communities: Enclave for the elites

Abuja is currently experiencing a proliferation of gated communities in different parts of the city. Gated communities are a type of fenced or walled-in housing estate that contains strictly controlled entrances for pedestrians and vehicles. The emergence and spread of these enclosed and guarded housing developments in both the Global North and South can be attributed to a variety of factors that include security, the provision of quality services and the desire to buy property that has value (Katrin 2009).

These spatial enclaves in the city have become the locus of intense modernity in terms of the provision of modern amenities. It is apparent that the gated communities of Abuja encapsulate a desire for spatial modernization and a modern way of life. The modern amenities include an uninterrupted electricity and water supply, paved roads, street cleaning, refuse collection, internet services, recreation parks, sports facilities as well as private security guards. Even though the Abuja municipality provides some of these infrastructures and services, they are not as regular and efficient as when they are provided by the developers of gated communities. As a result, Abuja's gated communities have become isolated spaces where residents enjoy full modern amenities similar to in the cities of high-income countries. Through walled housing estates, the wealthy elites of the city segregate themselves from the lower class and create a superficial social homogeneity based on wealth and social status.

In her study of 'African urban fantasies', Vanessa Watson highlights the fact that gated communities are part of an attempt to remake African cities in the mould of a utopian urban planning that 'prizes exclusionary and self-contained spaces that limit opportunities for interaction between different classes, while worsening marginalization of the urban poor' (2013: 14). It is arguable that this elevated social status that is defined by wealth has assumed a spatial identity through gated communities. The affluent classes imprint themselves physically on the urban structure through the formation of communities and clustering, as well as through the erection of boundaries and the establishment of distance (Fainstein 1994: 1).

Many of my lower class interlocutors criticize the exclusionary nature of Abuja's gated communities, as well as their new social value characterized by the neoliberal lifestyle of consumption. They perceive the lifestyle in gated communities as too artificial, enhancing class exclusion and incongruent with the communal values of Nigerian culture. As one of my interlocutors stated, 'I cannot live in such an enclosed environment where I spend most of my time indoors, from office to sitting room. To me, this lifestyle is too arid and stale, that is why I see it as artificial.'

A popular story that circulated on social media reveals this imaginary world of Nigerians concerning the lifestyle within gated communities and in Abuja in general. The story goes like this: A rich man living in one of Abuja's most expensive gated communities decided to take his three children to his ancestral village for the first time as punishment because they misbehaved. Contrary to his expectations, the children became enamoured with the new village environment. They were captivated by the simple life of the village: they played with the other children freely, enjoyed moonlit stories with their grandmother, collected water in the river and ran in an expanse of open space. When the father came to take them home after a couple of days, the children refused to go with him, saying that they did not want to go back to Abuja.

This story is not based on reality; it is only a romanticized view of an African village as typically depicted in folklore and epic Nollywood movies. However, the story is also a critique of the lifestyle in gated communities and contains an imaginary world that casts life therein as devoid of humour and interactions that underpin *conviviality*. The wealthy class people of gated communities are viewed as living in an illusion, an artificial life that lacks freedom because it is mired in excessive regulations, isolation and insecurity, which render such a lifestyle monotonous, without spontaneity, fun and joy. The story attempts to show that the residents of gated communities are living in an illusion because they have mistaken their affluent life as superior over the life of that of the lower class. This mistake is what drove the rich man in the story to take his children to the village as punishment, yet contrary to his expectations, the reality of the convivial communal village life shattered his children's illusion and unchained them from the shackles of regulated and isolated lifestyle.

Scholars such as Katrin (2009) make similar criticisms of gated communities by noting that good internal relations between residents do not seem to inevitably lead to strong feelings of community cohesiveness. They further indicate that everyday life within these enclosed spaces is highly regulated by legal contracts and the arrangements for self-governance by homeowners: 'These legal instruments undermine the concept of gated neighborhoods as voluntary communities able to develop their own informal controls and sanctions' (Katrin 2009: 229). Low (2001) also critiques gated communities in the context of the United States, as materially and symbolically contradictory to the ethos and values of community, as well as a threat to public access to open space, and responsible for creating yet another barrier to social interaction, the building of social networks and increased tolerance of social diversity. This scholarly criticism matches Nigerians' perceptions of Abuja's gated communities that see them as a strategy of the elites to set themselves apart from the poor in order to conceal their wealth and thus avoid the obligation to share which underscores the value of communal responsibility.

This imaginary world of the lower class that critiques the lifestyle of the residents of gated communities nevertheless masks a desire or dream among many urban residents to attain a similar high status. The desire to be rich is palpable in the activities of Abuja residents, from the prosperity gospel, Islamic success prayer books and the vast body of self-help literature, to large-scale corruption cases in government. The palpable desire for wealth and fancy consumer commodities coexists in the minds of many from the lower class in a paradoxical juxtaposition with the critique of neoliberal lifestyles. The ambition of the elites to create their own utopian enclaves in the form of gated communities and the lower class's ambivalent and covetous outlook towards them transform such places – gated communities, malls – into affective spaces.

It can be argued that these affective spaces render the Abuja cityscape a phantasmagoric collective dream world. This dream world overlaps with the neo-Pentecostalism that dominates Abuja's religious landscape. Neo-Pentecostalism emphasizes the prosperity theology, which teaches that financial blessings and physical well-being are always the will of God, and that faith, positive speech and donations to religious causes will increase one's own material wealth (Wilson 2007). Pastors of this brand of Christianity preach to their mass audiences and promise them blessings in the form of new jobs, cars, houses and protection from the 'curses of Satan', namely misfortune, unemployment, poverty and other impediments to success. These blessings can be acquired through faith and bountiful donations to the church (Gifford 2004: 48).

In Abuja, the prosperity gospel and neoliberal crony capitalism feed into each other. The prosperity gospel encourages the consumption of fancy commodities and preachers display an extravagant show of wealth through expensive designer clothes and automobiles as a sign of God's blessing. As one of the senior pastors of Christ Embassy stated in a sermon that I attended,

Many people look at the appearance. That is the reason why we dress well in the church. We live in good houses, drive expensive cars and fly in first class. Jesus said, 'Seek the kingdom of God first and every other thing shall be added unto you.' It is because we apply the principles of the kingdom that God blesses us. As far back as the year 2000, I have been receiving gifts of a brand new Mercedes-Benz and other expensive cars. (10 August 2014)

This statement clearly indicates a combination of neo-Pentecostal preaching and the neoliberal market economy that encourages consumption (Barker 2007: 1). As capitalism creates desire for commodities through the use of media, prosperity theology creates the same desire through the pulpit. The prosperity gospel in this regard works to advance the cause of modern capitalism by encouraging success, by which it means a life of neoliberal consumption (Barker 2007).

By promoting the desire for commodities and consumption, prosperity theology has embedded itself in the spectacle of neoliberal capitalism. However, neo-Pentecostalism does not only absorb the ideas and practices of capitalism, it also enchants the system. This enchantment is centred on the neo-Pentecostal idea that faith, rather than the production and distribution of goods and services, creates prosperity. As a result, the conflation of prosperity theology and neoliberal capitalism remains superficial, as their fundamental logics diametrically diverge from each other. Despite this essential difference, there is no doubt that prosperity theology cultivates and promotes desires that reinvigorate the force of desire for consumption in Abuja. Though there is hardly a Muslim equivalent to prosperity theology, some Muslim groups such as NASFAT and Al-Habibiyya do promote the use of special prayers to foster prosperity. Prosperity gospel and prayers empowered the phantasmagoric dream world of the city.

Sites of divine encounter: Religious buildings of the city

Some of the great landmark buildings of the city are Abuja Central Mosque and the National Christian Centre. The Abuja National Mosque, also known as the Nigerian National Central Mosque, was built in 1984 (ArchNet 2002). The mosque is located in the central area and is situated on Independence Avenue, across the National Christian Centre. This national monument consists of a huge aluminium dome that is covered with anodized gold. The mosque also has a small dome and four splendid minarets that dominate the skyline of the city. Residential quarters of the chief imam and muezzin are located adjacent to the mosque. The land on which the mosque is located is low-lying, so the building was erected on a high concrete structure so as to make the mosque visible from different parts of the city.

The National Christian Centre of Nigeria, previously called the National Ecumenical Centre, was built as the prime Christian place of worship in the capital city. It is an interdenominational church that comprises multiple Nigerian denominations. The building of the National Christian Centre commenced in 1989 but lay dormant for several years until 2004, when the Christian Association of Nigeria (CAN) organized a committee to ensure its speedy completion in October 2005. The Church is built in a neo-Gothic style and has several pivoted arches with a wide nave leading to the altar. The Church features stained glass windows adorned with the conspicuous mix of yellow, green and red colours that can be seen all around the building (Adeyimi 2011).

These two buildings dominate the centre of the cityscape, attracting the attention of passers-by. It is apparent that the intense competition that defined relations between Muslims and Christians in the political sphere has manifested in the realm of architecture. After the completion of the central mosque, the National Christian Centre lay incomplete for an extended period. This became a serious issue within the Christian community, with many blaming disunity in CAN for failure to complete the building. They always pointed to the National Mosque, complaining that if Muslims completed theirs, there is no reason why Christians could not do the same. The quibbles around the two monuments underlined the rivalry of visibility of religious symbols in the centre of the capital city. Competition between Muslims and Christians is not limited to verbal rhetoric alone but extends to claims over physical space.[3] Suvakovic (2014: 10) writes,

> Architecture is essentially a political and ideological practice that uses its techno-aesthetic and techno-artistic strategies to participate in the organisation of individual and collective human life, as well in representing the symbolic and imaginary field of visibility of a society for itself and others.

In this sense, the Central Mosque and the Christian Centre formalize and express the central role religion plays in the Nigerian polity. The two landmark buildings communicate the symbolic importance of Islam and Christianity in the life of Nigerians through staking imposing structures in the centre of the capital city. The buildings are clearly architectural political statements that reflect the competing struggle for public presence between Muslims and Christians. The magnificent structures of the two buildings portray dynamism and power wielded by Islam and Christianity in the country.

Figure 1.2 National Mosque, Abuja. Source: Author.

Another famous icon of the city is not a man-made structure but a tremendous work of nature called Zuma Rock. Zuma Rock rises spectacularly immediately north of the city along the main road to Kaduna and is sometimes referred to as the Gateway to Abuja. Zuma Rock is 725 metres (2,379 ft.) above its surroundings (Alofetekun 2008).[4] The indigenous people of the area believed that the rock is the abode of gods and spirits, and it was revered as a sacred site. If the Central Mosque and the Christian Centre are symbols of an entrenching presence of Islam and Christianity, respectively, Zuma Rock tells the story of the implicit presence of African Traditional Religion (ATR) that refused to die completely and continues to influence some practices of mainline religions. This subtle influence continues despite the overwhelming attack from Pentecostals and Islamic reformists on the minimal presence of some elements of traditional religions and practices.

The major Pentecostal churches in Abuja established branches in different parts of the city, including its most expensive areas. The Mountain of Fire and Miracle's Abuja headquarters is a massive two-storey rectangular structure located in a business district along Jabi Road. The ash-coloured marbles that cover the building make it sparkle and conspicuous. This building, like most

Figure 1.3 National Ecumenical Centre, Abuja. Source: Author.

of the other Pentecostal churches in the city, such as Lord Chosen, Dunamis and Redeem, break with traditional church architecture and experiment with varieties of modern design.[5]

Many religious organizations nowadays are engaged in building immense structures in Abuja and its surroundings. Some Pentecostal churches and Muslim organizations have initiated enormous religious campuses along the Masaka-Abuja highway. Living Faith Church has acquired huge areas of land in Masaka along the highway, where it has built a gigantic church, a university and a massive estate called Goshen City. Passers-by are greeted with a large billboard on which is written, 'Welcome to Goshen City'. The Redeemed Christian Church of God has bought another large stretch of land close to that of Living Faith, where hundreds of thousands of people gather during their annual Holy Ghost Congress. The Ahmadiyya Muslim Society has followed suit by building an enormous mosque on the same highway. As massive places of worship have emerged on the highway, the area is gradually becoming into what Janson and Akinleye (2015) call a 'spiritual superhighway' in describing a similar situation along the Lagos–Ibadan expressway, which was also transformed into a gigantic religious site. This appears to be a new trend of recently established mega-churches and mosques having to go outside the city to build huge religious structures that can accommodate the crowds that attend their mass religious services.[6]

Christ Embassy is one of the dominant churches within the Pentecostal spectrum that exists in the city of Abuja. Instead of building one enormous church that can accommodate tens of thousands, as in the case of its headquarters in Lagos, Christ Embassy built numerous churches in different parts of the capital city. The central church is the regional headquarters of the church and is located at Durumi, Area One. It is a huge and impressive structure designed like a modern secular building, possibly able to accommodate up to five thousand people (in my estimate). The stage is designed and decorated with small geometrical objects like cylindrical forms, pyramids and polygons coupled with colourful flower arrangements. The stage's main colour is blue, with a combination of other matching colours, such as gold and white. The entire stage is also illuminated by different colours of light.

Similar to Christ Embassy, NASFAT has about six branches in the FCT in places such as Karu, Nyanya, Dutsen Alhaji, Kubwa, Gwagwalada and Utako. The Utako mosque is its zonal headquarters in Abuja and is located in the city centre. The building is decorated with white marble inside and out. Numerous rows of white pillars inside the mosque enhance its aesthetic appeal. The mosque stands

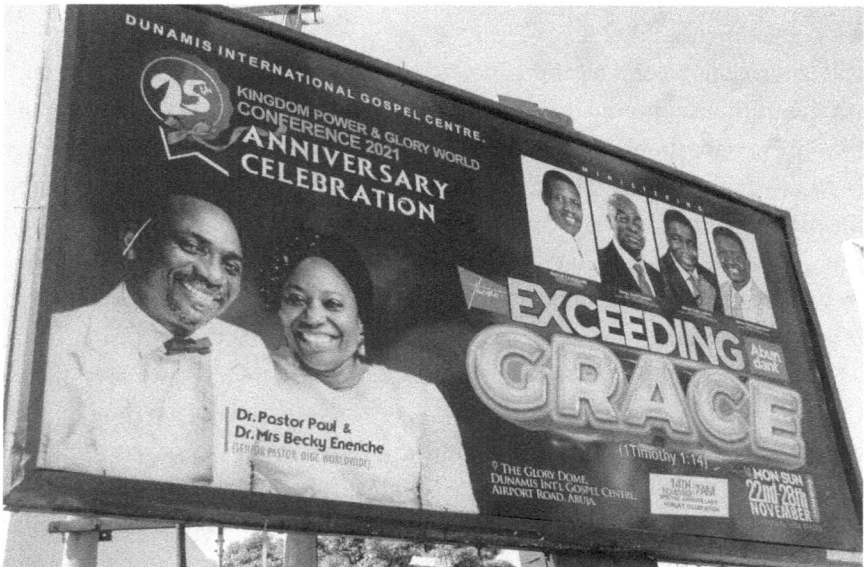

Figure 1.4 Pentecostal billboard in Abuja. Source: Author.

on three floors, with a gross floor area of 4,272 square metres, and has sitting capacity for about five thousand worshippers. The ground floor was designed to accommodate the male congregation; the first floor is reserved for women, while the upper floor is the conference hall, with a capacity to accommodate 1,500 people.

As places of worship and retreat, religious buildings offer a spiritual experience to the wider community, where the clamour of urban life can melt away in a space designed to be used collectively and individually for an encounter with the divine. Nevertheless, many of the religious buildings in the city of Abuja serve simultaneously as public spaces for the overall life of the community. Religious buildings in Abuja highlight the multiple ways in which people connect with and gather in public, ultimately showing how communities collectively share experiences and emotions.

The sensation of feeling attached to their respective places of worship was commonly expressed by both Christian and Muslim men and women in Abuja. As suggested by the statement above, this sensation is tied to the fact that places of worship are sites where people sense an emotional connection with the divine. Reckwitz (2012: 254) argues that 'every complex social practice – as far as it is always spatialising and necessarily contains perceptive-affective relations – implies a form of affective space. In modern societies, this spatialising often results in built, architectural spaces which are made for and correspond with specific practices.' People certainly engage in spectacular practices and create routine in places of worship in Abuja. Most Pentecostal churches, including Christ Embassy, hold services three times a week. Some members go to the church and pray almost every day. NASFAT and groups such as Al-Habibiyya hold special services on Fridays and Sundays apart from daily prayers.

Religious places of worship are centres of activities and participation that are inextricably connected with people's sense of identity and belonging. Through a range of affective practices, believers develop a strong connection to their religious spaces to the extent that the latter become an inherent part of their social identity. As places of divine encounter, religious spaces provide a sense of hope and security as well as producers of affect and emotion that shape religious spaces and urban landscapes in more general terms. It is arguable that religious places of worship in the enchanted Abuja landscape become affective spaces through spectacular embodied religious performances, which can therefore be understood as spatial practices. The aesthetically designed religious structures have added another layer on to the dream-like Abuja landscape, which has become entangled with the lures and enchantments of an 'aspiring city'.

The diverse religious landscape of the city

The mass migration that ensued with the establishment of Abuja as the federal capital has created a rich religious diversity. Christianity and Islam are the predominant religions, but there are also a relatively modest number of new religious movements[7] such as Hare Krishna and Eckankar, which add to the complexity of the religious landscape of the city. Intra-religious diversity is even more pronounced than the plurality of distinctive religious faiths. Churches have followed the migration of a vast number of Christians to Abuja from all parts of the country since 1992. Now churches are expanding, and new ones are constantly emerging in the city.[8] The mainline churches such as Roman Catholic, Anglican and Baptist have large numbers of followers and their big churches spread in the population centres. However, the most dominant churches are obviously Pentecostals. These churches run the gamut from smaller ones with few members to the ones whose members count in the thousands. Some of the largest Pentecostal churches in the city include Redeemed Christian Church of God, The Lords Chosen, Mountain of Fire and Miracle Ministries, Living Faith and Christ Embassy.

Muslims in the FCT are predominantly Sunni in the Maliki School, as in the case of the majority of Nigerian Muslims. Some of them are members of Sufi brotherhoods, a form of religious order based on more personal or mystical relations with the supernatural. The two main brotherhoods, the Qadiriyya and Tijāniyya, have played a significant role in the spread of Islam in the rural communities in the federal capital. The most active Muslim groups in the public sphere of the city include the Izala movement, which preaches against what its followers perceive as innovative practices and advocates a return to the *Sunna* of the Prophet. *Salafis* are also visible in the city, and many of the prominent religious leaders in the city belong to this category. Moreover, some minorities of other Islamic groups exist in Abuja such as Ahmadiyya, Tablighi Jamaat and Shi'ite.

Unlike many cities in Nigeria, almost all Abuja neighbourhoods have ethno-religious diversity. However, some groups or faiths tend to be predominant in particular areas. This is the case in both the lower class neighbourhoods in the outskirts of the city and the affluent gated communities in the city. This situation occurs probably because Abuja developed rapidly in the last two decades with people coming from all parts of the country almost at the same time. Abuja is unique among many northern Nigerian cities that are plagued by protracted ethno-religious conflicts.[9] In both the wealthy and poor neighbourhoods the fault lines in diversity did not transmute into a conflict that may disturb the peace in the city.

The responsibility for regulating religion and fostering harmony in the multireligious landscape of Nigeria which includes Abuja lies with the Advisory Council on Religious Affairs.[10] This department is under the Ministry of Internal Affairs, and the head office is located in the Federal Secretariat in Abuja. The Council consists of twenty-four members appointed by the president of the country that represent the Christian and Muslim population evenly. Some of the functions of the Council are to develop avenues for articulating cordial relationships among the various religious groups and between them and the federal government.[11] The Council is expected to devise means of consolidating national unity and the promotion of political cohesion and stability in the pluralistic Nigerian society. The Council also has the responsibility of assisting the federal and state governments by stressing and accentuating the position and roles religion should play in national development.[12]

The Council coordinates with the established religious organizations in Abuja for organizing programmes that aim to promote peaceful coexistence between Christians and Muslims. Most of the programmes of the Council focus on organizing interfaith dialogues, workshops and seminars on achieving sustainable peaceful coexistence. Despite the fact that the Council has engaged in various means of pursuing these goals since its formation in 1987 by the administration of General Ibrahim Babangida, the success of its programmes has been eroded by the incessant religious riots in many parts of the country. Nevertheless, the Council has contributed its fair share in effective management of religious diversity in the federal capital. However, despite the tension caused by the religious noise and road closure or disruption of traffic by some religious groups, the Council did not solicit the city authority to regulate these activities. The city authority has legal power to initiate rules to regulate religious activities, but so far it has not done so. Moreover, the Nigerian Constitution guarantees freedom of religion and prohibits all sorts of discriminations based on religious belief. It is apparent that this constitutional provision usually clashes with the attempt to regulate some religious activities. Religious groups often perceive regulation by state authority as infringement of their rights. Recently there was uproar in Kaduna state when the governor attempted to regulate preaching and noise from the loudspeakers of mosques and churches. Many Christian leaders accused the governor of violating their constitutional right to preach the gospel.

In Nigeria a tacit perception has developed that historical churches initiated by the European missionaries before or during the colonial era are regarded as established. By contrast, Pentecostal churches are regarded as new, even those that developed in the 1970s or 1980s. However, seeing Pentecostal churches as new does not imply lack of recognition by the federal government. The former president of CAN who left office in July 2016, Ayo Oritsejafor, was a Pentecostal pastor. All registered churches, whether those regarded as established or Pentecostals, have equal rights before the law and they are protected by the Constitution. Section 38(1) of the 1999 Constitution and Article 18 of the Universal Declaration of Human Rights, states, 'Every person shall be entitled to freedom of thought, conscience and religion, including freedom to change his religion or belief, and freedom (either alone or in community with others, and in public or in private) to manifest and propagate his religion or belief in worship, teaching, practice and observance.'[13] As a result, Christian missionaries are operating in the Muslim states, even those who declared *shari'ah* law. In the villages of northern Muslim states such as Kano and Katsina there are still minority populations of Hausa 'pagans', called *Maguzawa*, and both Muslim and Christian missionaries are presently competing in proselytizing them to either Islam or Christianity. It is only recently that some states (Lagos and Kaduna) have begun attempts to limit religious expression in relation to regulating noise pollution and preaching.

On the local level, the mainline religious leaders from the Roman Catholic Church, Anglican, Baptist, Presbyterian and other historical churches and Jama'atu Nasril Islam (JNI) are constantly working on various initiatives to optimize peace in the city. As they watched other neighbouring cities ravaged by ethno-religious riots, some started making concerted efforts for consolidating good inter-religious relationships. These initiatives are spearheaded by the Roman Catholic Church and the JNI, rather than Pentecostals and Islamic reformists. Pentecostals and Islamic reformists have a lukewarm attitude towards dialogue, and they often refused to participate.[14] These established religious bodies consistently organize interfaith dialogues to boost mutual understanding and mitigate the tension between Muslims and Christians.

Pluralistic religious soundscape of the city

A variety of religious sounds that emanate from different kinds of sources which range from churches, mosques and shops in the public space have created a rich and complicated acoustic ecology of the city of Abuja. In many parts of the city these religious sounds rise over the everyday cacophony of the city's environment, such as the noise of traffic, the wail of sirens, the clamour of construction, and voices of hawkers and vendors of various kinds. Itinerant Christian preachers also use loudspeakers early in the morning to preach to neighbours about the importance of repentance. On several occasions in Abuja, I was awakened by these male and female preachers, who preach loudly using strong language to declare that people should repent because Jesus is coming. These loud voices in the early morning hours evoke what Isaac Weiner (2014: 4) describes as 'aural aggression'. According to Brian Larkin (2014b), the use of loudspeakers in religious settings is not only a means of evangelism or *da'awa* but also a performance of presence-making. This announcement of presence through sound is precisely what causes competition between different religious groups in the same environment. Larkin (2014b: 5) quotes Jacques Attali that 'the imposition of one's noise is also a means of silencing others'. In the same vein, Stocker (2013: 66) asserts that 'sound is the physical signature of our dynamic surroundings'. This assertion helps us to understand the competition to drown out one another through loudspeakers between Islamic reformists such as Izala and Sufi groups in other northern Nigerian cities. Apart from announcing the presence, religious sounds that emanate from loudspeakers and other sources can be seen as an act of place-making. One can easily recognize the religious identity of a particular area of the city by the nature of sound ambience of the environment. Klomp (2020: 9) states, 'The feeling of "home" is strongly mediated by the soundscape of a region, and that the unique experience of a lifestyle, of a city's or countryside's atmosphere, is fundamentally determined in each instance by the acoustic space.'

Most neighbourhoods in the city have mosques and churches that use loudspeakers to amplify their religious services. It is a common practice for a wealthy man in a Muslim neighbourhood to build a mosque inside his compound and employ an imam who leads prayer, teaches and preaches to the neighbours who attend the mosque. Household worship among Christians is also rapidly increasing nowadays. Sounds that emanate from these religious practices help identify the religious character of the environment. Wrightson (2000: 10) writes, 'the idea that the sound of a particular locality (its keynotes, sound signals, and sound marks) can – like local architecture, customs, and dress – express a community's identity to the extent that settlements can be recognised and characterised by their soundscapes'. In this sense, sonic ambience can be seen as intrinsically connected to space (Klomp 2020).

As many young pastors establish their smaller churches, they use loudspeakers to reach the public. These new, smaller Pentecostal churches seem to lack the resources of bigger churches, hence their inability to broadcast themselves on commercial radio and television. As a result, a loudspeaker is the only means through which their preaching goes beyond the enclave of their church buildings. Apart from the sound that emanates from loudspeakers of the smaller churches, another sound arises from household worship. Most of the big Pentecostal churches have household fellowship meetings organized by members living in the close neighbourhood. This is a church service in small groups where people living close to each other perform a service in their houses that is accompanied by the heavy sound of worship and preaching. Some neighbours often complain and perceive this as noise that disrupts their rest. Isaac Weiner (2014: 2) observed a similar situation in New York:

> Each of these auditory outbursts has generated controversy and elicited complaint at various moments in U.S. history. As they emanated outwards from the more traditional spaces to which modern religion has been confined, these sonic expressions have reached multiple, heterogeneous audiences – both intended, and unintended, willing and unwilling – who have heard and responded to them in very different ways.

The controversy generated by religious sounds caused Lagos State Environmental Protection Agency (LASEPA) to intervene and enact anti-noise laws to curb noise pollution in the city. According to the LASEPA report, out of the 4,700 complaints it received in the year 2020, 50 per cent were from neighbours of religious houses. Another 20 per cent was due to religious activities in places that were not religious houses, making it 70 per cent. Violation of this law has caused the shutdown of several mosques and churches in the last decade.

In Abuja where noise is not regulated, many people quietly continue to complain about it. In my conversations with both Christians and Muslims in Abuja about this issue, they disclosed to me that they bitterly oppose religious noise but that they are afraid to voice their grievances for fear of being labelled as irreligious or unbelievers.

However, some people appreciate loudspeaker-mediated religious sounds and listen to them attentively. Weiner (2014: 4) quotes Hillel Schwartz, who aptly affirms in a similar vein that 'noise is never so much a question of the intensity of sound as of the intensity of the relationship'. It is, therefore, this relationship that defined sound as a sacred sonic expression that deserves attention or unwanted aural disturbance. For instance, most Izala members approved of preaching through cassettes played by Izala mosques with loudspeakers around four o'clock in the morning, even though it is one of the most controversial sounds. However, most Sufi Muslims perceived this sound of preaching as noise that violates their right to sleep, while at the same time they appreciate loudspeaker sound during *Maulud* (Prophet Muhammad's birthday), which vibrates throughout the night. Yet, even this issue of appreciating the sound due to the sympathy or religious affiliation with the source of the sound cannot be generalized. I encountered many people who complain about sound that emanates from their own religious groups. In my conversations with both Christians and Muslims about this issue, they disclosed to me that they bitterly oppose any noise that disturbs people and creates discomfort. Sani Musa is a Muslim who is working for a furniture company and resides in a house that is close to a Sufi mosque in Nyanya Abuja. He said he is highly disturbed by the sound of loudspeakers broadcasting daily from the mosque. Conversely, he tolerates the regular call to prayer because it is compulsory, but the other extra activities such as preaching and recitations of praise songs to the prophet or *zikr* (melodious invocation of God) that arise from the loudspeaker extremely disrupt his ability to rest and sleep at night. Sani said he wanted to relocate to a place far away from any loudspeaker but has not been able to do so due to his limited financial resources. Another interlocutor stated that in his view using loudspeakers apart from normal prayer calling was ethically wrong. He continued that there should be a religious ruling by Islamic jurists to prohibit such practices. According to him, denying someone's ability to sleep is tantamount to invading their personal freedom that God himself cannot approve. He suggested that all other activities, even long prayers during fasting in the month of Ramadan, should be performed without loudspeakers.

Moreover, some Christians I interviewed disapproved of the excessive use of loudspeakers even from churches. One interlocutor who lives in Nyanya, Abuja, told me that every day when he comes back from work, it was hard for him to rest due to the sound coming from a church close to his house. He said that even though he is a Christian and believes in God, in his view, the church should switch off the loudspeaker during service, since not everyone is interested in listening to the service. When I asked him why people like him are not complaining publicly or taking their case to the authority to express their dissatisfaction, his response was that he does not want people to see him complaining about religious activities. Another person, a thirty-four-year-old electrician in the city, told me that most of his Christian clients in Wuse area have relocated to other parts of the city. And many of them cited the discomfort they experienced as a result of the prevalent number of mosques that use loudspeakers in the area.

Larkin (2014b) argues that one of the means by which Nigerians cope with the regular presence of noise emanating from the loudspeakers is shifting their attention away from the sound – a situation he called 'techniques of inattention'. I want to disagree with Larkin here because most people that I interviewed and observed perceived the sound of loudspeakers as a noise that can be tolerated only with pain out of necessity. Many people complained that it is impossible for them to remove their attention from the irritating and unpleasant loud noise that makes them highly uncomfortable. When people have control over the sound, for instance, on radio, they choose the channels that suit their taste. I have witnessed many occasions where people quickly changed stations either on radio or television immediately when the programme of another religion comes on air. People select where to direct their attention if they have a choice, and if they do not have a choice they tolerate the unwanted noise. Nevertheless, some people narrated stories of what they heard from the loudspeakers of other religious groups and expressed their opinion whether in agreement, disagreement or even ridicule.

Visual markers of religion in the city

Public spaces in Abuja are saturated with religious posters on virtually every nook and cranny of the city. From a distance, they look like commercial adverts of consumer products, but at a close look, they appear to be adverts of different kinds. Almost all of them advertise Pentecostal crusades, revivals and other mass gatherings. They usually come with very dramatic captions such as the following: God of Miracle, Engaging the Supernatural Power of Faith, Grand Connect with Grace for Exploit, Break the York of Barrenness, God of Miracle, Prophetic Blast, Abuja Prophetic, Fire Conference, National Turn Around Crusade, This Mockery Must End, Unlocking the Ancient Harvest by the Spirit, Unstoppable Progress Summit, We Serve a Very Big God, It's Breakthrough Season, That Shrine Must Catch Fire.

The main visual displays of the posters almost without exception are pictures of the pastor whose church organizes the event. In many cases, the pastor appears with his wife beside him and sometimes with his associates. The verbal element of the posters consists of the dramatic and emotionally appealing captions I mentioned above. These two elements constitute the visual prominence on the posters. Pictures of the men of God in the posters have realistic details with shining faces, immaculate outfits (usually suits) and neat haircuts. The captions have very strong, conspicuous and attractive typesetting designs.

These posters that cover the structures of the city show the vibrant religious activities that are going on there and the desire to capture public attention. Their pictures being the most prominent element of the posters, it is clear that the men of God are advertising not only spiritual products but also their faces. The captions indicate that the main products advertised are protection, wealth, miracle for healing, security and power to overcome worldly problems. This implies that spirituality, particularly through the prosperity gospel, is used as a tool for effecting changes in the mundane world. Pentecostals are using bold and conspicuous images in these posters and other visual media as a strategy to capture the attention of the public.

Religious stickers are widely used on vehicles and in the offices, houses and even on items such as bags and computers. Many churches and Muslim groups produce stickers and distribute them to their members as forms of public relations. The conspicuous typescript and graphics of stickers as well as encoded messages make them highly attractive visual objects. This makes them an easy medium for advertising a religious organization or denomination. One of the most ubiquitous stickers that pervades the city of Abuja is that of the Living Faith (aka Winners Church), which contains the written caption, 'I Am a Winner'. Similar to Pentecostal churches, NASFAT's members embraced the use of stickers on their vehicles, bags, computers and houses. Different types of stickers that display NASFAT logos are sold in the mosque during Sunday worship prayers.[15] The present chairman of NASFAT central branch in Abuja told me that he came to know about NASFAT through a bumper sticker which he was seeing daily on passing vehicles. He said that initially he wondered whether NASFAT was a company that sells cars because of the many cars he had been seeing with NASFAT's stickers. This led him to begin enquiries about NASFAT and eventually he became a member of the movement. Stickers serve as visual markers of religious identity; they are communicating to the public the denomination or religious group to which the person displaying the stickers belongs. One controversial sticker that some Muslims paste on their bags or cars reads, 'If your God is crucified why not try Allah, he is ever living'. This causes grudges in some Christian circles while many ignore it without a comment. Some Muslims discuss the message of the sticker with amusement and spread the news about it. Religious images through posters, billboards and stickers permeate the structures of the city. However, because the authorities have not yet attempted to regulate religious activities and put in place an avenue of complaint, the posters, billboard, stickers and other visual markers of religion continue to spread throughout the city.

Religion and social capital in the city

This section attempts to show that the religious landscape of Abuja is a ground where many people engage in the constant struggle of building social capital. Pierre Bourdieu and James Coleman popularized the notion of social capital. The concept has captured the interest of many social scientists who extended and applied it to different circumstances. Bourdieu and Wacquant (1992: 119) define social capital as 'the network of more or less institutionalized relationships of mutual acquaintance and recognition'. According to Sander and Lowney (2006: 3), social capital focuses on the social networks that exist between us (literally who knows whom) and the character of those networks, the strength of the ties and the extent to which those networks foster trust and reciprocity. Places of worship in Abuja are a fertile ground for building social capital because scores of state officials and other influential people visit such places. This feature of Abuja makes it attractive to religious leaders and induces many of them to relocate their headquarters to the city.

As I was approaching Abuja from Jos for the purpose of starting my fieldwork, I was dazzled by the myriad of posters and billboards advertising Pentecostal activities in the city. Among them, I saw many posters of Pastor Joshua Telena who founded Shepherd House of God in Jos but who had now apparently relocated to Abuja. Joshua Telena is very famous for propagating the prosperity gospel and for his unusual techniques of taking money from members of his congregation. That evening, I went to the house of a friend of mine who had relocated from Jos to Abuja. As we were watching television, I saw one famous Muslim cleric, Sheikh Nura Khalid, preaching in the national assembly mosque in English. My host told me that Sheikh Nura had relocated to Abuja a long time ago, and now he had acquired huge amount of wealth and was driving expensive cars. He came to Abuja when he was expelled from Izala after a personal and theological dispute with the then leader of Izala, Sheikh Samaila Idris. As a result of his expulsion, he lost his position as the principal of one of Izala's secondary schools.

After talking with some people and observing the religious terrain in the city, I discovered that the cases of Joshua Talena and Nura Khalid are just tips of the iceberg. Many religious leaders are relocating to Abuja because there is a huge material benefit to be accrued as a result of networking with state officials. It is noteworthy that rich people and politicians in Nigeria give or donate a considerable amount of money to religious leaders and organizations. For example, *Premium Times* reported a story that the coordinator of the Conference of Islamic Organisations (CIO), Abdullahi Shuaib, revealed that two Islamic organizations were offered $3 million around February 2014 by the past administration to secure their support in the re-election bid of ex-President Goodluck Jonathan (Kayode-Adedeji 2015). There is also a similar report by the *Daily Post* that the former President Goodluck Jonathan in early 2015 offered about 10 billion naira (21,083,700 million euro) to some famous Pentecostal pastors led by Pastor David Oyedepo of Living Faith Church to support his re-election campaign (Daily Post 2015). Similar incidents happen all over the country but are more pronounced in Abuja. Religious organizations, both Muslim and Christian, organize fundraising in the city and invite ministers, National Assembly members and businessmen. For instance, in one capital raising of Izala that I attended, one politician donated 20 million naira (42,167 euro), and the former speaker of the National House of Representatives, Alhaji Aminu Tambuwal, donated twenty cars for running the organization.

Religious leaders in Abuja have more access to material benefits than their counterparts in other parts of the north. According to one of my interlocutors, many pastors have become wealthy and acquired houses and land due to their connection with state officials in the city. As a result, some pastors, particularly of Pentecostal strands, become powerful and influential people. My interlocutor told me that one pastor of Living Faith Church of God, who presides over one of the big branches of the church in the city centre, was transferred to another church in another state. However, the pastor resisted the transfer and clearly told his superiors that he could not afford to lose the material benefits available to him in the city. When the church headquarters in Lagos insisted on the transfer, the pastor disaffiliated with the church and established his ministry in another part of the city. Lin (1991: 31) affirms that 'the premise behind the notion of social capital is rather simple and straightforward investment in social relations with expected returns. Individuals engage in interactions and networking to produce profits.' In this vein, it is arguable that some religious leaders are reaping a benefit through their social network in the city.

It is not only the religious leaders who are struggling to build social capital, but many people who attend places of worship in Abuja also do so with the extra intent of establishing a network with top state officials either directly or through religious leaders. It is a widespread perception in Nigeria that access to government services is difficult unless one knows officials in charge of such services. People always repeat the familiar adage that 'merit does not count, it is whom you know that counts'. Incidentally, some people are drawn to religious places of worship for the purpose of networking to gain or enhance social capital, which became a motor behind religious affiliation. The larger the numbers of influential people, the bigger the congregation.

According to my interlocutors, persons who are looking for a job or government contract purposely go to churches where there are officers who may likely help them achieve their goals. My interlocutor is a university graduate who has been looking for a job for more than four years without success. When he told one of his friends about his problems, she instantly advised him to start attending her church because the then Secretary to the Government of the Federation (SGF), Anyim Pius Anyim, was worshipping there. She promised that she would help him get a duty in the church such as ushering that will make him visible so that he will be noticed by the State Secretary or other government officers that would help him find employment. He said almost at the same time another friend of his told him to start going to the legislative quarter's church where former Senate President David Mark worships. His friend had told him that if he became active in the church, the senior pastor might secure a job for him through the pastor's connection with the Senate President and other top government officials.

I discussed this situation with one of the pastors of ECWA Church located along Airport Road. He told me that in Abuja smaller churches have difficult times because most people prefer to worship in bigger churches that have wealthy and influential members. He said his small church is continually becoming depopulated as a result of people migrating to more prominent churches. He knows many individuals who are residing in the area close to his church but prefer to go to the far distanced Maitama branch of ECWA in the city centre because that is where they have the possibility of networking with influential people.

To follow up this trend in the Muslim community, I visited the Central Mosque in December 2013 to see the Chief Imam Sheikh Musa Muhammad (who passed away in 2015). Even though I could not interview him due to his busy schedule, I talked to some people who were waiting to see him outside the mosque. There were up to twenty people that morning waiting to have an audience with the imam. I initiated a conversation with one of them. He said the imam is a very influential person in the country and due to his position as the national imam he wielded influence over people of high authority in government, both Muslims and Christians. If the imam asked any favour from them on behalf of anybody, his demand is quickly considered. When I asked him what he wanted from the imam, he said that he was working with a government ministry as a driver. However, he lost his job and wanted the imam to intervene and talk to his superiors in the ministry to restore his job. I asked him whether he was sure that the imam knows the people in that ministry. He said it is not necessary whether the imam knows them or not, his position as a senior religious leader is enough to compel them to reinstate him back in his job. Another person told me that he wanted to see the imam to help him get back his plot of land that was seized by land grabbers in the Masaka district next to Abuja. On many occasions, religious membership is determined by the goal of gaining access to profitable social networks in places of worship. Sander and Lowney (2006: 5) maintain that bridging relationships was particularly important to creating a sense of unity across race, class or religion; to 'importing clout' into communities that lack clout; and to breaking down stereotypes. Bridging is the type of social capital that predominates in the religious scene of Abuja because religion has become a medium that bridges the gap between lower class people and high-ranking state officials that help them access services which otherwise would be difficult for them to enjoy.

Conclusion

This chapter has described the social ramifications of religious diversity in Abuja. As the federal capital located in the centre of the country, Abuja has attracted people from all corners and has become a religiously pluralistic city. It is the fact of this diversity and also the diversity of the nation as a whole that prompted the authorities to promote Abuja as a centre of unity. In my early days in Abuja in November 2013, I came across the Unity Fountain, which is a roundabout located in the heart of the city. The fountain contains the names of all the thirty-six states of the federation written on different angles of its structure. The fountain was apparently built to celebrate the symbolic role of Abuja in the Nigerian federation as a centre of unity. Moreover, the vehicle licence plate number for the FCT reads 'Centre of Unity'. The idea of unity always appears in the cityscape, particularly on the mass media. The authorities hoped that this idea of unity would enhance harmonious coexistence among the diverse ethno-religious groups. People from different religious backgrounds are unified under a single political, economic and legal system in the city. These people are bound to share and cohabit the same neighbourhoods and interact at different levels of social engagement. Unlike many other major cities in the federation, Abuja has successfully managed to preserve relative peace and unity through relentless effort of many religious actors and government institutions. Despite the existence of grudges and sound pollution, the relative peace has been sustained without degenerating into destructive conflicts.

It has been noted in this chapter that religious spaces are growing rapidly in Abuja and has become intertwined with the fabric of the city. It is arguable that religious structures have added another layer on to the dream-like Abuja landscape, which has become entangled with the lures and enchantments of an 'aspiring city'. Some places of worship, such as the National Mosque and the National Christian Centre, are landmark structures and aesthetically designed to make an impression on the onlookers. Moreover, the dominance of religious cacophonies in the city has generated mixed reactions, which sometimes depend on the listeners' relationship to the sources of the sounds. Sounds broadcast from religious places have enriched the texture and soul of the Abuja cityscape. However, these religious sounds that permeate the city often become sources of discomfort and distress to many people in both Muslim and Christian communities. The chapter argues that instead of removing their attention from these sounds, people of Abuja tolerate them out of necessity. Similar to sounds, religious images also permeate the city and even become mobile in the case of bumper stickers on motor vehicles that move around the city. Automobiles carry religious stickers with them to different corners of the city. This mobility increases the visibility of the stickers.

The manifestation of religion in the city is not only restricted to sights and sound but also extends to social relationships. A complex nexus of relationships exists among people of authority, religious leaders and members of religious organizations that affect religious participation in the city. Social forces in Abuja have made religious places of worship more than places where people meet for prayer, solace, repentance or ritual performance. The social structure of the city has generated a system of religious economy where religious leaders and their followers received material benefits from people of authority. Moreover, the system obliged them to reciprocate, as, for instance, in backing policies or voting during elections or rendering varieties of spiritual services such as prayer. As a result, a symbiotic relationship has developed between these two classes of society.

Although Christianity and Islam belong to different religious traditions, they produce similar pattern of responses to social situations, as in the case of an effort to establish social capital in places of worship and the use of loudspeakers and reactions they engendered in the city of Abuja. These similar patterns point to the fact that Muslims and Christians are not independent impervious entities that exist in their exclusive universes. These similarities can be explained by the fact of cohabiting the same environment and exposure to the same external social forces acting on society. Sharing living space also fosters mutual influences and similar responses to social challenges. The next three chapters will explore these mutual influences on religious practices between Christ Embassy and NASFAT.

Christ Embassy:
Being born-again without morality

Introduction

> The book of 2nd Corinthians 5:20 says that we are ambassadors for Christ. Like any other ambassador here on earth posted to another country. We are also ambassadors {representatives} of Christ to reconcile the world back to Him. We are posted into the world though we are not of the world. We are to win the world to Christ. Zion is our home country because we are on official assignment. In doing this, we give people's lives a meaning, i.e., salvation, healing, and peace. (Interview 10 January 2014)

These were the words of the instructor of the foundation class when he was telling me about the background of Christ Embassy and the origin of the name. Christ Embassy is among the successful Pentecostal churches in Nigeria, its branches spread throughout the urban landscape of the country. Seeing themselves as ambassadors of Christ in the world, members of Christ Embassy believe that they have the mandate to spread the gospel to the world and teach people techniques of maximizing health and wealth, which they believe are encapsulated in the gift of salvation.

Christ Embassy creates a self-image of a modern church that comprises members who are mostly upwardly mobile professionals. The expression of modernity in Christ Embassy can be seen in its sophisticated organization and the efficiency of its bureaucracy that is based on principles of motivation, which involve a comprehensive system of reward for an optimum performance. According to the teaching of Christ Embassy, a born-again believer has some special rights in Christ. These rights include success, health, wealth and victory over the enemies. The means through which one could achieve these rights involve a series of practices and techniques that aim to radically transform the individuals. The purpose of this chapter is to introduce the church through discussing some selected themes, such as brief historical background, organizational structure, membership, cell ministry, perception of the others, fundraising, significance of time and worship services.

When talking about Christ Embassy, I will constantly make references to Pastor Chris Oyakhilome because, as is the case with most newer Pentecostal church founders, he dominates all operations of the church.[1] In fact, he owns the church. His domination is not restricted to administration alone but encompasses the teachings and theology of the church. In Nigeria, many people refer to Christ Embassy as Oyakhilome's church. Ukah (2007: 15) writes about the founders of newer Pentecostal churches, including Pastor Chris, as 'bank of grace, repository of charismata, and a special bridge between his followers and God. He controls both charisma and cash; his word is law. He is an oracular instrument and initiator of doctrines and orientation. He alone holds a special privilege of interpreting the will of God to his people.' It is for this reason that one cannot do research in any of Christ Embassy's branches without substantial references to Pastor Chris. The larger-than-life pictures of Oyakhilome are displayed in all the branches of the church. The pastors almost repeat his preaching verbatim and consistently make references to him. His programmes are broadcast every Sunday, and his written materials are sold on the premises of all the branches.

Brief historical background of the Church

Pastor Chris Oyakhilome[2] is often addressed as pastor, teacher, man of God or healing minister, but his followers mainly refer to him as Pastor Chris. Pastor Chris is a celebrity pastor in Nigeria, and one of the most famous televangelists and best-selling authors in the country. Based on the information I acquired from numerous interlocutors, Oyakhilome was born on 7 December 1961 into a family with deep spiritual tradition that played a vital role in the formation of Pentecostalism in Nigeria. His grandfather was among the founders of the classical Pentecostal church, Assemblies of God of Nigeria. Pastor Chris is the eldest son of the family of Elder T. Oyakhilome, who was a renowned missionary in Benin during the colonial period. Elder T. Oyakhilome was a former member of the Church of God Mission International, which was founded by the late Benson Idahosa in Benin City. Idahosa was the pioneer of neo-Pentecostalism in the country, and he was often called the father of prosperity gospel who achieved international fame. Due to the influence of his family, young Chris grew up as a member of the Church of God Mission International and as a devoted follower of Benson Idahosa.

After his primary education, Chris attended the prestigious Edo College, one of the famous secondary schools in Benin City. He started preaching from his youth, holding large miracle meetings during his secondary school days. During the college holidays, he worked as part-time staff at the Church of God Mission in Benin City. This became an opportunity for him to interact with and appropriate the teachings of Benson Idahosa. Chris Oyakhilome initiated Believers' LoveWorld Ministry when he was a student of Architecture at Ambrose Alli University, Ekpoma, in Edo State in 1981.[3] It was known as the 'Youth for Chris'. The name later changed to 'Believers' Love World Campus Fellowship'. On graduating from campus, the young Chris Oyakhilome established Christ Embassy (the first church) in Benin and later handed it over to his disciple and assistant Rev. Tom Amenkhienan and moved to Lagos. In Lagos, Christ Embassy began in Adeniyi Jones in Ikeja, from where the church moved to Alausa and finally to Oregun Road.

From the time of its inception in the campus, Christ Embassy expanded gradually into most parts of Nigeria. Eventually, the church spread beyond the borders of Nigeria into many African countries such as Ghana, Ethiopia, Kenya and South Africa. Moreover, the church expanded into Europe, Asia, and North and South America. Pastor Chris now holds large meetings in the United States and has Healing School sessions in Canada and the UK. Due to his charismatic ministrations, he has won many followers from the corporate world and from upwardly mobile young men and women who are working hard to keep the church going. Despite the fact that there are numerous other pastors in Christ Embassy, members regard Pastor Chris as their first pastor and spiritual leader. They listen to his preaching and read his booklets. Other pastors serve only as supporting personnel for Pastor Chris.[4]

Anita Ebhodaghe was born in Benin to a wealthy Nigerian father, Mr. John U. Ebhodaghe, who was a former managing director and chief executive officer of Nigerian Deposit Insurance Corporation (NDIC). Her mother was from Switzerland. As a result, Anita holds a dual citizenship. Anita is the first daughter in a family of five. Anita Ebhodaghe was among the first students to join Pastor Chris in his newly established campus fellowship, Believers' LoveWorld Fellowship, when she was studying English Language at Ambrose Alli University, Ekpoma, in Edo State. It was through her active membership in the ministry during her student years that she later started courtship with Chris Oyakhilome and got married to him in Lagos in 1991. She has two teenage daughters with the pastor, Sharon and Charlyn.

Anita was a former member of the central executive council (CEC), which is the principal governing body of the church. She was the director of Christ Embassy International Office and one of the members of the board of trustees. Anita was the former head of Christ Embassy Church in the UK and neighbouring regions. In April 2014, Anita filed a divorce suit against Pastor Chris at London Central Family Court to end their twenty-year-old marriage. She accused her husband of misconduct and unreasonable behaviour. Pastor Chris denied the allegations and spoke on the divorce suit, on the evening of Sunday, 7 September 2014, during the monthly global communion service of the church. He said it is not biblical to divorce, but if his wife insists on it, he could consider it as an option. Presently the marriage has been dissolved and Anita has been removed from the website and publications of the church.

Anita Ebhodaghe co-authored Christ Embassy's daily devotional booklet, Rhapsody of Realities, which has been translated into over 250 languages all over the world. However, since the filing of her divorce case in London, Pastor Anita disappeared from the Rhapsody of Realities devotional and website of the church. She has authored numerous Christian books with her ex-husband such as *Unending Springs of Joy, Don't Pack Your Bags Yet, Confession for Living, a Handbook for Successful Living*, and many others. Presently she leads her new ministry in London which consists of many members of Christ Embassy who sided with her after the divorce.

Organizational structure

Christ Embassy is organized into regions which include several countries in a particular continent; zones comprise several states or provinces within a region; parishes or branches constitute a zone; central pastoral units and cells are the smallest units of the church which do not have enough members to form a parish. The leadership hierarchy of the church includes the president/ founder, the vice president, the board of trustees, the CEC, the international pastors conference, regional directors/pastors, zonal directors/pastors, group pastors, parish pastors, church pastors and coordinators. The national headquarters of Christ Embassy is located in Lagos along the Kudirat Abiola Way, Oregun, Ikeja, close to the Lagos State government house. The building is a mega-structure with an impressive architectural design which, according to one of my interlocutors, cost about two billion naira. The main auditorium of the building has the capacity to seat about forty thousand worshippers.

The building also contains the offices of pastors, administrators and chains of businesses.

The leadership of the church ensures strict discipline and total commitment in their various duties. Deep loyalty and respect define the relationship between members and leaders. The most powerful and influential organ of Christ Embassy is the CEC, which has about eight members, including Pastor Chris. Pastor Ken, his younger brother, is also a member of the CEC, and he is the head pastor of Christ Embassy in Houston, Texas. Another influential member of the CEC is Pastor Tom Aniekhanan, who is a cousin of Pastor Chris; before moving to South Africa, he headed many Christ Embassy branches in Nigerian cities such as Benin, Kano and Lagos. Pastor Tom is the director of Church Ministry and Organisation (CMO), the central administrative and co-coordinating office of all Christ Embassy churches worldwide. Other members of the CEC include Pastor Tom Obiazi, Pastor Tuoyo Edun and Pastor Ambrose Isesele.[5] The General Executive Council (GEC) is made up of all the pastors in the ministry. This comprises of the pastors of Christ Embassy churches, satellite church pastors, campus pastors and other ordained pastors in the ministry. They meet at the Pastoral Conference, which is held annually in November.

The Abuja branch is one of the most important branches in the northern part of the country. Abuja serves as the zonal headquarters of the north-central region. Pastor Chidi Okwonko is the senior pastor of the zone, and he oversees all six branches of Christ Embassy in the federal capital territory. Like all the pastors of Christ Embassy, Pastor Chidi also emulates Pastor Chris in both style and themes of preaching. The zonal headquarters in Abuja is a two-storey building that is close to the main church at Durumi in the Area One section of the city. When I visited the place for the first time, the atmosphere felt like a modern business environment. People who looked like chief executive officers of business firms, dressed in black suits, were moving around the building from one office to another. The offices are well-furnished with exquisite furniture.

According to one of the instructors of the foundation school, Peter Tseka, Christ Embassy has various organs. There is a Campus Ministry, which plays an important role in spreading the message of Pastor Chris among students. The ministry, as stated earlier, started from campus and Pastor Chris has a unique ministry for the youth, which is the reason that the church places great emphasis on working within universities. The church has fellowships in most of the Nigerian universities, polytechnics, colleges of education, and schools of administration. The name of the campus fellowship is Believers' LoveWorld Campus Fellowship. Peter Tseka told me that Christ Embassy established a

Figure 2.1 Christ Embassy Church, Karu, Abuja. Source: Author.

training school called LoveWorld Ministerial College (LMC). LMC is not a Bible school but a training ground for leaders since every member of the church is a potential leader. Tseka stated that LMC affords the leaders the opportunity to be trained on the doctrines of Christianity as interpreted and understood by the church, and the school offers courses from general studies (GS), church administration, lay pastoring and pastoral courses.

Another training programme in Christ Embassy is the LoveWorld Correspondence Bible Course. This is also a training course open to all. It is done by correspondence without a classroom environment. It is comprised of daily study, an audio cassette by Pastor Chris and a course manual. Tseka told me that the church organizes an annual International Pastors and Partners[6] Conference (IPPC). Pastors of all branches of the church are encouraged to attend this programme. The various churches and campus fellowship tender reports and prizes are awarded.

Members and membership

Before the conclusion of an enthusiastic church service on Sunday, 1 December 2013, at the Christ Embassy Church, Karu branch, Abuja, the senior pastor proclaimed, 'Anybody who comes here for the first time should stand up.' I and other four people stood up. Immediately as we stood up, the entire congregation began to sing for us.

'Welcome to Christ Embassy'
This is the place
Where you give your life a meaning
This is the place
Where the word of God does transform
You're at the right place, at the right time
You're blessed because you came (×2)
Welcome to Christ Embassy!

After the song was finished people came and shook our hands and embraced us with welcoming smiles and expressions of joy and love. The scene looked like an emotional homecoming for a family reunion. The pastor said, 'You should now follow the usher to the next room because we have a special package for you.' The ushers came and led us to another big room with plenty of plastic chairs. I saw different groups of people sitting at different angles of the room receiving a lesson from their instructors. We also sat at one angle and two people came and introduced themselves to us as Adewale and Tseka. Adewale stated,

You are welcome to Christ Embassy. You are not here by accident; you are here because you are led by the Holy Spirit. Before you become part of this church you are required to participate in a foundation school that comprises of six module courses. After the completion of the course you will write an examination and a long essay. You should not worry. The examination is very simple. It is based on what we are going to teach you. For the long essay we will ask you to go and win a soul and bring him [her] to the church and write your experiences. When you finished the long essay we will ask you to join a cell and become an active member of the church. We promise you great things in this church. You will know so many new things about the word of God. I promise that your life will never be the same as from today. Another important thing I want to ask is that if anyone of you is not baptised previously, after the course we can baptise the person. We usually go to swimming pool for the baptism because we believe in full immersion.

Adewale brought out small forms and distributed them to us. The spaces to be filled in the form include name, address, occupation and phone number. The form also includes the question, 'Are you born again?' Another question is, 'Do you want us to visit you?' Adewale explained the nature of the classes to the newcomers. He said the lesson is not a formal teaching where a teacher would go to the front of the class to teach. He continued that the school is like a private lesson because each participant is given a private tutorial by the instructor. And each participant is going at his own pace. Some finish the course in six weeks and some take more than that. One can arrange with the instructor to organize the classes to suit his/her time and schedule. He said one should buy an exercise book for taking notes during the lesson.

The first module of the course includes spiritual renewal through becoming a born-again believer. The module also includes the theme of salvation, dominion in life and forgiveness. The second module deals with the nature of the Holy Spirit and procedures for invoking its presence. Module three deals with the different doctrines of Christianity as understood and interpreted by Christ Embassy. The major doctrines discussed in the module are the doctrine of Christ, resurrection of the dead and baptism. Module four discusses evangelism, soul-winning, the importance of prayer and the techniques of effective prayers, and the great commission. Module five addresses the importance of growing a Christian character through Bible study and the Rhapsody of Reality, as well as attending extra-church services within the week and active participation in cell fellowship. Module six describes the concept of the church and the structure of Christ Embassy and its various ministry units.

Through the time of my fieldwork I understood that the foundation school is a means of retaining newcomers and guiding them in understanding the doctrines and practices of the church. In a short period, people are taught several things which otherwise would have taken them a long time to learn. The emotional welcoming of newcomers with songs and hugging is another clever strategy of establishing emotional tie with them so that they may have the impression of becoming new members in a loving and caring religious community. One newcomer (about twenty-five years old) told me, 'I was overwhelmed with the reception, and the brotherly love these people showed to me, it is beyond my comprehension. After some time in the church I felt that I am part of the family' (interview, 3 August 2014, Abuja). However, through my interaction with various people I noticed that not all people who joined the foundation school stay till the end of the classes. Many left at different stages and some never even came back after the introduction. This is because not everybody who comes to the church for the first time has the intention of becoming a permanent member. Some attend the church out of curiosity while others go with an open mind but find some beliefs and practices unacceptable to their taste and understanding and eventually left. However, for those who stay to the end, the school serves as a form of initiation. I noticed that most of the people who came for the first time and joined the foundation school were members of smaller Pentecostal churches and a few Catholics. I met a Muslim convert only once. When I asked him about his reason for converting to Christianity, he said Islam is very difficult for him because the rituals are cumbersome, and that was why he opted for Christianity.

Cell ministry

The cell is the smallest unit of organization within Christ Embassy. The term is derived from the biological cell which is the smallest structural unit of an organism that is capable of independent functioning. The sole purpose of cell units in Christ Embassy is evangelism or soul-winning, as it is often called in the church. Another purpose of the cell is to give members an opportunity to participate in the church activities. For instance, a person can be part of a choir or lead prayers in the cell if he/she is not comfortable doing so in the large congregation. The cell also gives a sense of belonging to the members. The cell provides opportunities for members to cultivate acquaintances and friendship in small groups. Cell members know each other, they pay visits to each other's homes and places of work. There is cell evangelism in Christ Embassy which they call 'cell outreach'. Members of a particular cell go into the city to preach the gospel in public places such as market squares and parks. Every member of the church must belong to one cell. The logic of assembling people from similar background and profession is based on the view that these people could help one another through advice and sharing of experiences.

Cells in Christ Embassy are created and organized based on varieties of criteria such as residential proximity, vocational proximity, gender and specialized professions. Some of the cells in the central branch of Christ Embassy Abuja include Avant-garde, Charisma, Citadel, Citizens, Cornerstone, Diamond, Favour, Glory, Dunamis, Eagle, Footballers, Joy, Lighthouse, Rhema, Oasis, Ruby, Sapphire, Agape and Foundation. The cell leader determines a convenient venue for the cell meeting, which could be restaurants, cafes, conference centres or the house of a member, among others. Cells in Christ Embassy do not have a minimum number of members, but the maximum is fifty. Once a cell reaches fifty members, the rule of the church requires that it should be split into two.

The cell leader pioneers a new cell with a vision of winning and training souls. A leader of a cell has responsibilities to guide and direct the members towards achieving the vision of his/her cell. A leader is required to cultivate a meaningful relationship with his/her members and motivate them through good behaviour and an impeccable moral character. Moreover, the leader keeps records of all the activities of the cell, such as the membership list, attendance at cell and other meetings, testimonies, programmes, financial dealings, correspondences, goals and objectives. These records are submitted quarterly to the coordinator of the church for evaluation and monitoring.

During my fieldwork in Christ Embassy, I attended meetings of two cells, one with the group of information and communication technology (ICT) experts, called professional cell, and the other with a group of bank employees. The bankers' cell is called 'Zenith cell' and the leader is Olu Johnson.[7] The cell holds its meeting in a café called Fountain in the outskirts of the city. The meeting commenced with the opening prayer, followed by worship songs, Bible study and preaching by the cell leader. The leader then introduced the newcomers and asked them about personal questions or need for prayer. After these activities, a general discussion is held about another issue concerning the group. During my first meeting on 8 February 2014, the group discussed the issue of organizing dinner for the church leaders. They talked about the cost of the dinner, the venue and the time. They also spoke of the next evangelical outreach and the location of the next outing. Finally, the cell leader asked me whether I want them to pray for me or pay me a visit, which I politely refused.[8] The cell leader replied it is alright since 'you are here for a research purpose; you are not bound by our rules'.

Nowhere is the principle of motivation in Christ Embassy more ostensibly manifest than in the Cell Ministry Award Day, which is held monthly. The award is designed to motivate members to work hard and achieve the objectives given to them by the leadership of the church. There is a long desk beside the entrance of the church building with about five young women leading the registration. Each person entering the church has to tick on the form the cell to which he/she belongs. At the end of the month, the officials in charge would determine the cell that has the maximum percentage of church attendance. From the register of the cell leaders, the individual who achieved 100 per cent attendance would receive an award during the award day. Moreover, a cell that reached maximum fundraising and one that won the largest number of souls would also receive an award. The full award categories are: Soul winner of the month, Outstanding mother, Outstanding father, Exceptional cell leader, Exceptional cell member, Financial commendation, Cell of the month (adherence to instructions, number of souls won, achieved financial target, attendance of church service, submission of report promptly), Super cell of the month (90 per cent participation and maximum number of first timers that the cell members brought to the church).

During the award day, which commences after the regular Sunday services, the church becomes like a football field. For each award announced the entire congregation would burst into yelling, clapping and jubilation. This practice encourages competition between the cells and serves as the prime motivational factor that propels the members into working extra hard for the attainment of the goals set for them by the church. The deployment of elements of competition in running some of the activities of the church boosts efficiency in the administration of Christ Embassy and makes it more competitive among myriads of Pentecostal churches in the country. It is partly for this reason that Ukah (2007: 17), in his categorization of Nigerian Pentecostal churches, places Christ Embassy under the category of 'firm-like structural organisation'. It is arguable that the exponential growth of Christ Embassy hinged on these practices that induce the members to work as efficiently as possible for the growth of the church.

Fundraising: The practice of sacred investment

There are three primary methods of fundraising[9] in Christ Embassy, which are tithes, partnership and free will seed offering. In every Sunday service ushers distribute envelopes for people who want to pay tithes and other fees. The payees go towards the front of the altar, kneel down, pray and drop the envelope there. A tithe is a mandatory giving of one-tenth of one's income to the church. Pentecostals view tithes as a form of transaction with the divine, for the purpose of reaping reward. Tithes, offerings, gifts to men and women of God, often cast as sowing and reaping, have become a virtual subculture within contemporary Pentecostalism in Africa. This practice resonates well with the concept of a successful ritual in African religion which is perceived as a form of gift to the gods that may be rewarded at the appropriate time (Asamoah-Gyadu 2013: 80). According to the teaching of Christ Embassy, as taught in the courses of the foundation class, one-tenth of one's income belongs to God. Therefore, it is compulsory for members to pay their tithes. Every time one gets an increase in one's income, one-tenth must be set aside to be given as tithe. However, the church does not enforce the payment with any disciplinary measure, but members are warned that refusal to pay incurred opening their doors to the Devourer (Satan), who is going to wreck their finances. Pastor Chris, in one of his preaching broadcasts during the Sunday worship service, preached on the dangerous consequences of refusal of payment of tithe. He stated,

> The Devourer comes in so many ways; he comes in like a thief, or sometimes you keep your money and the exchange rate goes up, or you saved money in a bank, and the interest rate goes up, you are losing. But when God kicked the Devourer out [through payment of tithe] you keep on progressing, you will be full of blessing. Let me tell you a story (because of paying tithes) I never suffered. I only have one story in my life; it is like this continually. I never been poor and I do not know what it is to be poor. I could not be poor. (26 August 2016)

Pastor Chris here gives an example of the benefit of paying tithes. He attributed his prosperity to the tithes that he had been paying to his church before he established Christ Embassy. However, there is a problem with paying tithes, which might cause a contradiction in the teaching of the church. This is because the tithes were part of the law of the Old Testament and Christ Embassy is vehemently de-emphasizing Jewish practices of the Old Testament period. Since Pastor Chris needs the money that comes from the payment of tithes, he attempted to resolve the contradiction that tithes posed to his teaching. Pastor Chris solved this problem by initiating a new theology which proposed,

> Practices in the Old Testament performed by men of faith such as Abraham, Jacob and Isaac, who came before the Jewish law, apply to the Christians. Men of faith in the Old Testament and Christians are linked by the principle of faith, not law. Since tithe was first practiced by Abraham who was the original man of faith; therefore, tithe is compulsory in the present dispensation of faith and grace. (26 August 2016)

By this argument, Pastor Chris reduces the dissonance that arises through his rejection of Jewish practices that may affect the church emphasis on tithe giving and thereby institutes it as one of the primary sources of funds for Christ Embassy.

'Partnership in Christ Embassy' is a pledge that a member could make to be paying a certain amount of money monthly for sponsoring church programmes, such as the publication of Rhapsody of Reality, upkeep or construction of church buildings, TV and radio productions and broadcasting, as well as a host of other activities of the church that demand regular financing. A member can name the programme that he/she wants to sponsor and continue to pay consistently without failing. 'First fruit' offering is also a percentage that one can remove from extra money apart from regular earnings such as salary. First fruit differs from tithes because it is not regular; it depends on the money one obtained through sources such as a bonus from work, inheritance or gift. The purpose of first fruit is blessing the rest of the money and showing gratitude to God.

A 'seed offering' is money given to the church by the members according to the dictate of their free will. The teacher of the foundation class told me that a seed offering is almost as important as paying tithes. According to the teaching of the church, the term 'seed' is a metaphor used to indicate that giving money to the church is like sowing a seed of any kind in the ground. Just like the seed grows to become a crop or giant tree, the money given to God will come back in bigger or multiple folds. Seeds could also be sown 'on the pastors of the church', particularly Pastor Chris. Sowing seed on the pastors means giving money as a gift to the pastor personally instead of donating to the church as an institution. This practice is highly encouraged especially during the meeting of small groups such as cells. During one of the meetings in the Zenith cell the leader told us that one day he gave 200,000 naira (421.674 euro) as a seed to the senior pastor of the church. And within two weeks God gave him twice that amount. When the members of the cell were organizing an outreach in the meeting in which I participated, the leader advised that they should be contributing money, and when it reached a substantial amount, they should send it as a seed to Pastor Chris so that God may bless the cell. Another function of seed offering is to solve protracted problems such as loss of fortune or sickness. During my lesson, the teacher stated, 'If you are facing any problem in life, pray and pay a seed to God, that problem will automatically vanish' (2 March 2014).

Seed sowing is tacitly projected as an investment that people can make so as to incur a significant profit. The stories and testimonies of people who invested and got a reward for what they had invested serve as one of the potent motivational and inspirational factors in seed sowing. The story of Bulus Michael would show the power of motivation in the investment nature of seed planting. His story goes as follows:

> Some years back, I had a successful transport business with many trucks. Then suddenly events began to turn upside down, and I found myself mired in debt until I became completely bankrupt. I had about ten trucks, but now all of them have gone. In fact, I owed banks a lot of money, and the interest is increasing day by day. One day my friend involved me to become a middle man in a multi-million naira trucks transaction. After the completion of the deal, I got a commission of about 500 thousand naira (1,054.19 euro). I decided to give the entire money to my church as a seed offering for my bankruptcy. I believed that God will look at my sacrifice to remedy my difficult financial situation.

From my discussion with this interlocutor, I found that he was apparently not interested in donating for the purpose of promoting the gospel. He was driven by the investment nature of seed offering. Since the money that he earned was not enough to solve his financial predicament, he decided to invest the money in the church so that God will reward him with enough to solve his insolvent situation. It can be argued that sowing seed in a desperate situation is sending a strong statement of faith to God. The believer is demonstrating to God the power of his/her faith through the act of tremendous sacrifice and self-denial that might attract God's attention and compel him to intervene in the life of the believer. In another sense, seed offering is a distress call to God that is useful in finding supernatural means of solving financial problems. This is one of the reasons many members of Christ Embassy resort to seed offering in times of financial difficulties. However, Michael has not yet reaped the fruit of his seed offering; he is still waiting, believing that it will come at any moment.

Writers such as Ojo (2006) and Bonsu and Belk (2010: 1) view this kind of practice as economic imperialism that promotes materialism and emasculates the economic conditions of members. Linda van Kamp (2010) understands this kind of excessive financial sacrifice in Pentecostal churches as an expression of economic individualism and individual autonomy from the family ties promoted by the church and a break from the old order. At the same time, the new order or life promised by the church usually remained in the realm of vision and unfulfilled aspiration. There is hardly any concrete economic improvement in the lives of the members despite the enormous financial sacrifice they made to the church. Many individuals end up blaming themselves and their faith when they failed to experience economic breakthrough promised by the pastors.[10] Gifford (2015) cites similar examples to critique some scholars who see a close correlation between Pentecostalism and development. He argues that the enchanted religious imagination among the Pentecostals impedes development by encouraging fear and mistrust, and diminishing human responsibility and agency. Gifford is of the view that the prosperity gospel of 'covenant wealth from tithes and offerings' is the antithesis of Weber's Protestant ethic, and usually ends up serving the interest of the pastor and magnifying his personality. In my view, the belief that prosperity can be achieved without increase in economic productivity is a magical thinking. Prolonged economic deterioration, crumbling infrastructure and lack of social investments in Nigeria make the dream of prosperity gospel difficult to realize. Yet, it is the same dire economic situation that propels the growth of prosperity gospel. In this scenario, the actual beneficiaries of prosperity gospel are the people who promote it and preach it to their followers.

Sacred temporality: The spiritual significance of time in Christ Embassy

After an extended period of praise and worship song in Christ Embassy, the senior pastor, who was already onstage, remarked, 'You should remember that 2015 is the year of triumph, therefore, endeavour to emerge triumphant in all your activities this year. God has already permeated the spirit of triumph in this period, it is in the atmosphere, all you need to do is to focus your attention and capture it.' This happened during the last segment of my fieldwork in Abuja between September and October 2015. This short remark by the pastor is a routine in Christ Embassy to remind the members about the intention of God for them in that particular year and month. This is because time in Christ Embassy is more than a cognitive formula for managing and reckoning mundane human activities. Postill (2002: 1) states that calendars regulate (directly and indirectly) the daily lives of people. However, the calendar in Christ Embassy creates rhythms of aspirations that change monthly and annually. It can be argued that Christ Embassy adds spiritual meaning to the Gregorian calendar. Lesnard (2014: 46) quoted Hubert as saying,

> The institution of the calendar is intended solely, and probably not even primarily, to measure time as quantity. It does not derive from the idea of a purely quantitative time, but rather the idea of qualitative [time] that is made of discontinuous and heterogeneous parts and that invariably turns on itself. Calendars crystallize and stabilize collective rhythm and activities. Unit of time is units of measurement but of a rhythm where oscillation between alternatives periodically leads back to the similar.

In a similar vein, the spiritual significance of the calendar in Christ Embassy creates rhythms of mental activities that oscillate and change with each unit of time. In another sense, units of time such as year and month have been marked and invested with a spiritual purpose that regulates the mental and physical activities of the members. There is a belief in Christ Embassy that the Holy Spirit reveals to Pastor Chris the intention and plan of God towards his people in the beginning of each year. They also believe that the Holy Spirit reveals to Pastor Chris numerous blessings he decided to shower on believers. For instance, on 31 December 2013, during the crossover service which was broadcast live in all branches of Christ Embassy worldwide, Pastor Chris declared the year 2014 as the year of 'greatness'. During the declaration, Pastor

Chris stated the following while people were in a state of elation, shouting and jumping in the church:

> I have this message for you from God. This day which begins this year, and therefore, this year 2014, the Lord will begin to magnify you in the sight of others, and they will look at you and wonder, who are these people? They will say, these are they that are filled with the Holy Ghost, these are they that are working in the light of God, and manifesting the victory of Christ … these are the chosen generation the royal priesthood, the peculiar people. Finally, God has said 2014 is the year of 'greatness'.

Then the shouting increased tremendously and immediately the pastor declared the spiritual theme of the year. The year of greatness required believers to change their mindset and think big in whatever they do. They should aim for great things and do great things and hold the mental picture of great dreams. In church services throughout 2014, pastors encourage members to repeat the words 'I am great' silently in their heart throughout the year and see greatness in all the people they encounter. This is because it was the intention of God to make people achieve great things in 2014. Furthermore, in the first Sunday of each month during the celebration of the Holy Communion, Pastor Chris reveals what he claims to be a message from the Holy Spirit regarding the spiritual theme of the month. Pastor Chris claims that God designates each month with a particular priority that he wants believers to focus their attention on, similar to the New Year. Below are the complete spiritual designations of the months of 2014 as declared by Pastor Chris during the Holy Communion services:

January: month of greatness
February: month of consolation
March: month of placement
April: month of laughter
May: month of open doors
June: month of prayers
July: month of visions
August: month of grace
September: more grace
October: month of supernatural help
November: month of strengthening
December: month of thanksgiving

In each worship service of the church, pastors remind the congregation about the intention of God for that particular month and year. On 1 December 2013, during my first visit to Christ Embassy, I saw a big screen above the altar of the church, and it contained the caption 'December Month of Special Grace'. Before the pastor commenced preaching, he stated, 'Remember that this is the month of special grace. Take this extraordinary opportunity provided by the Holy Spirit. I urge you to immerse yourselves in special grace, hold it, run with it, and live with it throughout the month.' This practice creates a peculiar kind of rhythm in the lives of the members. Each year and each month people struggle to materialize a different set of purposes which they believed permeate the atmosphere of that particular period.

The perception of time in Christ Embassy integrates the spiritual and material worlds. This view diverges from the concept of time proposed by Durkheim as developed through his analysis of Aboriginal societies. Lesnard (2014: 45) quoted Durkheim suggesting that 'time in these societies is a religious symbol that bifurcates sacred from profane, forming two homogeneous, alternating periods that punctuate the aboriginal calendar'. Rather than split sacred and profane, time in Christ Embassy unites the two realms of existence, in the sense that people are required to perceive and work towards achieving spiritual purposes encapsulated in time in all their secular activities. Furthermore, members of Christ Embassy perceive time as a sacred entity that flows with a different spiritual rhythm, which provides them with particular goals that reorient their activities in order to materialize the substance of each rhythm in their lives. One of my interlocutors told me his experience as follows:

> In April 2013, which is the month of laughter, I received healing from my chronic depression. Immediately our man of God declared the month of laughter I began to laugh. I practiced laughter, and I laugh at every funny incident and joke. I also learned how to make people laugh. I focus my mind on things and situation that give me laughter. As a result, many good things happened to me, and the greatest of all my depression disappeared altogether. (13 June 2014)

This person has claimed to achieve what God intended and invested in the month of April. Through a concerted effort, he reaped the fruit of the month and recovered from severe depression that defied conventional therapy. Time in Christ Embassy is perceived to be a resource but not in the sense of its optimum utilization as captured in the famous saying – time is money – but in the ontological sense. These resources are believed to be inherently embedded in the ontology of time that can be obtained with mental reprogramming. Apparently those who do not succeed in actualizing a particular temporal potential keep quiet and rationalize their failure on their lack of effort or negative thought.

Time of divine encounter: Sunday worship service and Holy Communion services

I am from a place where I had an intimate meeting with my Lord.

These are the words of my acquaintance Constance, a twenty-eight-year-old accountant employed by a company in Abuja. It was a Sunday afternoon when I accompanied a friend of mine to Court Road when I came across Constance. Constance is a member of Christ Embassy, and she referred to Sunday worship service as 'meeting with my Lord' when I asked her where she was coming from. Sunday worship service serves different functions in the lives of the members of the church. It is a time of an intimate encounter with God through prayer and praise and worship songs as well as study of Scriptures. Sunday worship also provides members with the opportunity for learning through listening to preaching in the church. In Abuja, there are similar services in the evening of Wednesday and Friday, but Sunday service remains the primary congregation of the church.

In most of the branches in Abuja, the service begins at 9.00 am and ends at noon, but in some branches where the church buildings are not large enough to contain the crowd, the service is split into two. The first runs from 7.00 am to 9.00 am and the other from 9.15 am to noon. Some people go to church very early; they come one hour before the service and pray in tongues fervently. The Sunday service begins with an opening prayer and then continues with praise and worship songs that last for about thirty minutes. Next is the reading of the Rhapsody of Reality. One of the junior pastors reads the Rhapsody of the day and asks the congregation to recite the prayer with him/her. This is followed by a broadcast of the Atmosphere of Miracle programme or a short sermon by Pastor Chris. Then another junior pastor comes on stage to make announcements, usually about upcoming events such as seminars, conferences and meetings. The second session of worship songs commences and at the same time people who are supposed to pay their tithes go to the front to drop the envelope that contains the money. They usually kneel down and pray at the altar before they drop the money. After singing about three songs, the pastor comes onstage together with the person who carries his tablet computer. The pastor would lead the next songs for about fifteen minutes, then he stops and preaches for about forty minutes. After the preaching, he welcomes the newcomers and asks them to follow the ushers who take them to the head of Department for the Foundation School. There is also a session for giving testimony where some members come onstage to testify about a miracle or blessing they claimed to have received from God.[11] Then the choir comes to the stage again for the final songs. The service ends with sharing the grace prayer which is uttered as follows: 'May the grace of our Lord Jesus Christ, and the love of God, and the fellowship of the Holy Spirit be with us all, now and ever more. Amen.'[12]

The Holy Communion (also called Eucharist or Lord's Supper) is a ritual practice to celebrate and re-enact the Last Supper of Jesus Christ.[13] Christians believe that Jesus instituted this practice when he told his disciples to eat the broken bread and drink the wine so they keep his memory. He referred to the bread as his body and wine as his blood. During the Holy Communion celebration, Christ Embassy celebrates and remembers the sacrificial death of Christ on the cross. I attended one of the Holy Communion services of Christ Embassy. Like all the major events and rituals of Christ Embassy, the Holy Communion is celebrated worldwide, with Pastor Chris leading the event in the church headquarters in Lagos. All branches of Christ Embassy transmit the service via live streaming in their virtual church service. Members also start fasting a night before the day of the communion and break the fast with eating of the bread and wine of the Eucharist.

After almost two hours of devotional worship songs, Pastor Chris appeared and joined the singing. Then he began to preach for nearly an hour about the importance of worship and identity of Jesus Christ. He recited many verses that reaffirmed the divine nature of Christ. He also cited many Old Testament verses that talked about the coming Messiah. When the time of the communion came, he went to the backstage and reappeared in priestly attire similar to a Roman Catholic liturgical vestment with two crosses on the breast. When he took the bread, he said that this communion can be taken only by born-again people. If anyone knows that he or she is not born-again, he or she should immediately drop the bread. He continues that the reason he said this is that Holy Communion is reaffirmation of one's acceptance of faith in the death and resurrection of Christ. He commanded all the people who joined the service to repeat the prayer he recited before they ate the bread. After eating and drinking of bread and wine, he announced the end of the Holy Communion. He finished the service with the announcement of the revelation he claimed to receive from the Holy Spirit about the promises of God in the coming period and the spiritual theme of the month. According to my interlocutor, eating the bread and drinking the wine of the Holy Communion connects people with the death of Christ. He said when disciples of Jesus broke and ate the bread and drank the wine, they represent all humanity and fulfilled the significance of Jesus' atonement death.

Miraculous healing performance

Miraculous healing plays a crucial role in Christ Embassy. A substantial segment of the church's theology is related to the issue of miraculous healing. According to Pastor Chris, a miracle is an inexplicable intervention by a supernatural power in the natural affairs of man. A miracle is something beyond the ordinary course of events. Usually, miracles are current events or happenings because they produce happy and fulfilling results. Miracle interrupts the normal sequence of events or regular habits of man (Daily Champion 2005: 1).

Pastor Chris built his pastoral career as a miracle worker. Many people are attracted to Christ Embassy in search of a miracle. And many claimed to have been healed by Pastor Chris. Scholars interpret charismatic Pentecostal healing in different ways. Jörg Stolz (2011: 4) summarizes how some anthropologists, such as Dow (1986), Csordas (1988, 2002), Geertz (1993) and Laurent (2001), interpret alternative healing, which includes Pentecostal miracle performances. According to Stolz, these anthropologists see alternative healing as a means of curing the 'selves' through 'symbolic manipulation'. This means illness in the framework of a given symbol system. Through some forms of rituals, the healers convince patients to change the meaning of their illness. As a result, meaningless pain is metamorphosed into a manageable burden. The ritual performances also empowered the patients and helped them feel capable of overcoming their malady. The patients may further become integrated into the religious groups of the healer, a process that might equip them with social capital. These procedures may help the patients feel relieved or eliminate their sickness. Furthermore, Stolz (2011: 1) argued that some 'social techniques' (e.g. suggestion, rhythm, music), context factors (e.g. audience size and beliefs) and causal mechanisms (e.g. probability-, latency- and selection effects) are combined in an ingenious way to produce miracles and healings. In this section, both these two approaches to the understanding of Pentecostal miracle healing will be applied in the analysis of the healing performances of Christ Embassy.

There are three ways through which Pastor Chris performs healing miracles. Christ Embassy operates a healing programme called Healing School Ministry.

The school events are held in Lagos, Johannesburg, Charlotte, Essex and Toronto. If a believer has a sickness that defies conventional medicine, he/she can apply and register online to attend the Healing School. The programme runs for two weeks and within this period, the patients are drilled on the Christ Embassy's principles of faith healing. On the final day of the exercise, a church service is organized where the miracle seekers line up in the front of the church carrying a placard that describes their health condition. Then Pastor Chris appears and begins to blow his breath in their faces, and immediately they fall to the ground. The blast of breath signifies life-given breath of God. Many report healing during the last sessions. Oyakhilome (2001: 8) claims that through the Healing School 'blind receive sight, the lame walk, the deaf hear, the dumb speak, and all manner of sicknesses, diseases and infirmities are destroyed'. Pastor Chris claims to heal all types of illness, including HIV and AIDS. This claim of miraculous healing of HIV/AIDS causes a lot of uproar in the media. Many people criticized the pastor and urged him to desist from this claim. Some call for government intervention on miracle workers who claimed to heal HIV.

Each Healing School service is recorded and broadcast in the satellite television programme of the church titled Atmosphere of Miracle.[14] In the programme, the host interviews healing seekers before they enrol in the Healing School. He asks them to describe the illness that makes them seek miracle healing from Pastor Chris. The clip of the programme shows the same person during the healing service. The next interview is after the person received healing and offers thanks to Pastor Chris for receiving miraculous healing through him. This programme is played during Sunday worship in Christ Embassy in all the branches of the church worldwide. The worshippers yell and clap to Pastor Chris when the miracle seekers yell and jump to express gratitude for the healing.

Another important miracle healing performance of Christ Embassy occurs during the Night of Bliss crusade. Night of Bliss is an annual spectacular religious service organized by the church. It is different from normal or regular church service because it is a public spectacle event that is attended by thousands of people. People from all over the country, both members and non-members of Christ Embassy, attend the Night of Bliss crusade. Night of Bliss consists of three episodes of hyper-emotionally charged religious performances. These are worship songs performances by the crowd, followed by fiery preaching and miracle healing by Pastor Chris. The event is rotated between cities in different countries. I have met many members in Abuja who attended Night of Bliss in different cities at different times. It is common to see people throwing away their wheelchairs and crutches during Pastor Chris's miracle performances. Many people claimed that Jesus healed them through Pastor Chris. It can be suggested that the first step in understanding the healing practices of Pastor Chris is to look at his theological understanding of disease. It is through his theology of disease that Pastor Chris's reinterpretation of the meaning of sickness comes to light.

According to Pastor Chris, in the book of Exodus 23:25 God made a promise to the people of Old Testament that if they obey his commandments and worship him, he would not afflict them with any disease. Pastor Chris (2001: 17) argues, 'people of the Old Testament were given the gift of health based on certain practices of worship and obedience, but Christians receive health on the condition of faith alone'. In this viewpoint, a Christian is not supposed to be sick. If sickness attacks one, it means there is a problem with one's faith. Pastor Chris teaches that diseases do not come from God because only good and perfect gifts come from God. God could not cripple and destroy his beloved children through sickness. But the question is, where does the disease come from? According to Pastor Chris, sickness descended into the world through the fall of man in the Garden of Eden as a consequence of deception by Satan. The fall of man caused spiritual death and severed man's fellowship with God. Spiritual death came with its companion, which is sickness. Moreover, Pastor Chris suggests that Satan is also behind the danger of pathogenic microorganisms – such as viruses, bacteria, insects and animals – that harm or kill human beings. He elaborates as follows:

> God made all insects to suck nectar, and bacteria and viruses were not made to bring sickness to anybody. But after the fall of man, when the devil stole man's dominion, he infused them with death – which is his life. That is the reason they harm those that are under his power till today. (2001: 17)

In this theology, Satan is behind all afflictions since he engineered the downfall of Adam and Eve that precipitated the advent of disease and went ahead to genetically re-engineer some creatures and infuse them with poison that is fatal to human beings. The last sentence of Pastor Chris implies that victims of a virus attack or even snake bites are living under the dominion of the devil. Their faith is weak. That is the reason for becoming victims of an attack by dangerous creatures.[15]

Pastor Chris redefined the concept of disease by attributing sickness to the actions of the devil. Since the devil inflicts diseases on human beings, Pastor Chris provides a teaching that empowers believers with tools of managing the devil themselves. Pastor Chris proposes that the death of Jesus on the cross has vanquished the devil, who introduced sin and sickness into the world. Jesus has restored fellowship with God and people's dominion over all creatures in the world, including disease. Jesus has reinstated life, which was lost through the sin of Adam and Eve, which paved the way for incipient death. Moreover, incipient death is the cause of all kinds of disease (2001: 149). Here the disease has become more manageable when the devil is tamed through faith in Christ. Equipped with these ideas, it is easy for patients who participate in the Healing School or miracle crusade to feel relieved from their afflictions during the healing session. This is even easier since as man of God, Pastor Chris is perceived as possessing more power to handle the devil.

Moreover, the social techniques highlighted by Stolz further facilitate the healing process. The miracle performance of Christ Embassy is set in a huge gathering. Millions of people throng the Night of Bliss spectacle. The final process in the Healing School, during which the miracle takes place, is also organized as a huge church service with a large number of participants. The huge crowd and loud music that engulf the site generate the significant affect and emotion that overwhelms the pain experienced by the patients. During the healing session Pastor Chris repeats, 'You are healed, miracle is taking place here.' Patients accept these remarks and convince themselves that the miracle is taking place in their bodies. Most people who attend healing services already go with the mindset that they would receive healing from God through the medium of Pastor Chris. Christ Embassy's stance towards biomedicine is ambivalent. The church does not reject it openly but they are always reiterating that if one has faith, one does not need biomedicine. So, it is a tacit rejection. Failure of faith healing is always explained as lack of sufficient faith on the side of those receiving.

Despite the highly publicized miraculous power of Pastor Chris and voices of the people who were healed from the media of Christ Embassy, there still exist the silent voices of individuals who did not receive the miracle healing. I met Winifred Elaigwu, who recounted to me her story:

> I was working as an accountant with an NGO that deals with the issues of good government, conflict, and economic empowerment. One day I woke up with a pain in my hips. Gradually the pain increased until I found it difficult to walk without help. I was taken to a clinic and admitted for two weeks, but without any improvement. I was constantly in pain, and it had become unbearable. A friend of mine told me that Pastor Chris is coming for healing crusade. I asked my aunt to take me to the crusade which was organised in a stadium. My aunt and my colleague from the NGO where I work took me to the crusade. I was brought to

the front, and Pastor Chris prayed for us. He kept on telling the devil of sickness to vacate our bodies, but nothing happened to me. To cut the story short my problem became worse because I was trampled and squeezed in the huge crowd of people. (Interview, 5 January 2014, Abuja)

A friend of Winifred, Constance Enaifoge, told me that Winifred was taken to a healing home run by a traditional healer in Nasarawa State. But her condition deteriorated after some weeks and she passed away at the healing home. The church did not care to follow up on the health conditions of people who seek healing from them or even those who claimed to be healed. There are many people like Winifred, but they do not go and give testimony on the stage. Only the persons who claimed to receive healing are allowed onstage. I even met a young woman whose leg was damaged as a result of an accident, and when she was taken to the healing crusade, the officials and ushers refused to allow her to go to the front. The rejection of people with visible health problems such as injury poses a question mark on the healing power of Pastor Chris.

The 'Atmosphere of Miracle' is a carefully recorded film with state-of-the-art equipment. The programme is also carefully edited to give the impression that Pastor Chris heals everybody he touches. For maximum effect, the programme is saturated with loud background music and sophisticated editing. The editing removed any instance of failure, such as the case of the lady I mentioned above. However, due to the secrecy and suspiciousness of outsiders, the technical crews of the church do not want to reveal the details of how they construct the programme. A former member of the church told me that he took his father, who had a serious injury as a result of a car accident, to the healing crusade in Abuja, but the officials refused him access to the stage. The absence of such people on the programme means that those who are intended to be visible are carefully selected.

There are people who are riddled with doubt and other forms of discontent, but the church does not provide avenues for such people to articulate their disapproval. Such people express their discontent among their circle of friends and some of them leave the church if they fail to resolve their doubt or discontentment. Dissenting voices are not given avenue to express their view publicly in the church. Usually dissidents in Christ Embassy opted to quietly disaffiliate and move to another church. In addition, grudges, quibbles and rivalries between members, particularly office holders, also take place. These things exist but hardly are they allowed to come to the surface and destabilize the institutions of the church.

Conclusion

During one of the foundation class sessions I witnessed an instructor who asked a young newcomer whether he wanted to be born-again. When the young man replied in the affirmative, the instructor laid his hand on the newcomer's head and said, 'Repeat this prayer after me.' After the conclusion of the prayer, he said,

> You are now a new creation. A born again Christian is a new creation. He or she is one who never existed or pre-existed, altogether a new man or woman, with a new kind of life and this life comes directly from God. Your past does not exist anymore. You are as pure as white paper before God. All the sins you have committed in the past has been forgiven.

This idea of 'new in Creation' which Pastor Chris justified from the Scripture is central to the church's theology and it is also behind the radical individualism in Christ Embassy. The concept of a 'new creation' comes in line with what Meyer (1998) describes as 'making a complete brake with the past' in the discourse of Pentecostals in Ghana. Moreover, the self-image of modernity projected by Christ Embassy is embedded in this idea of new creation (breaking with the past) and individualism. New creation implies breaking with the perceived shackles of the traditional past that a believer left behind as well as previous limitations of the old personality. Christ Embassy promises new life to the individual believer that is beyond the constraints of economic, cultural and political realities. There is a connection between the 'new' and the 'modern' in Christ Embassy. When a believer emerges as a 'new creation', he/she has been emancipated from the past and is ready to move into the future, which is clearly the prosperous lifestyle of consumption promised by the neoliberal economic imagination. The church conceived the newly born-again believer as an independent, modern individual who is free from sin and disease and has full responsibility in his/her life. The flamboyant lifestyle of Pastor Chris and his associate pastors reinforces and sustains the hope of their members in achieving the envisioned modern life they believe is their right in Christ.

However, in my observation the techniques of prayer and principles of faith and other practices encouraged by the church as the basis of realizing the vision of perfect new life do not always yield results. The money that members often invest in the church as a seed offering, in order to reap in multiple fold in the future, does not necessarily improve the financial condition of believers, and the faith healing of the church, as I have shown earlier, is mostly symbolic. Some people left Christ Embassy when their expectation failed to materialize after an extended period of time and moved to another Pentecostal church. I also met some people who left Christ Embassy because they became dissatisfied with some of the teachings and practices, particularly methods of raising money. However, many people stay in the church and continue with the hope of realizing the vision of the new life.

The spectacular worship service and prayers of the church and the exhilarating preaching of Pastor Chris prove to be attractive to many urban youths in Abuja. Many members in the church claim to have found truth and meaning in their lives through participating in worship services and the prayers that provide immediate experience with the Holy Spirit. Like other Pentecostal churches in the country, a variety of youth programmes attract a considerable number of young people to the church. The programmes provide the youths with social space to meet and interact in the extra-church activities that create bonding and opportunity for meeting life partners.

Members of Christ Embassy see themselves as ambassadors of Christ in this world. As ambassadors, they often say that their vision is to win souls, build them and send them. And they also want to take the manifest presence of Jesus Christ to the people of the world with signs, wonders and miracles via the agency of the Holy Spirit and the word of God. This drive to evangelize the world as well as the great ambition of Pastor Chris transformed Christ Embassy into a truly global church with hundreds of international branches. The church employs modern digital media, including satellite broadcasting and the internet, to propel itself into the global arena. This confirms Afe Adogame's point (2011) that Pentecostalism is an integral part of the globalization process, as well as a product or consequence of it. This global outreach of Christ Embassy could also be partly explained by how the church is run as an efficient business enterprise with motivational regimes that optimized productivity of the members who are part of the bureaucracy of the church. The success of Christ Embassy in achieving large-scale national and international outreach and its effective use of new media certainly extend the influence of the church to the wider Nigerian public. Christ Embassy is unique, somehow, and enigmatic among Nigerian mega-churches. The church apparently achieved a remarkable success in terms of membership, generating revenue, social visibility and media use as well as spread in certain parts of the world. However, the church seems to fail in delivering the promise of health and material bounty to some of its members. Christ Embassy is a sacred corporation that dispenses sacred bounds, but the most important target clients and customers are not the sick or poor but the healthy and rich or aspirant rich.[16]

The influence of Christ Embassy and other successful Pentecostal churches on the Nigerian public sphere is not limited to non-Pentecostal Christians but also pertains to Muslim communities. The next chapter will demonstrate how NASFAT responds to the domination of the public sphere by Pentecostalism in the country.

NASFAT: Pentecostalizing Islam

Introduction

In October 2013, I met the chief imam[1] of NASFAT Abuja central branch and after a long conversation with him, he told me that one of the pioneers of NASFAT and national chairman board of trustees (BOT), Alhaji Ganiyu Majeed,[2] was residing in Abuja. The chief imam connected me with Ganiyu Majeed, who agreed to meet me in the evening of the next day at the Islamic centre. When I arrived at the centre in the evening, Majeed gave me a warm reception and I noticed that he was a humble and easy-going person. Majeed told me that one of the most important reasons for the establishment of NASFAT was due to the challenges posed by Pentecostalism on Muslim communities in the south-west. Majeed continued,

> In the circle of young Muslim professionals we noticed lukewarm attitude toward Islamic practices. While at the same time we have been seeing Pentecostals with aggressive energy and dynamism flourishing throughout the country. To our most dismay we found out that many young Muslims are attracted by these Pentecostals. Many Muslims watch their activities on television, some attend their crusades and some even convert to Christianity. I and my friends we decided to launch an Islamic organisation that could revitalise Islam in the region and arrest the attraction of the young Muslims toward Pentecostalism. Within short a period, NASFAT has achieved great success. Our *Asalatu* programme [Sunday worship] has played a vital role in revitalising the spirit of Islam in the south-west and other parts of the country. Many people now are experiencing spiritual rejuvenation through participating in NASFAT programmes. As a result, the organisation is growing and expanding on daily basis. (Interview, 4 November 2013)

Given the words of Majeed, it is apparent that NASFAT has been established with the Pentecostals in mind. The activities of Pentecostals have repercussions on Muslim communities that elicited reactions which led to the rise of NASFAT and other similar groups. This is because the complex ecology of religious belonging in Nigerian urban spaces has generated mutual influences, borrowing, as well as clash and tension. This chapter argues that the pre-eminence of NASFAT hinges on its ability of consciously negotiated borrowing of the forms of Pentecostal practices. As a result, NASFAT provides spectacular religious practices and socio-economic services that respond to the emotional and social needs of urban Muslims. Where applicable the chapter will examine the influences of Pentecostals in some practices of NASFAT as well as similarities and differences in some activities between NASFAT and Christ Embassy. However, the comparison between Christ Embassy and NASFAT does not assume equal terms. This is because NASFAT, in order to avoid the loss of young people to the Pentecostals, accommodates Pentecostal forms to a much larger extent than Pentecostals adopt Islamic elements. In fact, there is a Pentecostal hegemony in the public sphere of the city of Abuja.

Historical background of NASFAT

When I asked Majeed about the origin of NASFAT he stated that NASFAT is an acronym of the Arabic phrase, Nasrul-Lahi-li-Fathi, translated as 'there is no help except from Allah'.[3] He continued that in March 1995 he and seven of his colleagues decided to initiate a prayer fellowship[4] in his sitting room in Lagos. He said that other colleagues also became interested and joined the prayer. Gradually the number increased to the extent that his living room could not contain them. The number of those attending increased progressively over a short period. The group moved its prayer headquarters first to the old secretariat mosque of the Lagos State government, and later, due to the phenomenal increase in attendance, to the new secretariat mosque where it now meets every Sunday between 8.00 am and noon. At a certain point, the leadership decided to expand the fellowship and the first branch of NASFAT outside Lagos was established in Offa, Kwara State. The reason for creating the Offa branch was that some of the founding members who were working with the Polytechnic in Offa had to commute to Lagos every Sunday for the prayer. Due to the risk of travelling on Nigerian roads, these members were permitted to form the Offa branch. From one branch in Lagos in 1995, NASFAT now has about 290 branches worldwide (Bello 2013: 2).

However, Majeed did not tell me about the roots of NASFAT in the Yusrullah prayer group in Ibadan. But, when I asked Mustapha Bello, the deputy national secretary of NASFAT, he told me that NASFAT founders were all members of Yusrullah before the year 1995. One of the reasons for the formation of NASFAT was the inconvenience of travelling to Ibadan every week for collective prayer. Adetona (2012) outlines this early beginning and he suggests that the desire to create a new Islamic identity among the elites and the agenda for salvation and prosperity led Alhaji Murtada Akangbe to initiate a prayer group for Muslim professionals in July 1984. The prayer was taking place in the house of Sheikh Akangbe in Ibadan who at the time was working with Wema Bank in the city. This group became successful to the extent that it attracted a considerable number of people from as far as neighbouring states such as Lagos, Ogun and Osun. As the membership continued to grow, the leadership decided to expand the branches to other cities so that people could pray at the centres close to where they live.

According to Adetona (2012), when Lagos-based members of Yusrullah formed NASFAT in 1995, the new society achieved phenomenal success beyond the expectation of the founders. In less than four years, its membership strength had surpassed 1 million, and it established branches beyond the south-western states of Nigeria. In Lagos alone, it has branches in all the local government areas, and each of these branches also records a very high turnout, without affecting the activities of the central prayer meeting at the new secretariat mosque. The first missionary and spiritual head of the group is Sheikh Mun'im Taiwo Tijani.

Abuja zone is one of the most important zones in the country due to its size and the calibre of its members.[5] The zone has six branches that include the central branch in Utako in the city centre, Karu branch, Dutsen Alhaji branch, Nyanya branch, Kubwa branch and Gwagwalada branch. Based on the information I gathered from the administrative secretary and Ganiyu Majeed and the secretary of the youth wing, NASFAT in Abuja started on 29 October 2000 at plot 720 Panama Close, off IBB Road, at Maitama, the residence of the NASFAT BOT Chairman, Ganiyu Majeed, with about seven members in attendance. Within a few months the venue was shifted to the residence of the chairman of Abuja NASFAT, Lanre Ipinmisho. The venue was relocated again to the Tofa House premises at the Central Business District. As a result of the immense growth in membership, the Tofa House could not contain the worshippers and so the decision was reached to move to the National Mosque of Abuja.[6] The NASFAT Abuja zone was inaugurated on Saturday, 27 September

2001. The event marked a turning point for NASFAT as Muslims from all ethnic groups trooped en masse to embrace the society.

In May 2007, NASFAT bought plot 313 in Utako District measuring 7,153.02 square metres from the Federal Capital Development Authority (FCDA) in order to develop an Islamic centre. NASFAT engaged some architects in the city to design the centre. The drawings specified the mosque, an Islamic school, offices, an ablution area, a generator house and a security post. The architectural design was submitted for approval to the Department of Development Control in October that year. Having secured the necessary approval from the Abuja Development Control, construction work on phase one, the main mosque building, commenced in 2008. The building has three floors, with a gross floor area of 4,272 square metres and a seating capacity of about 5,000 worshippers. The ground floor was designed to accommodate the male congregation, the first floor for the female congregation, while the third floor is the conference hall with a capacity of 1,500 people. During the development of the mosque, construction workers with high expertise were employed, quality materials were used and experienced professionals were engaged to supervise the project.

The Zonal Board formed a mosque completion committee that was headed by former NASFAT Chairman Tosho Y. Alabi. The committee then embarked on fundraising to commence the project. Several members of Abuja zone donated substantial amounts for the project. The Zonal Board also asked the committee to start collecting voluntary donations from members every week after the *Asalatu* prayer on Sundays for the mosque project. Since an enormous sum of money is required to build a two-storey building in Abuja, the committee sought funds from Muslim politicians in Abuja and beyond. Among the politicians that contributed significantly were the governor of Nasarawa State Umar Tanko Almakura, the governor of Osun State Rauf Aregbesola, who is an active member of NASFAT, and the former governor of Lagos Raji Fasola, who is the current Federal Minister of Power, Housing and Works. Despite their donations, the mosque was not completed until 2016, when it was commissioned by the Sultan of Sokoto Muhammadu Sa'ad Abubakar in a big ceremony. Currently, the project has cost 180,000,000 naira (379,507 euro).

Organizational structure and membership

On a warm Monday morning in early November 2013, I visited the office of the administrative secretary of NASFAT. The office is located adjacent to the mosque

Figure 3.1 NASFAT Central Mosque, Abuja. Source: Author.

inside the premises of the NASFAT Islamic centre. Prior to this visit I met the secretary on Sunday and asked for an audience with him. He said I should come on Monday in the morning. I entered the office, and the first room was a reception area where I saw two women working, who told me that the secretary was waiting for me inside. I entered and met the secretary in his cosy and neat office. The office is well-furnished with a desk, chairs and file cabinet. I saw stacks of files on his table and on top of the cabinet. The secretary told me that he runs most of the activities of the organization under the supervision of the zonal chairman and zonal executive council (ZEC). When I asked him about the objectives of NASFAT administration, he replied,

> NASFAT want to create an efficient administrative system to run the organisation in such a way that it will become a model for other Muslim groups. The main reason for the efficiency of NASFAT administration is because the founders and present leadership are from professional backgrounds. There are many bankers and civil servants from executive and managerial cadres. NASFAT benefited from the knowledge, skill, and experiences of these people in building strong and efficient administrative system. We want to make NASFAT more efficient than Pentecostal churches. (Interview, 5 January 2014)

The end of the secretary's remarks indicates that NASFAT is keenly conscious of Pentecostals and their activities. This conscious awareness of Pentecostals was encapsulated in the expression of the desire to outsmart them in the game of efficiency. The secretary further indicated that since NASFAT has grown and expanded, there is need for better management coupled with dedication and hard work to make it run smoothly. He affirmed that bad management can affect the entire edifice of NASFAT and it may even affect the religious programmes which form the core of NASFAT activities. The secretary referred me to the NASFAT constitution for detailed explanation on how NASFAT is organized and the distribution of powers within the organization.

NASFAT is organized into four levels: international, national, zonal and local branches. There are international branches in West Africa, Europe and North America. The structure of control of NASFAT includes the BOT, the management council, the spiritual[7] (religious) council and the advisory council. NASFAT's constitution states that the BOT shall be the highest organ of the organization. Some of the essential functions of BOT at each level of the organization include acting as the custodian of the values, ethics and philosophy of NASFAT (NASFAT Constitution 2007). According to the constitution, the management council of NASFAT includes the following organs: the national executive council (NEC), ZEC and the branch executive council (BEC). The advisory council of NASFAT consists of the national council of elders (NCOE), and their counterparts in the zones and branches. The constitution emphasizes that the mission board should work towards the realization of the aims and objectives of NASFAT and provide guidance on all religious matters as it relates to the organization. The national mission board in collaboration with the education committee designs Islamic and Arabic education programmes for the general members of the organization (NASFAT Constitution 2007).

The administrative secretary told me that active participation in NASFAT required formal membership. The organization has laid down procedures for a membership application. The secretary said one can join religious programmes of the organization without being a member, but one could not gain a membership card and could not enjoy certain benefits that are restricted to only registered members. The benefits include special financial assistance or job opportunity where members are considered first. He continued that membership requires payment of a monthly fee. He said NASFAT is open to all Muslims from all parts of the world who share the aims and objectives of the society and have agreed to be bound by the provisions of its constitution.[8]

A prospective member is required to obtain a registration form after the payment of a prescribed fee. The applicant has to be sponsored by at least two active, registered members and must have attended at least five *Asalatu* (worship service) sessions before his/her application is considered. The zonal chairman is in charge of making sure that members abide by the rules of the organization, including membership.

It is apparent that educated professional elites such as medical doctors, lawyers, bankers and top-ranking civil servants form a significant portion of NASFAT's membership, especially in Abuja branches. It is important to notice that NASFAT was founded by middle-class professionals who wanted to provide a forum where professionals could engage in Islamic fellowship. Musa Adeniyi (2013: 326) describes a situation during the early period of NASFAT where the leadership deliberately made an attempt to attract Muslim professionals and the middle class. He stated that some members were given a target of numbers of bankers, academics and medical doctors they were expected to attract to NASFAT. However, as the society grew and membership expanded to hundreds of thousands, it can be safely affirmed that people of lower class background constitute the majority. Most of the present leadership of the organization is still dominated by the upwardly mobile professional class.[9] The current national president of the organization was an engineer and former director general of the National Television Authority (NTA). The national education secretary of the organization is a permanent secretary at the Federal Ministry of Education. The zonal chairman of Abuja is S. O. Q. Giwa, an attorney, who runs an influential law chamber in Abuja.

Even though NASFAT has spread to most of the urban centres in Nigeria, membership in the group among the ethnic Hausa population is minimal. This lack of acceptability may be informed by different religious cultures between Yoruba and Hausa Muslims. Yoruba Muslims developed denomination-like organizations (such as Ansar-Ud-Deen, Nurudeen and Nawaruddeen) that were formed in response to the Christian missionaries in the early twentieth century. Many Yoruba Muslims identified with one of these groups, worship in their mosques and participate in their social programmes. However, these organizations are non-sectarian and non-ideological in nature. NASFAT followed the example of these older Islamic groups but added some elements to respond to Pentecostalism. Lack of development of such denomination-like religious organizations among Hausa Muslims in the north, coupled with linguistic and cultural barriers, restrict Hausa membership in Yoruba Muslims organizations, including NASFAT.

Engaging with the 'other' in NASFAT

NASFAT expresses great concern about Muslim–Christian relationships and perceives Christians as closer to Muslims in theology and world view than African Traditional Religions. NASFAT's chief imam during Sunday preaching stated, 'Christians are not infidels; they are people of the book. Christians are close to Muslims because they believed in the past revealed Scriptures and prophets.' This idea of Christians as people of the book elevates the status of Christians among the members of NASFAT. Moreover, NASFAT is making a concerted effort to improve Muslim–Christian relations in the country through interfaith programmes. As part of its numerous interfaith programmes for peaceful coexistence, NASFAT organized a joint action initiative called 'Walk for Religious Harmony' in 2015. Churches such as the Redeemed Christian Church of God, Foursquare Gospel Church, Christ Embassy and Newborn Apostolic Church and other churches are invited from time to time, particularly in Abuja and Lagos, to send their members to walk with Muslims for about one hour while having informal conversations. It is believed that this kind of activity would enhance mutual understanding among diverse religious communities. On fostering peaceful coexistence among followers of other faiths, NASFAT president, Bolarinwa (Adeyeri 2016:1), said,

> Peace is achieved through promoting understanding of one another. And if you are a true Muslim with proper understanding of the Holy Quran, you have no reason not to respect, for instance, Prophet Isa [Jesus] because he is a prophet of God, you must respect the Bible as a Muslim, and most importantly, our religion enjoins us to love our neighbours, to be at peace with our neighbours. And that we have successfully preached to our members, so, anywhere, our members are of best behaviour, because they live the saying of the Prophet [SAW] that the best among you is one with the best conduct. This concept is even reflected in the motto of the society, and that is why we are what we are. (*The Guardian* 2016)

NASFAT leaders always remind Muslims that Jesus Christ, who is the central figure in Christianity, is one of the great prophets of Islam. The leaders see this as a strategy to create a positive link between the two religious communities. The leaders hope that through respecting Jesus Christ, Muslims would extend that respect to Christians. They remind Christians that Muslims respect their saviour; as a result, the leaders hope that Christians would respect Muslims in return. The positive responses from the Christians indicate that this initiative has achieved relative success. I talked to some young Christians who participated in the walk and they said that it had opened up their mind and drastically reduced their bias towards Muslims.

The assistant national secretary for the youth wing, who resides in Abuja, related to me (interview, 10 September 2014) that the wing organizes interfaith dialogue and programmes with the Christian youths in the city. He said that most religious conflicts in the country involved youths. Therefore, it is imperative to encourage understanding and cooperation between Muslim and Christian youths through dialogues. He continued that many sessions of such dialogues have taken place, and the success of the events in Abuja has drawn the attention of the national executive of the organization. The executive now has decided to make youth interfaith dialogue a national programme to be carried out by all the branches of NASFAT in the country.

However, NASFAT faces the same dilemma as Christ Embassy, which is the desire to proselytize while at the same time attempting to maintain a good relationship with Christian leaders. Attempts of *daʿawah* become particularly problematic when Christians are targeted by self-acclaimed Muslim Bible preachers who want to validate Islam through biblical verses. The greatest point of contention is that these preachers use the Bible to challenge the basic Christian doctrines such as Trinity and salvation through Christ.[10] NASFAT invites such preachers (a notable example is Yusuf Adepoju) regularly to preach either on Sunday or during important events to draw the attention of Christians about the truth of Islam and to further enhance the faith of Muslims. The polemic preaching and debates of Yusuf Adepoju and Zakir Naik are reproduced and distributed in both audio and video formats on Sundays in the NASFAT Islamic centre. These preachers use what Martha Frederiks (2010: 267) refers to as 'vicious polemic' to argue their case against Christians. Frederiks also notes that these preachers are influenced by the famous South African Muslim polemicist Ahmed Deedat, who debated many Christian evangelists in the 1980s and 1990s. Many Christians who come across such a form of preaching perceive it as an attack against their faith. A thirty-four-year-old male Christian who is self-employed in Abuja told me that such preachers, particularly Yusuf Adepoju and even Ahmed Deedat, do not have proper understanding of the Bible and the knowledge of biblical hermeneutics and exegesis.

The desire on the part of NASFAT for peaceful coexistence and *daʿawah* practice, which is regarded as religious duty, creates a dilemma which NASFAT has been unable to resolve. This is because the polemical nature of the *daʿawah* is often interpreted by Christians as distorting their Holy Scripture to fit the Muslims' proselytizing agenda. Some Pentecostals, particularly members of

Christ Embassy whom I interviewed, harboured suspicions about some NASFAT joint action initiatives as part of the hidden *da'awah* agenda. However, this dilemma of the intersection between evangelism and coexistence also occurs in Christ Embassy. As I show in Chapter 6, some pastors of the church cast Islam in a negative light.

NASFAT differs from other Islamic movements in its goals, orientation and practices. However, despite their differences, NASFAT leadership does not oppose or condemn other Islamic organizations. NASFAT differs from Sufi groups in the sense that it does not approve the religious hierarchy prevalent among the Sufis, hence its emphasis on equality among Muslims (Soares 2009). NASFAT diverged from Islamic reformists because its overall vision is not to reform Islam from impurities or innovations or even return Muslims to the pristine form of Islam that was practised by the Prophet and his companions. Instead, the organization focuses more on reinvigorating the practice of Islam, making it compatible with modern life and protecting Muslims from what they perceive as an external threat from Pentecostalism. Furthermore, leaders of NASFAT attempt to negotiate how to be a pious Muslim in a neoliberal urban setting. This situation is similar to the finding of Marloes Janson (2014) about the processes of renegotiating Muslim identity among Tablighi Muslim youths in Gambia and their struggle to reconcile faith with a modern lifestyle.

It is part of the policy of NASFAT to foster a good relationship with other Islamic organizations. In the do's and don'ts of NASFAT and the shared values of the organization, promotion of brotherhood and equality of all Muslims have utmost importance. The NASFAT president had this to say on this issue:

> We are always in touch with [Islamic organisations], and there is something that was formed recently in the South-West – the Muslim Umma of South-Western Nigeria. It is just a group made up of all the Islamic groups in South-Western Nigeria to bridge the gap between them and the Supreme Council for Islamic Affairs so that things will run smoothly and there will be no issues with the people of Northern Nigeria. Apart from that, anything any Islamic organisation wants to do, NASFAT will be there in so far as we are invited. We know, and they also know that as far as the South-West is concerned, if not Nigeria today, you cannot just say you are talking about Islam without NASFAT. (Orikeye 2009: 2)

It is for this reason that when NASFAT organizes events such as seminars or conferences, Muslim scholars from other organizations, including northerners, are invited to deliver lectures. In the month of Ramadan, the NASFAT Abuja zone organizes weekly lectures. Prominent Islamic scholars from all over the country are invited to deliver lectures on different aspects of Islamic topics in English.

Whenever NASFAT leaders find an opportunity to talk to the media, they always emphasize that Islam is a peaceful, tolerant religion that is compatible with modern life. It is apparent that NASFAT attempts to project an image of Islam as a modern religion that can coexist peacefully with others in the pluralist Nigerian urban environment. It is also in line with this agenda that NASFAT leaders engage in constant condemnation of terrorist activities of Boko Haram and reiterate that Islam prohibits violence against innocent, unarmed civilians. During a world press conference to mark the twenty-first anniversary of the organization, NASFAT President Abdulahi Yomi Bolarinwa lamented the adverse effect of Boko Haram on the image of Islam and failure of Muslim leaders to face the challenge of violence in the name of their religion:

> Unfortunately, Muslim leaders have not risen as one to challenge this mindset and condemn terrorism perpetrated by groups of psychopaths who masquerade as Muslims. By their deafening silence and indifference, they unwittingly create the impression of support for these terrorists. It is time for Muslims to unite in the face of this changing world that aspires to change the creed of Islam and eliminate its core values and laws. And for us at NASFAT, our 21st anniversary provides a unique opportunity for new partnerships for public enlightenment and mass education of people on what Islam actually stands for. And we wish to challenge the mass media to take up the challenge. Clearly then, a religion that places such high premium on good, orderly behaviour will not and does not approve violence. This is common knowledge. Religion doesn't promote terrorism; neither do race or ethnicity. It is people who perpetrate acts of terrorism. (Bolarinwa 2016: 1)

NASFAT's leadership expressed disappointment with the mainstream Muslim reactions to Boko Haram violence in the country. According to NASFAT, to extricate Islam from terrorist activities, all Muslim leaders need to condemn Boko Haram publicly. The leadership is not satisfied with the current condemnation of Boko Haram by the Sultan and other Islamic religious figures. In their attempt to portray Islam as a peaceful religion and dissociate it from violence, the leaders call on media to refrain from calling Boko Haram an Islamic sect. In one of his sermons during Sunday worship I attended in Abuja, Ustaz Abdul Rashid Balogun stated that every Christian is a potential Muslim; therefore, killing Christians is denying them a future opportunity of converting to Islam.

The rapid growth of NASFAT and its conspicuous presence in the public sphere have attracted the attention of other Muslim organizations, as expressed by the secretary of Nurudeen. NASFAT certainly pose a challenge to the older Islamic organizations similar to the Pentecostal challenge to historical mission churches. These older organizations feel the need to reorganize in order to stay competitive. However, in the far north Izala and *Salafi* do not show excessive concern or fear of competition with NASFAT. Sani Yusuf, a thirty-eight-year-old official of Izala, told me that NASFAT is one of the most successful Yoruba Islamic organizations to engage in charity works. The northern Islamic groups admired the social engagement of NASFAT, from charity to education and media programmes that are visible in the Nigerian public sphere. Even though there are criticisms of NASFAT for what some believed to be blind imitation of Pentecostals from different angles, particularly in the north, most of the other Islamic groups view NASFAT positively.

According to John Peel (2011) there has been an increasing search for religious authenticity and attempts by some Muslim leaders to get rid of innovations from Yoruba Islam. These attempts are spearheaded by *Salafi* groups and even the Muslim Students Society of Nigeria (MSSN). So, practices that aligned with Yoruba traditional religion are being reviled as anti-Islamic and allegedly need to be discarded. Even though NASFAT is not a *Salafi* movement, it has the attitude of demonizing the practice of divination and charms associated with traditional religion. Many aspects of traditional religion are regarded as *shirk* or polytheism by NASFAT. Therefore, indulging in some practices associated with indigenous religion is considered a grave sin against Allah.[11] NASFAT as an organization prohibits its members from dabbling with the vestiges of traditional religion. The most visible forms of vestiges of traditional religion are *babalawos* in Yorubaland and *bori* in the north among the Hausas.

The issue of dabbling in the vestiges of traditional religion is not relegated to the level of private sin against God, but it is seen as an offence against the organization. It is clearly written in the dos and don'ts of the organization that member should not engage in polytheistic practices. Despite this rule, NASFAT does not engage in policing the members concerning involvement with *babalawos*. The punishment for visiting *babalawos* is also not specified. Even though it is possible that there are members who might secretly visit such medicine men, I have not come across any evidence of this during my fieldwork period. In the view of NASFAT's leaders, traditional religion is an evil 'other' because it is based on polytheism, which is the most serious offence in Islam. They also believe that traditional religion incorporates magical practices or even deals with demons. As a result, similar to Pentecostalism, African Traditional Religion and its remnant practices are reviled and demonized thoroughly in NASFAT.

Youth, wings and the caliphate system

Youths have played a significant role in the dynamism and progress of NASFAT in recent years. As one of the most widespread Islamic religious groups in the country, NASFAT has one of the largest youth members. According to the youth secretary, the youth wing in NASFAT was developed in the year 2004 at the national headquarters in Lagos, and all the zones and branches were asked to initiate the wing. The sole purpose of establishing a youth wing is *da'wah*, or propagating the message of Islam and helping the youths to be responsible members of society.

The secretary of the youth wing in Abuja central branch told me (interview, 14 July 2014) that at the national level they organize an annual national youth conference. The conference is rotated among the zones nationwide. Each zone that intends to host the conference can apply, and the national youth secretariat assesses their capability and security of the place before issuing approval. Usually influential people are invited to the conference. For instance, at the conference that was held in Minna branch, dignitaries such as the former emir of Kano Alhaji Sanusi Lamido, emir of Bida Alhaji Yahaya Abubakar and former military head of state General Abdul Salam Abubakar were invited as guests.

In July 2015 Lai Hussein, who assisted me during my fieldwork in NASFAT, told me about the youth camp programme and advised me to attend. He told me that the programme takes place in the months of September for zones and December for branches. The camp usually is held in the secondary school during holidays, and it lasts for three days. The programmes of the camp range from preaching, teachings on Islamic tenets and doctrines, night vigil prayers, melodious recitation prayers, seminars and skill acquisition programmes. Experts and technicians who specialize in different kinds of skills are invited to teach the participants both theoretical and practical aspects of the skill. I attended the camp as part of my fieldwork. I noticed that when people registered, the officials gave them blue t-shirts with NASFAT's logo and an inscription on the back that reads, 'NASFAT Youth Camp 2015 Zuba'. And women were given a white *hijab* with a blue NASFAT logo on it.

Once one registered and had been assigned a bed, it was difficult to go out without strong reason. There were guards at the gate who made sure that the participants remained inside till the end of the programme. I observed that the officials were very strict about the observance of ritual prayer (*salat*), particularly the dawn prayer. The officials went to the hostel around 5 o'clock in the morning to wake people up. They usually shouted, 'Wake up for prayer, if you are sleeping you are wrong.' The programme ran for three days with intermittent periods for rest, recreation and socialization. I participated in a workshop on making perfume. Moreover, they also taught poultry and fish farming and different kinds of skills to help youths achieve self-reliance in their lives.

Another important programme item is the singles forum. All the participants converge in a hall and discuss the issues of life as a single, causes of late marriage and polygamy. Two assistant imams of the central branch led the programme, and I witnessed heated debate when it came to the discussion about polygamy. Most of the male participants supported it, but the female members expressed disapproval. The officiators tried to convince them to stop opposing polygamy since it is permitted by *Shari'a* and also has many advantages. The women who opposed the idea raised their hands and when given the opportunity to talk, they expressed their opinions. One of the rationales behind this forum is to create opportunity for dating between the singles that would result in marriage. The secretary told me that this arrangement was very successful because it resulted in thirty-three marriages in Utako branch alone. There is a realization among the youths that some singles came to NASFAT for the sole purpose of finding life partners.

Another subgroup is the caliphate system, which is the smallest unit of organization in the NASFAT of Abuja.[12] All the members of the branch are assigned into different groups named after the companions of Prophet Muhammad. Each group has a coordinator, secretary and treasurer. The group raises money through weekly contribution by the members. The coordinator has the comprehensive list of his members, their home addresses and personal information. The groups meet fortnightly and discuss issues related to fundraising, mutual assistance, individual problems and many other matters regarding the groups. For instance, caliphate renders financial assistance to a member for marriage, naming ceremonies, bereavement, bankruptcy and other life challenges. Group members pay courtesy visits to individuals. A member can also bring an invitation letter to his/her group during important events such as wedding or naming ceremony.

The caliphate system is similar to the cells of Christ Embassy and other Pentecostal household fellowship. As is the case with other practices, it is possible that NASFAT has borrowed this practice from the Pentecostals. Other Muslim organizations do not have this kind of system. Therefore, NASFAT did not get the idea from them. But since Muslims are exposed to Pentecostal activities and programmes and live side by side with Christians in the city as neighbours, it can be assumed that NASFAT has borrowed the idea of caliphate system from the Pentecostals.

The youth and the caliphate system bind the members together and create a cohesive religious community. These activities also exact pressure on the individual members to maintain their participation in the organization. If an individual misses the service for one day, another member asks him/her reasons for not showing up. Intensive participation in smaller group units creates double obligation for the members to uphold their loyalty to their religious organization. The first obligation is based on their personal religious commitment, beliefs and conviction, and the second rests on the desire to fulfil the expectations of their group. Since the congregation is large it might create a strong sense of social bonding, as is the case with smaller groups.

These activities provide social networking among young men and women in NASFAT. The cell activities in Christ Embassy also serve a similar function of granting an opportunity for social networking among the youths of Christ Embassy. Similar to NASFAT, the cell activities in Christ Embassy also afford the young people opportunities for dating and marriage. Both the leaders of NASFAT and Christ Embassy constantly encourage the youths to marry among their own religious groups. In both Christ Embassy and NASFAT, youths derive enormous benefits from this social networking. The group activities and interactions amplify youths' ability to share experiences and care for each other. Social networking among youths in both Christ Embassy and NASFAT gives them an opportunity to receive support from like-minded individuals, and to locate other avenues for assistance and for giving or receiving career or personal advice.

Sources of funds and social projects

Running a big organization like NASFAT requires a stable source of funds. As a result, NASFAT devises several means of getting funds for the effective running of the organization. The primary source of funds comes from monthly membership contributions. The organization also receives aid, grants, donations, *Zakat* and endowments by members and non-members. In January 2014, during Sunday service, the imam announced that a businesswoman made a donation of 1 million naira (2,108.37 euro). Since NASFAT has initiated many business ventures, the organization receives income, profit and dividend from such initiatives. Another source of revenue is sending letters of financial request to prominent businesspeople and politicians, many of whom respond positively. Through these kinds of requests, it was announced during Sunday service that the governor of Nasarawa State in 2015 donated 10 million (21,083 euro) naira to the organization.

NASFAT puts great emphasis on economic empowerment because the leadership believes that economic empowerment is imperative to spiritual development. They are of the view that ethical reform goes hand in hand with economic empowerment (Soares 2009: 193). Highly spectacular religious performances in NASFAT serve as a transforming force for individual members. However, NASFAT's piety is not a world rejecting mode of religiosity. Instead, it is highly world affirming. In fact, NASFAT's engagement with the world gives rise to numerous socio-economic programmes.

The combination of piety practices and socio-economic development initiatives makes NASFAT a formidable social force in many Nigerian urban centres. However, Christ Embassy does not emphasize socio-economic development through pragmatic social programmes. Instead, the church opts for providing mental techniques for individuals to help themselves. Even though members of Christ Embassy contribute significant money to the church, members of NASFAT benefit more from their financial donation than members of Christ Embassy. Christ Embassy's radical individualism betrays a lack of a coherent socio-political vision and socio-economic activities. The fervent obsession with individual material success and prosperity irrespective of the economic and political condition of the country makes its mode of religiosity individualistic.

Furthermore, NASFAT has given urban educated Muslims a social space to interact and acquire a new sense of belonging to a big family of spiritual community. In an environment where there is an absence of social welfare and any social safety net by the government, NASFAT provides different kinds of financial assistance to its members through the *zakat* funds. The assistance ranges from business start-up capital, scholarships and even payment of hospital bills. For this reason, Soares (2009) asserts that NASFAT is an Islamic social movement that challenges some conventional terms and categories of analysis of Islam.

Times of divine encounter: *Asalatu,* Tahajjud and Lailatul Qadr

Apart from socio-economic activities, NASFAT has introduced many structured Islamic devotional practices that are highly spiritually and emotionally appealing to urban Muslims. One of these practices is called *Asalatu* or Sunday worship service, the structure and form of which are very similar to Pentecostal Sunday worship. This service involves prayer, reading some portion of the Qur'an, Islamic teachings, preaching, prayer requests and testimonies, and announcement of job vacancies. According to Majeed (14 December 2013), one of the purposes of Sunday worship service is to keep Muslim youths busy so that they will not accompany their Christian friends to church service and to give them a forum to pray and socialize.

To give a picture of a typical Sunday *Asalatu* programme, here is a description of the one I attended on 24 November 2013: The 7,500 square metre mosque in Utako was full with worshippers and was vibrating with the loud voice of worshippers reciting the NASFAT prayer book. Similar to Christian worship, the congregants were highly excited, exhibiting a high sense of devotion as they recite the prayers. Whenever the name of Muhammad is mentioned in the prayer, their excitement would immediately heighten, and they would raise their arms in salute and respect to him. When they reached the last portion of the prayer, they repeat the name of Allah or *zikr* several times. The tempo of the sound suddenly increases, and the mosque is reverberating with the sound 'Allah, Allah, Allah' continuously for an extended period.

One of the assistant imams came forward and gave a talk about the importance of Hajj in Islam. He said some wealthy people are travelling from one place to another, but they do not bother to perform the pilgrimage. He warned these people that their struggle and money will be in vain if they refuse to go on pilgrimage. He recited many verses from Surah al-Lail that show the importance of Hajj in Islam. The next session after this short talk about the importance of the Hajj was the Qur'anic recitation. The chief imam led this session, and everyone opened their copy of the Qur'an, and as the imam recited they repeated after him. The session went on for about twenty minutes.

Next was a preaching by the chief imam which was undertaken with a loud voice and agile body language. He taught about faith in Allah and holding up to it no matter the circumstances one found oneself in, whether good or bad. Two people were behind him who recited verses for him and reiterated a particular section of the verse which the imam wanted to emphasize. He quoted a verse in the Qur'an which says, 'Those who have unwavering faith in Allah and remember Allah daily, Allah will give angels to protect them, and the angels would always tell them not to be afraid and not to be fearful.' He continued that all the wealth of this world was vanity without faith in Allah. And everything in this world is transient, and it will go back to earth. Therefore, the only significant thing in this world is faith in Allah.

After the preaching by the chief imam came the time of prayer request. One of the assistant imams moved to the podium and announced many prayer requests. He said a brother has been promoted to the level of permanent secretary by the president of the country, and he wanted the congregation to pray for him in order to succeed in his new position. The assistant imam asked the congregation to recite Surah *al kauthar* for him and led the recitation (*al kauthar* is a short chapter in the Qur'an, usually recited for success). He said another member was also promoted in her workplace and sent a prayer request for success in the new responsibilities. He continued that another brother has experienced many failed promises by his colleagues and friends; he needs prayer for Allah to compel them to fulfil their promises to him. Another brother required prayer about his current position at the recently privatized Power Holding Company of Nigeria (PHCN) because many of his colleagues were laid off after privatization. The next was the period of an announcement. The man in charge of this session announced various vacancies in the NASFAT national administration. He said there is a vacancy for executive secretary, and the requirement is a university degree with fifteen years of working experience in a similar profession.

The chief imam led a new session to welcome newcomers. He said, 'Whoever comes here for the first time should stand up.' Then about four people stood up. Immediately the congregation welcomed them with *takbir* or *Allahu Akbar* (God is great). The imam asked the congregation to recite Surah *Qulya* for them while at the same time pointing their fingers towards the newcomers. *Qulya* is a chapter of the Qur'an that is often used for protection against evil. The congregation was apparently praying for the newcomers' protection as a symbol of expressing care and concern about their lives. A newcomer told me,

> NASFAT is a place to be. I am very happy with the reception I had when I prayed with them for the first time. The warm welcome I received and the prayer they offered for us made me feel special. From that day I decided to continue attending the prayer and eventually join as a full member. (Interview, 13 November 2014)

In Christ Embassy the congregation sings the welcoming anthem for the newcomer while in NASFAT the congregation recites the chapter of the Qur'an as prayer for them. However, both the song and the prayer serve the same purpose. As the above statement indicates, the purpose of collective welcoming of newcomers in the two groups is to make them feel special and cast a positive impression of the two groups on the newcomers. It is arguable that NASFAT borrowed this practice of welcoming newcomers from the Pentecostals. This practice is likely one of the examples of NASFAT's borrowing of Pentecostal practices.

The next session was about the mosque building project. The chairperson of the committee came forward and announced the current situation on the completion of the Islamic centre in Abuja. He said the project was initiated three years ago. Now, what remained were the finishing touches. He also said the reason why the project has been stopped is that the project manager travelled. He commended the members of the committee for the endurance and sacrifices they made for the mosque project. The chairperson asserted that all the achievements made so far were due to their devotion and passion for the success of NASFAT mission. He also thanked Allah for his help. The chief imam said all recent returnees from Hajj should stand up and come forward. He asked the congregation to pray for them. As a result, all of them donated money to the organization. One Hajia Wasilat donated 50,000 naira (105.419 euro). After a long speech by the imam in the Yoruba language, he asked everybody to stand up for the recitation of Surah *Ya-Sin*. Immediately when the surah was concluded, people started greeting each other while moving towards the door.

The *Asalatu* worship of NASFAT has notable similarities with the Sunday service in Christ Embassy. It is noteworthy that all the sessions of Christ Embassy worship have their counterparts in the NASFAT Sunday service. They all commence with prayer, preaching, announcements, prayer request, testimonies, welcoming newcomers and end with prayers. It is arguable that NASFAT takes the structure of Pentecostal worship as a template which they fill with Islamic contents. Larkin and Meyer (2006) explore a similar trend in Pentecostalism and Islamic reform movements in West Africa with particular focus on Nigeria and Ghana. Meyer and Larkin argue that, despite the almost diametrical differences between the two groups, by looking deeper one can see the two groups shared many similarities. Even though NASFAT does not fall into the category of Islamic reformist, it shared the same goals with Pentecostalism much more than the reformists. However, NASFAT borrowed more from the Pentecostals than vice versa.

Dressing in white during Sunday worship services by NASFAT members attracts curious attention from other Muslims. Some of my friends both in Abuja and Jos expressed their curiosity to me and wanted to know more about NASFAT when I told them about my research. They wanted to know why NASFAT members pray on Sundays and dress in white during prayer. This curiosity is more common among the Hausa Muslims in the north. As a result of these enquiries, some decided to join the movement.

Other NASFAT members also told me that their journey into NASFAT began with curiosity. Even some Christians sometimes become puzzled about NASFAT Sunday worship and asked me questions about it. As NASFAT is becoming more proactive in its social engagement and its visibility, particularly in the media and charity works, other Muslims begin to become more accustomed to its practices and see it as a mainstream Islamic organization. Some new groups are appearing recently which emulate NASFAT practices and styles. In Abuja a new elite Muslim group called Al-Habibiyya has been formed, which introduced Sunday worship services and several practices that are apparently inspired by NASFAT.

Apart from the Sunday service, NASFAT holds *Tahajjud* prayers or night vigils during the night of every first and third Friday of the month. Most Muslim groups hold *Tahajjud* only during the last ten days of Ramadan and many, such as Sufi groups, do not even do it at all. For sustaining spiritual rejuvenation, NASFAT leaders decided to introduce monthly *Tahajjud*. Night vigil prayer begins around 10.00 pm, and lasts till about 4.00 am. The prayers consist of a long *nawafil* or supererogatory ritual prayer and varieties of melodious recitation led by the chief imam and his assistants. Many members testified to me that the night vigil prayers make them nearer to God and better Muslims. Members believe that their prayers of supplication are more efficacious during night vigil performances, and it is an important period to pray about some pressing needs and problems. Members who could not attend could send their prayer requests in writing, accompanied by any amount of money they could afford to give.

Christ Embassy and many Pentecostal churches practice night vigil prayers for the same reasons as NASFAT, which is spiritual rejuvenation and prayer of supplication. The question here is whether NASFAT borrowed the monthly night vigil from Pentecostals. The answer is probably positive. This is because Muslims do not have this tradition of collective prayers in the mosque as night vigils. There is no doubt that Islam has encouraged Muslims to wake up at night for supererogatory prayer because there are some Hadith of Prophet Muhammad that say God is closer to his creatures around 3.00 am than at any time of the day. But this is only for private prayer, not congregational prayer.

It is apparent that the monthly night vigil is a NASFAT initiative inspired by Pentecostals' night vigils. Amidu Sanni (2006) maintains that provision of prayers which provide utilitarian values in healing and power accession is another means through which NASFAT and related prayer groups meet the challenges of Pentecostals.

Another significant spiritual practice in NASFAT is Lailatul Qadr. According to the teaching of NASFAT and Islam in general, Lailatul Qadr is the night of majesty. It is a special night in which God showers his blessing, mercy and forgiveness on his people. The night occurs on any day during the last ten days of Ramadan, but it is more likely to occur on the twenty-seventh day of the month according to Hadith of the Prophet. NASFAT decided to hold a special night of prayer during the last days of the month of Ramadan, hoping that the prayer would coincide with the Lailatul Qadr. This special prayer is the pinnacle of NASFAT spiritual performance, and members hold it in high regard. Branches all over the country conduct this prayer, but the largest gathering of such prayer is the one taking place at the NASFAT Village along Lagos–Ibadan expressway. Adetona (2012: 104) had the following to say about this prayer:

> NASFAT annual Lailatul Qadr, which is often held towards the end of the Muslim fasting period of Ramadan, has been a remarkable spectacle to be held in the last four years. When the main bowl of the National Stadium could not contain the participants at the all night event in the year 2000, the group moved to its open and undeveloped prayer land, NASFAT village, a vast expanse of land on the Lagos-Ibadan expressway.

Many members of NASFAT prefer to travel to Lagos to perform the Lailatul Qadr there. One of my interlocutors told me that he enjoys the Lailatul Qadr prayer in such a gigantic gathering because it often results in powerful religious experiences. He said that in 2013 they experienced a miracle during Lailatul Qadr; as the prayer was going on thousands of unusual white birds descended on the prayer ground from nowhere. He continued as follows:

> The sight of thousands of people all dressed in white praying and invoking the name of Allah at the same time was a great transforming experience to me. Suddenly beautiful white birds began to descend on the prayer ground. I felt a strong sensation all over my body, coupled with the feeling of overwhelming joy, bliss, and ecstasy. I started to feel as if I was in a dreamland; God is present in that place. From that time every year, I perform my Lailatul Qadr in Lagos. (Interview, 22 February 2014)

NASFAT Lailatul Qadr has strong resonance with spectacular Pentecostal religious gatherings such as crusades or revivals. The major Pentecostal churches in the country hold an annual religious gathering at the end of the year. I already mentioned the Night of Bliss of Christ Embassy, which is led by Pastor Chris. Living Faith Church organizes annual end of the year gathering called Shiloh, and it takes place at the church's headquarters at Canaanland in Ota close to Lagos. Millions of people converge at Canaanland every year for the Shiloh event, the purpose of which is to give people the opportunity to experience the presence of God. The Redeemed Christian Church of God holds an annual Holy Ghost Congress with millions in attendance at the Redemption Camp, at Lagos–Ibadan Expressway. The 2015 Holy Ghost Congress was tagged 'Floodgates of Heaven'. Through Lailatul Qadr prayer, NASFAT has provided Muslims with something similar to Pentecostals' massive public religious performance where hyper-emotion is generated, and people claim to experience divine encounter. These huge emotional performances provide transcendent experience on a massive scale.

The practices of Sunday worship and night vigil prayer and melodious Qur'anic recitation are spectacular religious performances that resonate with what Birgit Meyer (2012) called sensational form. These spectacular practices have a notable affinity with a Pentecostal, emotionally charged mode of worship, which is based on the bodily experience of the Holy Spirit. Meyer (2010b: 742) describes the place of experience of the Holy Spirit among the Pentecostals as follows:

> The all-pervasive presence of the Holy Spirit goes along with the valuation of the body as a vessel for divine power. The Holy Spirit is an experiential presence that invokes feelings. One of the most salient features of Pentecostal/charismatic churches is their sensational appeal; they often operate via music and powerful oratory, through which born-again Christians are enabled to sense the presence of the Holy Spirit with and in their bodies, wherever they are, and to act on such feelings.

This kind of sensational bodily experiences of the divine presence appeals to many urban dwellers and plays a vital role in the success of Pentecostalism. During my fieldwork, I asked a young girl who moved from the Roman Catholic Church to Christ Embassy about her reason for joining the Pentecostal church. Her response was that the 'Catholic mode of worship is too stale and formal, but Pentecostal worship is more attractive to me because it allows me to sense the presence of the Holy Spirit' (Interview, 21 February 2014, Abuja). There is no doubt that this experiential dimension also plays an important role in the remarkable spread of NASFAT in the Nigerian urban environment. Nolte (2015: 12) highlights the disquiet experienced by Yoruba Muslims as a result of the domination of the urban public sphere by Pentecostalism. With the failure of Islamic reformists to take root in Yorubaland, some movements emerged to resist the threat of growing Pentecostalism.[13] Nolte continues that the most popular among these was NASFAT, which practices an intense emotional personal engagement with God.

The similarity between the forms of NASFAT and Pentecostal Sunday worship and NASFAT's use of the term 'born-again' to describe their practices of spiritual transformation clearly reveal some level of Pentecostal influence on the organization. NASFAT uses the doctrines of necessity in Islam to negotiate and justify some of their practices that are seemingly similar to Pentecostal practices. The doctrine of necessity or *dharura* in Islam is a law that permits unlawful things or actions, and it can be applied in a situation when observing the law becomes too challenging and unbearable. NASFAT leaders applied the doctrine on the ground of checkmating Muslim youths' attraction towards glittering Pentecostal activities. They argued that if Muslim youths are provided with something similar but rooted in Islam, they will not be attracted by the Pentecostals. They maintain that the danger of losing Islamic faith far outweighs the discomfiture with some practices that resonate with Pentecostal activities. In one *Asalatu* I attended, the imam said, 'Those who are complaining about our Sunday worship and said we are copying Christians are sitting in their homes now watching Pentecostal programmes on television, which is more wrong, watching Pentecostal programmes at home or worshiping and praying in the mosque' (2 November 2013). It is probably because of these practices that some people called NASFAT 'born again Muslims' or 'Muslim Pentecostals' (Hasan 2015: 46). Bello (2013: 8) elaborates on this issue:

The decision to drive [NASFAT]into the minds of the Muslim professionals and youths through activities rather than engaging in the building of mosques and other religious institutions was a direct response to the yearnings of the Muslims at the time of its emergence. The Muslims of that era were under the siege of Pentecostal Christianity with its powerful ministry in form of praise worship, healing and deliverance services as well as counselling. The existing Muslim organisations such as Ansar-ud-Deen and Nawair-deen Society particularly in a cosmopolitan city of Lagos could not provide an alternative to what was considered an onslaught which was beginning to take its toll on the religion by the conversion of some Muslims to [a] Pentecostal brand of Christianity. NASFAT therefore, came to fill this vacuum of a platform for Muslims particularly on Sunday which was hitherto considered a Christian day of worship.

This attempt to negotiate borrowing some forms of Pentecostal practices was put to the test when some NASFAT imams celebrated the 'crossover night' by observing all-night prayers to welcome 2013, arguing that if they would not do so, Muslim youths would follow their Christian friends to the church. This infuriated the national leadership to the extent that they warned the rest of the leaders that there should be a limit on what to emulate from Pentecostals. As a result, they organized a meeting at the national headquarters to draw a line about new practices and to initiate programmes on training imams. NASFAT leaders often highlight that they have achieved relative success in meeting the challenges of Pentecostal churches by reducing their attraction on Muslim youths.

Conclusion

This chapter has suggested that the remarkable spread of NASFAT in the urban Nigerian landscape in general and Abuja in particular is based on the ability to provide effective social services and spectacular religious performances that respond to the needs of urban dwellers. It is noticeable that NASFAT provides religious and socio-economic services on a scale that few if any other Muslim religious groups can match. NASFAT leaders are seriously concerned with the image of Islam. They hold the view that the image of Islam has been tarnished by decades of religious conflicts in the north and the destructive insurgency by the radical Boko Haram. The leaders set a mission for restoring that image through media campaign and preaching. Hardly would a NASFAT leader give a public talk without attempting to dissociate Islam from violence and emphasizing its teaching about peaceful coexistence. Another way that NASFAT tries to portray the positive image of Islam is through public work or contribution in community development. NASFAT leaders always claim that through various social projects and charity which they extend to non-Muslims they have positively increased the visibility and understanding of true Islam. The far-reaching outreach of NASFAT is an indication of the appeal of its programmes to the Nigerian Muslims. Even though NASFAT has not yet penetrated the Hausa population in the far north of Nigeria, partly due to language barriers, other ethnic groups in the north such as Igalas and Igbiras have joined the movement, particularly in Abuja. The success of NASFAT also prompts other groups to imitate its programmes, especially in Lagos and Abuja.

Similar to Christ Embassy, NASFAT has a self-image of being a modern, sophisticated religious organization led by upwardly mobile professional elites. Like Christ Embassy this desire to be modern is predicated on the attitude of breaking with the past. NASFAT not only distanced itself from the cultural past related to traditional religion, but the leaders often reiterate that there is a gulf between the modern educated Muslim youths and their elders who are traditionally oriented. And this chasm may hinder effective communication and understanding between the two generations. Hence the need for modern forward-looking organizations like NASFAT to cater to the spiritual and material needs of the modern young Muslims and help them overcome a myriad of urban challenges.

4

Communion with the divine:
Prayer as performance of mediation in
Christ Embassy and NASFAT

Introduction

During my fieldwork in Christ Embassy, I had a personal lesson in the foundation class about the subject of prayer with my instructor, Pastor Adewale. After the general Sunday worship service we went to the Children's Room and sat opposite each other.[1] He said, 'As usual we are going to start the lesson with prayer, so let us close our eyes and pray.' After the opening prayer, the foundation class instructor asked me this question: 'What is prayer?' I replied, 'Prayer is a form of request to God.' He said, 'No, prayer is a communion with God.' Adewale continued: 'Communion is an act of personal communication between a believer and God. God reveals himself with love to an individual through communion. This joyful and loving communication that occurs within the interior of the individual is what constitutes the essence of prayer.' There is similar understanding of prayer in NASFAT. One of the deputy imams in Abuja told me that 'prayer is an act of appeal to God that requires the full conscious participation of all the mental faculties and body of the one praying. When a believer engages in prayer he [she] is in direct connection with God who hears and understand everything the supplicant says.' These notions of prayer as an act that involves 'communication' or 'connection' with the divine resonate with the view of Meyer (2009: 11) that posits religion as a practice of mediation. She also emphasizes the role of media in the process of mediation and extends the notion of media to include varieties of things from modern media technologies to substances and even the human body. In line with this understanding, this chapter views prayer as a religious medium that mediates between a person and a suprahuman/metasocial entity who may be God, gods, deities, angels, spirits, ancestors and so on.

There are different genres of prayers in Christ Embassy and NASFAT, but they are not clearly defined and categorized in the two groups. For the purpose of this study and comparison, I select and examine three different genres of prayers in Christ Embassy and NASFAT. I categorize them as prayers of adoration, prayers of aesthetic speech and prayers of instrumentality. Prayers of adoration, called 'praise and worship' in Christ Embassy, refer basically to collective prayers performed in congregational setting. These prayers comprise praises to God expressed in the form of songs and music. In NASFAT, prayers of adoration are performed in the congregational recitation of NASFAT's prayer book. Most of my interlocutors across the two groups told me that they enjoy reciting these prayers in private, particularly during leisure times. The term 'prayers of adoration' has been adopted because the word 'adoration', as defined by the Oxford Dictionary as 'deep love, respect, worship, veneration', covers the nature and contents of these prayers.

The second genre of prayers discussed in this chapter is special prayers which I call prayers of aesthetic speech – glossolalia (speaking in tongues) and *zikr* (repetitive invocation of God's name) in Christ Embassy and NASFAT, respectively. I call them aesthetic speech because in these prayers, the emphasis is on the sound of the prayers rather than complete sentences of ordinary language. These prayers are also practised in both collective and private settings for the purpose of invoking or communicating with the divine through the medium of what is perceived as sacred sounds (glossolalia and the names of Allah).

The third and final genre of prayers discussed in the chapter is prayers of instrumentality, which in Christ Embassy is known as affirmative prayers and in NASFAT simply as *du'a* (which means prayers). This is because these prayers serve as instruments for actualizing individual needs through their proclaimed unique spiritual potency and agency. I will analyse these three genres of prayers through the concepts derived from speech act theory and semiotic ideologies, as well as the notion of spectacular form so as to understand different potent powers and meta-level significations attributed to them and how they are understood to operate. The chapter argues that prayers of adoration and prayers of aesthetic speech in Christ Embassy and NASFAT facilitate the process of mediation by orchestrating bodily experiences of affect, which members recognized as a 'divine touch' or 'the presence of God'. Furthermore, the chapter also argues that prayers of instrumentality in the two groups attempt to establish communication with the Divine and achieve the desired goals through the performative power and semiotic systems ascribed to the language of prayers.

Theorizing prayer

Edward Tylor is one of the earliest scholars to attempt to theorize prayer. However, his approach to prayer is rooted in the social evolutionism that characterized his entire study of religion. Tylor sees prayer as a desire that proceeds from the human spirit which is expressed verbally or non-verbally and directed towards the supernatural. In short, prayer is the address of personal spirit to personal spirit. Tylor suggests that this notion of prayer, which is found in 'primitive culture', has been modified in the process of social evolution into a more mechanical routine. He argues that 'prayers, from being at first utterances as free and flexible as requests to a living patriarch or chief, stiffened into traditional formulas whose repetition required verbal accuracy, and whose nature practically assimilated more or less to that of charms' (Tylor 1873: 371). This social evolutionist perspective of Tylor could not be subjected to empirical observation as both aspects of prayers could still be found in the so-called higher modern religions. In both Christ Embassy and NASFAT, people practise prayers as a heartfelt desire or request towards God as well as structured or mechanical prayers that require verbal accuracy.

Marcel Mauss diverges from Edward Tylor's individualistic and psychological approach to prayer. Mauss conceived prayer as an aspect of social reality that performs functions similar to social institutions. According to Mauss, prayer is a considerable set of acts that show the characteristics of a particular religious rite (2003: 35). Mauss bases his argument on the ground that prayer is an efficacious act as well as an effort of physical and moral energy in order to produce certain effects. In another instance Mauss suggests that prayer is a means of acting on sacred beings, which are influenced and changed by prayer (2003: 37). In line with the argument of Mauss, this chapter discusses certain kinds of prayers in Christ Embassy and NASFAT which are performed as regular religious rites that invoke the divine for the purpose of acquiring spiritual or material favour.

In her study of Navajo prayer Gladys Reichard (1988) proposes a symbolic and structural approach to the interpretation of prayer. She used alphanumeric designations to chart rhythmic word and phrase patterns in order to identify a structural division that corresponds to her interpretation of the Navajo prayer. As a result, Reichard made several distinctions in the form and content of the

Navajo prayer. Reichard highlights distinctions such as invocation, benediction and petition. At another point she identifies repetitive patterns such as address to the deity, the symbols of the deity, the behaviour of the deity and the concern expressed by the deity. Finding repetitive patterns and structures in NASFAT and Christ Embassy will be helpful in revealing the similarities and differences in their performance of prayers.

Thomas Oberlies (2017) identifies prayer as an address, or appeal, to the gods or other supernatural beings, predicated on the possibility of direct human–God communication. This also implies a considerable overlap with hymns, ritual incantations and devotional recitations. Oberlies further affirms that prayers may exhibit variable degrees of formality that apply both to written prayers that are highly formalized and conform to stylized and conventional patterns, and to prayers that involve action. According to Oberlies, prayer and its language could be formulaic, repetitive, redundant, spontaneous or non-spontaneous, and usually marked by meticulous precision. Many of the features of prayers, such as devotional recitations and repetitiveness mentioned by Oberlies, have appeared in the three genres of prayer discussed in this chapter.

The economy of canonized prayer books

Prayer is at the centre of NASFAT's and Christ Embassy's religiosity and it forms the basis of most of their worship practices. The most important source of prayer in Christ Embassy is Rhapsody of Reality. Rhapsody of Reality is a daily devotional booklet written by Pastor Chris Oyakhilome that is published monthly. The booklet is available in 156 languages and distributed all over the world. It contains small chapters that centre on the principles of prosperity gospel and the affirmative prayers for the day.[2] It is expected that one reads one chapter every day, preferably in the morning, and recites the prayer after reading. The book also contains a recommended Bible study for the day. Members of Christ Embassy believe that daily reading of the book and reciting the prayer nourish their spirit and help them remain steadfast as born-again Christians. One member told me, 'I see the Rhapsody as my little angel, because I don't miss reading it and reciting the prayers. Whenever I miss it for one day I will see the difference in my affairs of that day' (interview, 24 February 2014, Abuja).

On 3 November 2013, I attended the Sunday worship service at the central branch of Christ Embassy located at Durimi, Area 2, Abuja. In the middle of the service the pastor said it was time to read from the Rhapsody of Reality.

A well-dressed woman went to the altar to read the chapter for the day and recite the prayer. But before she began the pastor said,

> It seems to me that some people did not buy the Rhapsody for this month. Those who bought the Rhapsody should raise it up and let me see how many people have it. The number is not encouraging. Where are the ushers? Come and distribute to all those who do not have it. Remember daily reading of the Rhapsody is integral part of your spiritual growth. Even the author of the booklet, our man of God Pastor Chris, reads the Rhapsody daily. So, it is a must for members of this church to be buying and reading the Rhapsody.

One of the ushers, a young woman, handed me a copy of the book and asked me to pay 100 naira (0.21 cent). The pastor was using subtle psychological coercion to impel people to buy the book. During my session at the foundation class Pastor Adewale explained to me in detail the meaning and concept of prayer in Christ Embassy.[3] As he was talking, he was partly reading from a booklet about prayer authored by Pastor Chris. He said prayer is not just a means of religious communication with God; it is a form of fellowship. He continued, 'prayer helps to season our spirits as a dependable receptacle for God's Spirit and power. Then we can connect to his ideas, visions and leadings more easily in order to change the world.' Two tropes about prayer could be discerned in these remarks. Prayer has been portrayed as a medium of making contact with God through unlocking of human spirit to receive the power or anointing of God. Adewale also conceived prayer as a medium of making changes in the life of believers. It can be argued that prayer draws the power of God through communion with him for the purpose of achieving pragmatic effects.

NASFAT's constitution clearly states that the 'efficacy of prayer' is part of the shared values of the organization. In fact the prime motive of the establishment of NASFAT is to provide a forum where Muslims would gather and pray together. The NASFAT prayer book is the most important source of prayers in NASFAT's Sunday worship service. The book was written by former chief missioner of NASFAT Alhaji Akingbode. It contains prayer verses from the Qur'an, prayers taught by Prophet Muhammad, ninety-nine sacred names of Allah and different kinds of *salat* which are praises and prayers to the Prophet. The book contains Arabic text, transliteration, English and Yoruba translations. The first time I attended the Sunday service in NASFAT, I sat at the back watching the congregation melodiously reciting the prayer book. As I was sitting a man approached me. He held a number of books and said to me, 'Where is your

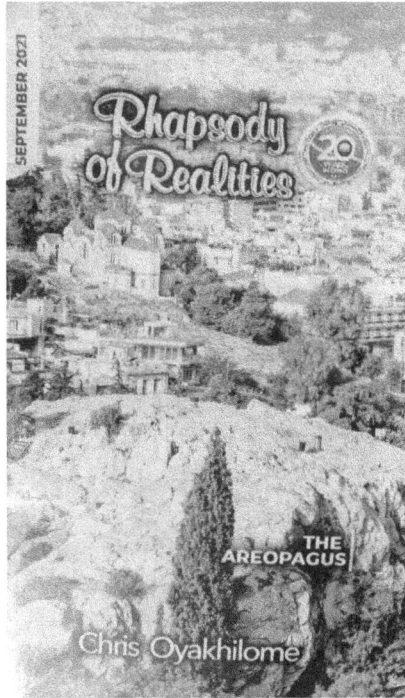

Figure 4.1 Rhapsody of Reality. Source: Author.

prayer book?' I responded, 'I do not have one.' He handed one of the books to me and said it cost only 200 naira (0.42 cent). I gave him the money and he moved on, looking for congregants who did not yet possess the book.

Clearly in both Christ Embassy and NASFAT the leaders are taking extra measures to make sure that people buy the prayer books. The NASFAT prayer book is different from Rhapsody of Reality in the sense that the content remains the same for a long time before a new edition is published with usually minor changes. But a new version of Rhapsody of Reality comes out monthly with a new set of lessons and prayers. The two books provide a canon of prayers and members are expected to recite them for spiritual benefits. The books provide authoritative prayers which are believed to be extremely efficacious because they are written by highly regarded religious authorities. These prayers differ from the spontaneous individual prayer because they have to be recited word for word as they appear in the texts. On the other hand, printing and distributing both NASFAT prayer and the Rhapsody generate substantial amount of revenue into the coffers of the two movements.

Prayer of adoration: The practices of sacred emotion

'Because God is a mighty being, whenever I feel his presence during worship songs, I feel intense emotion coupled with goose bumps all over my body' (interview, 13 February 2014, Abuja). This is a statement from one of my interlocutors Sade Patrick, a twenty-nine-year-old self-employed woman in Christ Embassy, expressing her feeling about the prayer of adoration. Prayers of adoration are performed as a form of worship to God and show veneration to religious figures such as Jesus and Muhammad. Adoration prayers exalt, esteem, bless and honour God. They also describe his character as holiness, goodness, love, mercy, power, grace and dominion in a melodious and poetic language. Praise and worship songs in Christ Embassy and melodious recitation of the NASFAT prayer book constitute prayer of adoration in the two groups.

Prayers of adoration or praise and worship songs play a central role in the worship of Christ Embassy. The choir has its leaders who guide the group and instrumentalists such as drummers and pianists. Choir membership is free to all who have a forte for music. A choir member told me that as the choir is one of the most influential groups in the church, anyone who wants to join has to be prepared for the responsibility of membership. She said this is the case because the devil pays particular attention to members of the choir and targets them because he was a member of the choir in heaven before his fall. Christ Embassy has about eighty different types of worship songs, and most of the old members memorize all the songs. Oyakhilome (2012: 33) stated this about the worship songs:

> When you worship God in spirit and in reality, there is union and drinking together of spirits. It is called the communion of the Holy Spirit. It is not just in our singing or in the words of our prayer, but in the communication and transportation that take place in the realm of the spirit. Worship transports you to lofty divine realms. This is why you feel enraptured as you worship sometimes; it is as though you are taken away from the earth realm into the warmth of God's spirit. You find yourself completely oblivious of everyone and everything around you as God's glorious presence envelopes you.

Worship services in Christ Embassy on Sundays and Wednesdays start with praise prayer songs that last for thirty minutes. During the singing people stand up, lift their hands up, and sing with a full show of emotion and devotion. Many close their eyes and gesticulate with their arms and faces. Pastor Chris (2012: 35) expresses the meaning of lifting of hands during worship songs:

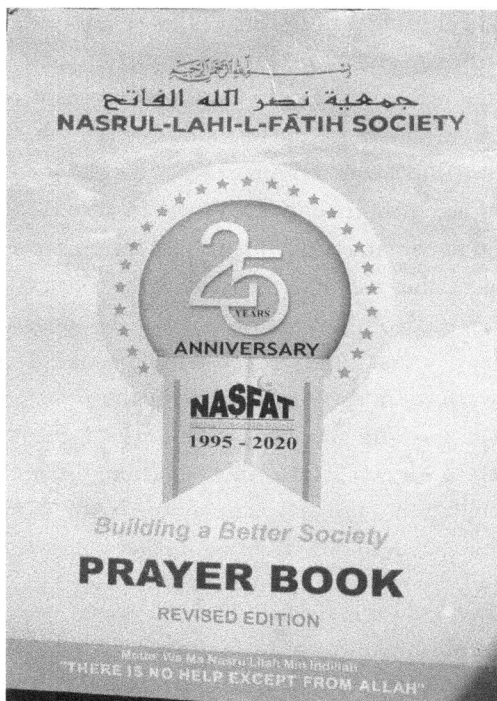

Figure 4.2 NASFAT prayer book. Source: Author.

When you lift up your hands, it is not just a sign of worship; it is the most beautiful thing to behold when God's people lift their hands to him in worship. As you speak forth words of praise to God and lift up your hands to heaven, you are sending incense of a sweet-smelling savor to him. The lifting of your hands has taken the place of the burnt sacrifice, and your prayers, the burning incense.

Lifting of hands in this explanation is a practice of symbolically carrying the substances of the worship to heaven. It is a symbolic means through which the essence of devotion will reach God. In this sense, lifting of hands during worship songs highlights that prayer is not restricted to the spoken words but also engages the human body in reaching out to the divine. It is further indication that worship song is an embodied practice performed with both human voice and body.

Some songs are sung with soft emotional music, while others genres of songs are accompanied by disco music and people dance with jubilation in the church. They usually seem to be overwhelmed with the emotion of joy and euphoria. The songs contain praises to God and Jesus and expression of love and devotion.

The song invokes God using phrases such as awesome God; we worship your majesty; your presence is comforting; king of kings; Lord of lords; your embrace calms my heart; your presence is power; worthy is your name.

In my interviews with several members of Christ Embassy, most of them asserted that the worship songs were the cornerstone of their spirituality. This is because they claimed that the songs keep them close to God and sustain their faith and help them remain in touch with his presence. They often mention that when they are singing, they feel what the lyrics of the songs say and this invokes the 'real presence' of the Holy Spirit in their body. The songs also remind them of the great sacrifice of Jesus Christ for the sin of humankind and how fortunate they are to be saved from sin and eternal death by the atonement of Christ. The most important aspect of NASFAT Sunday worship is the recitation of the prayer book, which is led by the imam. It takes about one hour to finish the book. Below is an example of an English translation extract from NASFAT prayer book; while the prayers are presented in English translation, they are recited in Arabic.

> Oh! Lord of heaven and earth, the Lord that provides for those in heaven and earth, the Lord we worship both in heaven and earth. Let us be steadfast in Islam. We cherish the prophets are protected from all distress. The distress experienced by those who have not come into contact with Islam. We are conscious of living unholy life for fear of not meeting up with the teachings of the Prophet of Islam Muhammad (PBUH). Oh, Allah! You are my Lord; there is no deity except You. What Allah wishes will be, and what He does not wish will not be. And there is neither authority nor power but with Allah, the Most High, the Supreme in Glory. (56)

The recitation of the prayer book plays a paramount role in the devotional lives of the members. They recite it loudly with vigour and intensity. I noticed that some members have memorized the entire book. There is an outpouring of devotion during the recitation: some close their eyes with their heads and hands up, some members become very jittery. There was a time during the youth camp when the tempo of the recitation was so intense that two young women fainted, and they had to be taken out of the mosque. Afterwards, I asked one of the youth leaders what happened to the young women. He said, 'It is called *jazabu,* it was the spirit of the *zikr* or invocation of God that descended on them.' This was the first time I heard such a statement; I think he wanted to say that the women were overwhelmed by the presence of God. He continued that sometimes it happened to him during the recitation that he would feel a strange cold permeate his body, but he usually resisted fainting. This practice can be described in the words of

Gottschall (2004: 2) as a 'sacred sound performance' because the prayers and the Qur'anic verses are taken as the sacred words that have the capacity to transform both the internal and external lives of the performers.

Remarkable similarities exist in the performance of adoration prayer in Christ Embassy and NASFAT. The two kinds of adoration prayer are highly structured religious performances designed for the purpose of cultivating closeness with the divine. In NASFAT the congregation is required to wear white robes, often with a small white cap. The leaders emphasize that white is the official dress code for the service. Thousands of worshippers sit close to each other chanting and praying in synchronized ways. In addition, the members of the choir in Christ Embassy wear special uniforms aesthetically designed with conspicuous colour combinations. As Scheer (2012: 211) notes, 'Other people's bodies are implicated in practice because viewing them induces feeling. These effects are stored in the habitus, which provides socially anchored responses to others.' The arrangement of bodies in uniform dress, engaged in embodied religious performances, generates affective relations among the participants. In both Christ Embassy and NASFAT these practices are recorded with video cameras. In the big churches of Christ Embassy, the service is projected onto a big white screen on top of the stage. The appearance of larger-than-life, live images of the stage on to the big screens and amplifying the sound with public address systems reinforce the emotional impact of the religious performance. In both Christ Embassy and NASFAT, prayers of adoration take place in places of worship. In both groups, Church and Mosque are houses of God because they harboured his presence. As places of worship and retreat, religious buildings offer a spiritual experience to the wider community, where the clamour of urban life can melt away in a space designed to be used collectively and individually for an encounter with the divine.

Prayers of adoration express affection and praise in the form of melodious recitation in NASFAT and songs and music in Christ Embassy. The melody and music enhance the emotional touch of the prayers. Poetic invocation and glorification of God rendered in melody and music with emotional undertones can create a sense of the divine presence. Many members of the two groups told me about these highly emotional experiences during group worship. One of my interlocutors, a thirty-four-year-old male civil servant in Abuja from Christ Embassy, said the following about his experience of the worship songs:

Not only has it changed my life, but I also discovered that the secret of songs is that when you are building your spiritual life, the word of God is the block; the

Figure 4.3 NASFAT *Asalatu* (Sunday prayer service). Source: Author.

worship songs are like cement that stuck the blocks together. Without songs, the word of God will not hold to you. You can forget it tomorrow. But through worshiping God, those songs stay. (Interview, 7 January 2014)

One of the members of NASFAT had this to say about his experiences with NASFAT prayer book:

Whenever we start the recitation of NASFAT prayer book, I feel joy in my life. When we invoke the name of Allah and praise him, I feel his presence all around me. This practice increases fear of God in my heart and keeps me in God's remembrance constantly in my life. Recitation of the Prayer also increases love and respect to the messenger of Allah Prophet Muhammad. (Interview, 9 January 2014, Abuja)

The articulation of devotion, petition, invocation, veneration and benediction to God through melodious recitation and worship songs arouses affective or emotional presence of God as expressed by these individuals.[4] The entire practice of this form of prayer can be described in the words of John Corrigan (2004: 16) as a 'performance of emotion'. This is because the purpose of the worship service in both Christ Embassy and NASFAT is to glorify God and to feel his presence. Feeling the presence of God, according to my interlocutors, always comes with strong emotions. This emotional experience of the divine can be seen in what Scheer (2012) describes as emotion-as-practice. This encapsulates practice as dependent and intertwined, such as speaking, gesturing, remembering, manipulating objects and perceiving sounds, smells and spaces (2012: 209).

To invoke Reichard (1988) and Oberlies (2017), repetitive terms can be discerned in the two samples of Christ Embassy and NASFAT mentioned above, with the appearance of the terms mighty, glory, majesty, awesome and throne in the songs and prayer excerpts. Many of my interlocutors told me that they feel what they are saying in these performances of worship or prayer. They affirmed that they had these experiences as a result of addressing God in a poetic language with strong words coupled with the emotional melody. They feel the power and glory of God as they recite or sing the prayer.

The emotion generated in the practices of adoration prayer is reinforced in a situation similar to the group dynamics effect. This is because emotional practices in most cases are enshrined in a social setting. It is noteworthy that 'other people's bodies are implicated in practice because viewing them induces feeling. These effects are stored in the habitus, which provides socially anchored responses to others' (Scheer 2012: 211). It is apparent in prayers of adoration in Christ Embassy and NASFAT that emotion is distributed among the individuals. A dramatic exhibition of emotion is encouraged in the worship services of the two groups. Therefore, some people display intense emotions in the service to the extent of falling to the ground, particularly in Christ Embassy. This display of hyper-emotion becomes contagious and affects other members. It can be argued that these group performances and experiences, as well as the exhibition of emotions which accompany divine presence, cannot be separated. Prayers of adoration express affection and praise in the form of melodious recitation in NASFAT, on the one hand, and songs and music in Christ Embassy, on the other. The melody and music enhance the affective and emotional touch of the prayers. Poetic invocation and glorification of God rendered in melody and music with emotional undertones create the sense of a divine presence. It is apparent that music (in Christ Embassy) and melody (in NASFAT) help generate affect during worship. Shouse (2015: 1) argues that 'music provides perhaps the clearest example of how the intensity of the impingement of sensations on the body can mean more to people than meaning itself'. It can therefore be argued that it is emotion that facilitates the role of the prayers of adoration as religious media that connect believers with the transcendental realm.

Glossolalia and *Zikr*: Prayers of aesthetic speech

Glossolalia, which is also called speaking in tongues, is a religious practice characterized by the fluid utterances of speech-like syllables that do not have any readily understandable meaning, which is believed to be a divine language unknown to the speaker (Martin 1995). Glossolalia occurs most often as an ecstatic utterance in religious groups, which provoke trance or religious ecstasies during their usual rituals (Koic et al. 2005: 1). Many linguists have become fascinated with the phenomenon of glossolalia and produce plenty of works on the subject. William J. Samarin (1972: 82) argues that glossolalia consists of syllables made up of consonants and vowels taken from the speaker's native language or a foreign language known to him, with much repetition, alliteration and rhyme. However, the syllable stream does not fall into words.

Praying in tongues is one of the markers of Pentecostal Christianity (Asamoah-Gyadu 2013: 48).[5] Glossolalia, according to the teaching of Christ Embassy, is a spiritual gift granted by the Holy Spirit to born-again Christians. Moreover, it is regarded as the language of angels. In every congregational service in Christ Embassy, there is a special session for speaking in tongues. On many occasions when someone is called on stage to lead prayer, he prays in tongues, and when the pastor is preaching, and it becomes very intense, he begins to speak in tongues. Pastor Chris (2012: 31) had this to say about speaking in tongues:

> We speak divine mysteries and alter destinies through this supernatural effusion.
> Even though man is a spirit he does not dwell physically in the realm of the spirit.
> He lives on earth and relates with the material world. Yet there are certain things
> we cannot communicate or express with the earthly languages we have learnt.
> This is the reason God imparted on us the ability to speak in other tongues so
> we can have the right language to communicate with God. You must realize that
> there are not enough words in human vocabulary to express ourselves to God.
> This is why it is absolutely necessary for a Christian to speak in tongues.

While other Protestants view glossolalia as a spiritual gift that is given to the selected few, Christ Embassy sees it as a natural right of every born-again believer. Remi Moses, one of the teachers of the foundation class, told me that speaking in tongues occurs when the Holy Spirit descends on the individual believer. He continued that it was one of the most effective and superior forms of prayer. This is because while speaking in tongues the Holy Spirit identifies a pressing problem of the speaker and prays to God the Father on the person's behalf in the unknown language. A person who engages in speaking in tongues many not know the problem identified by the Holy Spirit and the problem would be solved without his/her knowledge.

Is glossolalia a learned skill or something acquired intuitively through inexplicable circumstances? Many scholars who observe the phenomenon see it as a learned skill. According to Samarin (1972: 73), glossolalia is a learned skill, 'yet not learned as foreign languages are learned. The tongue speaker is the product of considerable instruction, whether or not glossolalia comes suddenly or gradually.' Peer pressure in Christ Embassy prompts many new members to learn how to speak in tongues. As a sign of the baptism of the Holy Spirit and born-again status, new members desire to have this concrete evidence of this novel spiritual status. In my interactions with members of Christ Embassy, I witnessed the struggle of some members to acquire the ability to speak in tongues. Some newcomers to the church attempt to learn glossolalia through mimicry and internalizing set of sequences or patterns of randomly organized syllables. I observed how one member called Chidi Okafor learned his skill through practising with a few syllables which he apparently imitated from Pastor Chris. But gradually he increased his syllables and achieved proficiency in a short period.

Newcomers to the church of Christ Embassy are inspired to speak in tongues in the foundation class after the lesson about the Holy Spirit. I witnessed the event after we concluded the second class. The two teachers asked the students to rise; they said that they will pray for them in tongues. If they become filled with the spirit they will touch the students and the student should utter whatever comes from their mouth; if they succeeded they should continue but if they failed to take up, they should pray at home and ask the Holy Spirit to give them this ability. While praying, they should always try to utter something different from the known language. Instead of uttering anything that comes to their minds, new members try to imitate the tongues of the instructors. I observed that most members learned to speak in tongues through this kind of imitation.

Many new members experienced frustration when they failed to speak in tongues. When they finally overcome the hurdles and achieve fluency, they become overwhelmed with happiness and a sense of release because they had tangible evidence that they are born-again. Sarah Omale is a very dedicated member of the church. She said for months she had desired to speak in tongues, but it kept on eluding her. She reached the point where she was feeling spiritually inadequate because some people that came to the church after her were able to speak in tongues quickly. She told me that her frustration was due to the fact she believed she is a born-again person and, therefore, wondered why she could not speak in tongues. Her frustration ended after she gradually acquired fluency through imitation of others. When she achieved full mastery of tongues, it became an exhilarating experience. She said her entire body responded; she was feeling an intense sensation flowing through her. Even though she could not understand what she was saying, she knew she was communicating with God. That experience was a turning point in her life; she became more committed and more devoted to God.

Glossolalia is a religious 'sound form' with intonation and rhythm, produced as a special prayer performance. But glossolalia differs from other prayers in the sense that it lacks communicative or intelligible meaning of ordinary language. Glossolalia cannot be understood by the speaker or listener since it is believed to be an angelic language that proceeds from human tongues through the inspiration of the Holy Spirit. Glossolalia is one of the prime examples of religious mediation. This is because the body of the person praying in tongues is transformed into the medium of the divine spirit. Weiss expresses a similar view on the function of glossolalia. 'Glossolalia is a language where the relation between sound and meaning break down; it is the realm of pure sound, the manifestation of language in the realm of its pure materiality' (1989: 118).

The expression of divine language through the medium of human tongues depends on the peculiar glossolalic use of speech utterances.[6] The performance of glossolalia involves the pre-discursive expression of affective experience. This is because both glossolalic expression and the affect it generates occur 'prior to explicit language categorisation' (Knudsen and Stage 2014: 19). Glossolalia itself remains at a pre-discursive state since it is a sound form that lacks the communicative or intelligible meaning of ordinary language. Members of Christ Embassy believe that the sound of glossolalia is evidence of the presence of the Holy Spirit in the human body.

Zikr

Comparing *zikr* and glossolalia is like comparing an apple and an orange. In this section I do not claim that *zikr* is analogous to glossolalia in the sense of sharing similarities in structure and meaning. I am only interested here in the act of devotion or prayer that does not involve linguistic communication, but rather depends on spiritual potency of the uttering sounds. Glossolalia here is compared with the type of *zikr* that involves repetition of one name of Allah where the rapid repetition causes the blurring of the proper sound of the word. *Zikr* in Arabic means remembrance (of Allah); it is a devotional practice in which a believer chants one of the ninety-nine attributes of God or short phrases silently or aloud. A verse of the Qur'an says, 'Verily, the Muslims (those who submit to Allah in Islam) ... and the men and the women who remember Allah much with their hearts and tongues. Allah has prepared for them forgiveness and a great reward' (33:35). *Zikr* can be performed melodiously in a group or privately by individuals in the form of chanting. In NASFAT, both group and individual chanting are accepted and performed. The NASFAT prayer book contains different names of Allah that are melodiously chanted during worship services.[7] On some occasions, when the imam was leading the melodious recitation of the NASFAT prayer book and he came to the point where one of the names of Allah was mentioned, he would turn it into *zikr* and chant it with the congregation melodiously for several minutes before he moved on. For instance, the congregation would keep on repeating the name of Allah melodiously: 'AllahAllahAllahAllahAllahAllah'. The chanting usually became highly emotional and was mirrored in bodily gestures. One of my interlocutors stated that 'calling the sacred names of Allah [purifies] the heart from spiritual disease and also increases *taqwa* [or fear of God], and moves one close to Allah' (interview, 13 March 2014). This is the reason that group invocations of the name of God generate affect that is interpreted as religious experience in NASFAT.

Glossolalia and *zikr* resonate with each other in the sense that they are both forms of sacred aesthetic sound. *Zikr*, like glossolalia, does not contain a language structure that communicates meaning. Members of NASFAT believe that the spiritual significance of *zikr* is encapsulated in the sound of the attributes of God. *Zikr* is not a prayer that demands the satisfaction of needs from God but rather the sound that is embedded with spiritual potencies to invoke the presence of God. *Zikr* is an instrument for generating divine presence that is usually experienced as affect in the body. Most of the members of NASFAT with whom I interacted told me that they felt happiness, joy and a sense of accomplishment when they experienced the presence of God through the performance of *zikr*. Sharafuddeen Shola, a thirty-five-year-old resident of Abuja, stated,

The 99 names of Allah describe different attributes of God such as *Ar-Rahman* the All-Compassionate, *Ar-Rahim* the All-Merciful, *Al-Aziz* the Victorious. Each name carries within the sound the power of that attribute. In addition, each attribute of God is also assigned with angels that possess the nature of that attribute. The moment one begins to utter one attribute, one will be instantly surrounded by the angels of that attribute to give one protection, peace and maximum contact with God. Whenever, life turns upside down and I became low in spirit, I practice *zikr* for one or two hours. This practice usually elevates my spirit and helps me experience the special tranquility that comes from the remembrance of Allah. In addition, when I am in need, I chant a name of Allah that relates to my problem. For instance, if I am broke, I chant *al-Mughni* (The Enricher) for hours, every day till my financial need has been solved. (Interview, 29 November 2013)

Religious performances of glossolalia and *zikr* are embodied practices because they heavily engage the human senses and bodily movement.[8] Furthermore, glossolalia and *zikr* could be placed within the framework of the notion of sensational form because they are regular embodied performances that generate emotion, which is interpreted as the presence of the divine in human body.

'I Claim It in the Name of Jesus': Prayer of Instrumentality in Christ Embassy

Joseph Nanfa is a civil servant and long-time member of Christ Embassy. I first met him at the University of Jos and we met again when I visited Christ Embassy in Abuja. One day in February 2014, we stood beside the road after the Sunday service. He noticed that I was staring at an attractive car that passed by. He asked me, 'Did you like it?' I said, 'Yes, it looks good.' He said, 'Well, you can claim it.' I said, 'How?' He replied, 'In this church we have a belief that whatever you like, you do not need to beseech God with a weak voice to give you. You should engage in loud affirmative voice claiming that, that thing is yours. If you persist with unshakable faith that it is yours, it will manifest in the physical realm and become yours.'

Speech act theory or performativity was developed by J. L. Austin in the early 1960s and is concerned with how speech performs an action. According to Austin (1962), performativity highlights how the words we use to express ourselves in right circumstances become a means by which we enact ourselves (1962: 16). According to Austin, the striking example of words and authoritative statements performing action are: 'I name this ship,' or 'I now pronounce you man and wife.' Austin shows that all utterances perform actions, even apparently constative ones, and he presents a three-level framework – locutionary, illocutionary and perlocutionary – to explain the process.

A locutionary act is the performance of an utterance, and hence a speech act. The locutionary act also refers to the ostensible meaning of speech expressions related to the verbal, syntactic and semantic aspects of any meaningful utterance (Austin 1962). The illocutionary force of an utterance is the speaker's intention in producing that utterance. An illocutionary act is an instance of a culturally defined speech act type, characterized by a particular illocutionary force. Austin (1962) indicates that a perlocutionary act also is a speech act, which is centred at the level of its psychological outcomes, such as enlightening, persuading, inspiring, convincing, scaring or otherwise getting someone to do something. A perlocutionary act is in some sense external to the performance, and it can be considered, in a sense, as the product of the illocutionary act. For this reason, when investigating perlocutionary acts, the effect on the hearer or reader is emphasized (101).

An instrumental prayer which is also called affirmative prayer in Christ Embassy is a form of prayer that focuses on a positive outcome rather than a negative situation. This prayer dwells on the desired state of the desired intention as if it has already happened rather than identifying the problem and then asking God for help to eliminate it. In Christ Embassy there is a belief that one can change things through one's words.[9] One can experience victory after victory, success after success, if one learns to value and practice speaking in line with God's words. They believe that the proper use of words is the easiest way of guaranteeing success, prosperity, health, peace and progress.[10]

Pastors of Christ Embassy regularly teach that God reveals himself through his words. However, that revelation alone would not change circumstances of life; it is the *Rhema* which means spoken or creative word.[11] They urge that prayer should consist of declarative language because words have the potential to materialize in the world and believers should declare that it is impossible for them to be sick, broke or afflicted. If things are not going well at home, it is certainly the work of Satan, and born-again Christians have the power to exercise dominion over him through affirmative prayer. This idea of Christ Embassy that words perform actions on the material world resonates with the concept of performativity. The ways and manners in which the utterance is constructed play a role in the effectiveness of the intended consequences of the speech. The concept of performativity is useful to better understand how they understand prayer. The following samples of prayers culled from *Rhapsody of Reality* (September 2013 edition) reveal performativity of their language.

Dear Father, I boldly declare that I live in joy, prosperity, health and peace continually. The blessings of the new creation, as revealed in your word, are fulfilled in my life today. The transcendent life of God and the supernatural effect of His righteousness are working vitally in my spirit, soul, and body. I experience growth development, progress, deliverance, prosperity, and health because I am walking in the reality of who I am in Christ, taking full advantage of His grace and awesome presence in my life. Glory to God!!

The language of these prayers is unambiguously performative as they involve declarative and command phrases. The locutionary speech acts of these prayers are series of utterances that express varieties of claims, declarations as well as various expressions of commands. The illocutionary force of the utterances in the prayers is the assumption that what one has declared and commanded already materialized. When a performer of the prayer said *Dear Father, I boldly declare that I live in joy, prosperity, and health*, he believed that his words perform an action of materializing joy, prosperity and health. Therefore, this prayer is performative because it acts in the world. The perlocutionary act or psychological effect of the prayer acts on the performer, and it resides in his/her feeling of firm conviction that the prayer has been answered, which creates the sense of the presence of the desired states.

According to Austin (1962), effectiveness of performative speech depends on the authority of the speaker. For example, the fulfilment of the act of saying 'I pronounce you husband and wife' required a licensed minister before two people who are prepared to wed. In Christ Embassy, the authority of an individual believer to declare his desired state in prayer comes from using the phrase 'in the name of Jesus'. Oyakhilome (2004: 35) affirms, 'We have the power of attorney to use the name of Jesus; He gave us the legal right to stand in His stead and act on His behalf.' He further asserts, 'When we speak or make declarations in the name of Jesus we are taking His place or standing in His stead as master over all things' (40). It is important to notice here that the phrase 'in the name of Jesus' is not a magical phrase that performs a miracle; it is also not invoking the non-present spiritual agent like Jesus himself to act as a medium between the believer and God. What the phrase does is to transform and elevate the ontological status of the prayer performer into the superior position of Jesus himself during the time of prayer. As the authoritative declaration of a minister concluded the bond of marriage between a couple, members of Christ Embassy believe that whatever they declared in their prayer is bound to materialize because they have assumed the authority of Jesus during the moment of prayer.[12]

Affirmative prayer diverges from the traditional way of praying in the mainline churches where believers feel small and insignificant in front of the divine. The most significant point of divergence is that here it is the performer of the prayer who engages in the creation of an object of his needs through his words as opposed to imploring God to gratify the needs through his powers. Members of Christ Embassy approach God in their prayer with self-confidence and a sense of authority. The believers do not humbly beseech God for any favour as in the regular prayer of supplication in the mainline churches. Most historical churches do not recognize this form of prayer and regard it as an infringement on the sovereignty of God.

Another important difference with traditional forms of praying is that affirmative prayers work in reverse as opposed to the prayers of supplication which request God to do something. Here it is assumed that the desired situations have already been gratified. For instance, *I thank you, dear heavenly Father, for granting me the spirit of wisdom, understanding, and knowledge, which enables me to deal excellently in the affairs of life*. This prayer starts with thanking God for already granting the desired results of the request. One of the most important criteria for the efficacy of affirmative prayer in Christ Embassy is absolute conviction that the prayer has been answered. Thanking God is a way of expressing that conviction. In one of his sermons, Pastor Chris stated that one of the greatest problems among Christians is the prevalence of unanswered prayers. He identified the source of the problem as the weak conviction on the part of the believers. He told the audience that as soon as they finished praying they should immediately burst into jubilation that their prayer has been answered. It is this conviction that makes the affirmative speech of the prayers more effective. What constitutes the structure and form of affirmative prayer is a declarative statement, emphasizing the end result, coupled with absolute conviction on the gratification of the prayer. These three elements constitute the formula in which all wishes of the believers must be expressed.

In prayers there is power: Prayers of instrumentality in NASFAT

Each Sunday the chief imam of Abuja central branch gives to the congregation a prayer for solution to different personal problems such as health, finance or employment. On 30 September 2015, the chief imam of the branch gave a prayer for couples who could not bear children. He said whoever has this problem should recite Surah *Fatiha* and verse Q 25:74 seven times after each morning and night prayer for seven days. After the seven days, the person should give *sadaqa* of 50 naira (0.10 cent) note to a baby carried by its mother in the street. The imam said youth should prepare because next week he would give special prayers for those who are looking for employment.

This form of prayer is seldom practised by members of Izala and *Salafi* groups in northern Nigeria except if the prayer instructions come from Hadith. Sufis apply this kind of prayer in their daily lives but their leaders rarely share them with the public. They take it as a secret property to be shared only to selected individuals. But NASFAT leaders, together with some authors, share these forms of prayers with the Muslim public, thereby removing the wall of secrecy which Sufis build around them.

Another source of instrumental prayers in NASFAT is a series of booklets distributed on Sundays that present varieties of instrumental prayers for solving problems or achieving good things in life. A twenty-five-year-old interlocutor in NASFAT showed me an instrumental prayer book written by Sheikh Muddathir Ajaliye. The book contains prayers for breaking the yoke of barrenness, finding a life partner, taming delinquent children, achieving success in examination, finding employment opportunities, gaining job security, having luck after job interview, offering prayer against transfer from safe to dangerous places for employees and offering prayer for curing health conditions that defy medical solution. I had a conversation with one of the leaders, Yusuf Kabir, about his view on these genres of prayers. He told me that he has a firm conviction about the efficacy of Islamic prayers, and he practised them regularly. He affirmed that he got tremendous knowledge of prayers from the books of Sheikh Muddathir Ajileye (2011), who is one of the most prolific writers of prayer books in the south-west. He continued that this sheikh teaches people about the evil of this world and the ways of countering them through prayers. According to Kabir, many people live in constant fear of the 'powers of darkness', because they believe that these forces cause misery and destruction to human life. He said people nowadays have devised various means of overcoming evil forces by wearing an amulet, visiting spiritualists or drinking a magical potion for protection against such invisible dark forces. Kabir continued,

> Islam affirms the real existence of satanic and demonic forces and their powers. But at the same time, Islam has provided Muslims with means to protect themselves from evil forces. Through confidence and trust in Allah coupled with fervent prayers, the powers of darkness can be defeated. There is power in the

name of Allah, and one must have faith in him wholeheartedly before one can experience his power and liberation. With his name every form of evil can be overcome. (Interview, 22 December 2013)

These words show a remarkable resonance with Pentecostal rhetoric about the invisible world with its evil denizens. If one supplants the name 'Allah' with 'Jesus', this discourse could be attributed to any Pentecostal pastor in Nigeria. Both Christianity and Islam have the notion of the dark forces of the invisible realm, but the style in which this idea is articulated here reveals a Pentecostal influence on the speaker. The statement that there is power in the name of Allah invokes the Pentecostal statement of 'power in the name of Jesus'. Even though Muslims revere the names of Allah and use them in different forms of prayer, they still seldom use the statement that there is 'power in the name of Allah'. According to Kabir, there are many special Islamic prayers that can be utilized for all kinds of problems. Kabir described some of the applications of *Ya-Sin*, which he claimed to apply with practical results on so many occasions in his life.[13]

For seeking good employment recite Surah Ya-Sin once and in each verse of the surah recite Surah Fatihah (Q1:1–7) once. This process should be repeated after each five daily obligatory prayers with fasting for seven days and with intention. Follow up with *sadaqa* after the seven days. For overcoming evil plans of the enemies, Surah Ya-Sin and at each seven *mubina* of the surah recite the following verse, Q4:45, once for seven days as follows: *Allah has full knowledge of your enemies: Allah is enough for a protector, and Allah is sufficient for [a] Helper.* After the seven days, one should make *sadaqa* with something sweet to young children. These are just a few examples of numerous applications of Surah Ya-Sin. (Interview, 13 December 2013, Abuja)

Kabir concluded that it is because of the importance of Surah *Ya-Sin* that it is recited every Sunday as the final act in NASFAT's worship service. He added that the Surah *Ya-Sin* is the only chapter that is written in the NASFAT prayer book in its entirety. It is for this reason, Adetona (2012) argues, that NASFAT makes available to its lay members possession of mysterious powers by giving them special prayer formulas. Adetona states that in NASFAT once devotees can recite or perform the prescribed recipes or litanies, they become their own therapist. So, the legitimate procedure for the individual to access spiritual power is achieved not through the tenacity of the master–disciple relationship as found in Sufi organizations but through a guided leadership of a missionary authority.

Some Muslims in northern Nigeria, particularly from Sufi orders, believe that Surah *Ya-Sin* has magical potency that can be used to harm others. *Zan ja maka Yasin* is a common Hausa saying in northern Nigeria, meaning 'I will recite Yasin for you.' When somebody says this to his enemies, one means he/she is going to harm the enemy with the magical power of Surah *Ya-Sin*. In northern Nigeria people of Maiduguri, the capital of Borno State, are famous for their knowledge of the semi-magical formulas of Surah *Ya-Sin*. As a result, believers in the magical power of *Yasin* fear their *mallams* who specialize in such formulas. And many go to the city to seek solutions when they are facing serious problems that involve powerful opponents or seemingly insurmountable challenges. A friend told me that people circulate messages on WhatsApp Messenger that members of Shi'ite group are reciting Surah *Ya-Sin* to President Muhammadu Buhari to revenge the loss of lives they suffered in their clash with the Nigerian army and subsequent incarceration of their leaders in December 2015. As a result, mainstream Sunni Muslims are encouraged to recite Surah *Ahzab* (Q 25:5) to protect the president from the harm of *Ya-Sin*. This application of Surah *Ya-Sin* is quite similar to the imprecatory prayer[14] of Pentecostals, which they use to shout fire to the enemies and forces of darkness.[15]

Semiotic ideologies, sensational forms and the functions of prayers of instrumentality

The performativity of Christ Embassy's instrumental prayer speeches highlights how prayer is understood to perform actions in the material world. However, since the prayer is fundamentally directed at the spiritual world, we need to examine higher functions ascribed to the prayers of instrumentality speeches and their perceived effect on non-material reality. Understanding the ascribed semiotic functions of the instrumental prayers in Christ Embassy and NASFAT requires examining their semiotic ideologies.

Webb Keane (2008) propounds a theoretical analysis on semiotic ideology which he conceives as a culture's modes – or perceived ideal modes – of communication through language and objects (16–18). Keane points out that semiotic ideologies include both linguistic and non-linguistic signifiers – 'music, visual imagery, food, architecture, gesture, and anything else that enters into actual semiotic practice' – in which particular moral and political interests are endowed (21). According to Keane, this form of ideologies most commonly operates below the subject's level of self-conscious awareness, appearing as normal processes of life. According to Keane, Western semiotics posits a radical disjuncture between signs and their referents. In this Western model, signs have meanings that are supposed to be decoded; words and things are to be rationally manipulated as tools of communication without containing inherent power or agency. Through historical analysis Keane attempts to bring to light the Western denigration of materiality and fervent objectification of the world. Keane wants to break away from this tradition and to restore the salient importance of materiality to its semiotic subordination.

Instrumental prayers in Christ Embassy are imputed with spiritual agency and different forms of significations. For instance, consider the semiotic analysis of the following prayer expression: *I boldly declare that I live in prosperity and health.* The speaker in this prayer is stating that he or she lives in a particular state or condition characterized by prosperity and health. These circumstances are described by the signifier of 'prosperity', which denotes a state of thriving and flourishing material abundance, especially in a financial respect. And the signifier 'health' denotes a general condition of the body or mind in relation to the absence of illnesses, injuries or impairments. However, the relationship between signs (words) and their referents (desired objects) in Christ Embassy's affirmative prayers assumed a radically different mode of signification than the one describe above. The signifiers (words such as prosperity) in this respect are not restricted to referring or standing for particular denotation or state of prosperity or well-being; instead, the signifiers call their referents into existence from the spiritual world. For instance, uttering of 'prosperity' and 'health' goes beyond merely signifying certain conditions but rather creating those conditions. In this form of prayer, words have the power of creation because they are imputed with a spiritual agency which grants them a special ontological status that links them with the invisible realm. The process of creation begins in the invisible realm and remains in a latent condition there until the right time for materialization in the physical plane. Oyakhilome (2005: 7) explains the mechanics of this process: 'When we pray, we make tremendous power available, dynamic in its working, causing changes in our favor. Certain prayer sessions are specially designed by the Lord to help straight [en] things out for us in the spirit-realm regarding our immediate or later future as individuals, families or ministries.'

The implication of this explanation lies in the fact that the prayer speeches are inextricably connected with both the physical and the transcendent world. One of the most important findings by Webb Keane in his in-depth study of Calvinist missionaries and Sumba people of Indonesia is that ideas can never be separated from materiality and word forms. This is one of the reasons he states, 'semiotic ideologies required material instantiation' (Keane 2003: 80). Thus, it is arguable that semiotic ideologies encoded in affirmative prayers are entangled with the materiality encapsulated in the desired results of the prayers. However, it is important to note that the efficacy of the affirmative prayer depends on the accuracy of the speech expression. This is because the wrong expression of the prayer language may result in adverse manifestation. For instance, in NASFAT if the formula of prayer required repeating a certain verse of the Qur'an or name of Allah ninety-nine times, one has to do it exactly for the prayer to be efficacious. In Christ Embassy the language of the prayer must be performative and end with 'in the name of Jesus'. In NASFAT the Qur'anic verses selected to form the instrumental prayers are ascribed with semiotic functions, hence their ability to make changes in the empirical world. The relationship between the Arabic texts of the verses and the messages they refer to (commentaries and exegesis) is suspended and replaced with a semiotic system that has a unique set of referents.

It is important to notice that most common personal problems and needs have their instrumental prayers specifically designed to address them. In looking at these prayers, one can easily detect a connection between the problem or need and the literal interpretation of the Qur'anic verse that serves as the basis of the prayer formula. For instance, one of the deputy imams in NASFAT told me that prayer against opposition and protection requires one to recite the following verse: *Sufficient for Us Is Allah, and an Excellent Guardian Is He* (Q 3.173).[16] The verse should be repeated 450 times daily with the intention and 133,000 times for seven days if the situation is serious. In this example, the link between the need for protection against the machination of the enemies and the reliance on God who is stronger than the enemies and invoking his excellent guardianship is clearly established. Qur'anic verses in these prayers act as a sign system with the problems they refer to as their referents. In NASFAT as opposed to Christ Embassy, ordinary human speech does not possess a unique ontological status that grants it an agentive capability, but the recitation of Qur'anic verses, as the sacred word of God, encompasses such agency.[17]

Another important feature of the instrumental prayer in NASFAT is the rhythmic repetitive recitation. These prayers require repeating certain verses or names of God several times, usually at night. Apparently, repeatability is part of the structure of the prayer formula. Repeatability plays a vital role in creating the intended pragmatic effect and facilitates its physical manifestation. The example of a NASFAT prayer given above that requires 450 times of repetition – and

133,000 times if the problem is 'serious', such as an enemy who wants to kill oneself through spiritual attack or witchcraft – highlights the function of repetition in the performance of prayer. The sheer volume of repetition would overcome the seriousness of the situation.

Instrumental prayers in Christ Embassy and NASFAT can be analysed in the framework of the notion of sensational form, which calls attention to the human senses in regular and structured performances that are believed to be a communion with the divine. Meyer (2011: 29) asserts, 'Sensational forms are relatively fixed modes for invoking and organizing access to the transcendental, offering structures of repetition to create and sustain links between believers in the context of particular religious regimes.' In Christ Embassy, bodily gestures are important aspects of affirmative prayer performance. The prayers are uttered in a loud voice with agile body movements. During prayer, believers often move back and forth with their eyes closed and with their hands moving up and down. This form of prayer engages the entire human body and senses of the believers in the act of praying. The instructor of the foundation class Adewale asserted that for prayer to be efficacious and effective one has to immerse oneself thoroughly in the act of prayer and do it with utmost confidence and relative aggressiveness. This practice is to guarantee a quick materialization of prayer.

On many occasions instrumental prayers in NASFAT require performance of *nafila*, which is a *salat* that is non-obligatory but performed either to please God or to accompany different types of non-ritual prayers of supplication. Ritual prayer (*salat*) is one of the essential constituents of Islamic worship. In Islam, it is believed that anyone who engaged in the ritual prayer is in direct connection with the Creator. Apart from *nafila*, instrumental prayers have fixed structures and follows strict rules which must be followed as a precondition for the efficacy of the prayers.

Material sacrifices: Keys to the portals of prayers

Material sacrifice is the final stage of performing prayers of instrumentality in both Christ Embassy and NASFAT. Material sacrifices called *sadaqa* in NASFAT and seed offerings in Christ Embassy are given to the needy after successful completion for the speedy gratification of the prayer request. These offerings can take the form of money or any material item that has value and is cherished by the giver. Some prayers of instrumentality in NASFAT required a specific type of item known as *sadaqa*, and this may be a particular food or cloth. And sometimes even people who are supposed to receive *sadaqa* are specified and may include children, disabled or old women. For instrumental prayers to be efficacious, the rule of the *sadaqa* must be followed to the letter. Christ Embassy does not usually specify a particular kind of offering, but it is emphasized that one should give something dear to one's heart. In Christ Embassy the offering is invalid if one gives out something that has no value to oneself. In Christ Embassy, as in many other Pentecostal churches, all forms of prayer need to be backed up with the seed offering. During services in Christ Embassy stories of people who made a big offering and received a great reward are told and repeated over and over again. These stories play a vital role in encouraging people to give money to the church for the purpose of getting quick results from their prayers.

Material sacrifices are understood as keys that open the portal to the invisible realm and facilitate the materialization of the prayer. When I asked one of my interlocutors in NASFAT about the importance of *sadaqa*, he told me that whatever the power of the prayer, its result would remain latent and un-manifested. It is the *sadaqa* and its value that can open the door for it to manifest in the physical world. The larger and more valuable the *sadaqa* is, the bigger the result of the prayer. My teacher in the foundation school in Christ Embassy said something similar when he told me that whenever one prays, one should make sure to follow it up with a big offering for the purpose of getting a quick result.

It is arguable that *sadaqa* and seed offerings are not given to please the receiver; neither does the giver expect something in return from the receiver. Even though the material sacrifices are items of value given out to others, these valuables still are symbolically directed towards the transcendent realm. The believers who offer *sadaqa* or a seed offering expect reciprocations from the spiritual ream, not from the recipients of their offerings. It is through this symbolic sacrifice that seed offerings and *sadaqa* bridge the gap between the visible and invisible worlds. The two worlds are conjoined by the material offerings which have the capacity to act in the invisible world and elicit dormant desired situations into the physical realm.[18] Sometimes in both NASFAT and Christ Embassy there is a relationship between the specified material offerings and the objectives of prayer. For instance, the *sadaqa* of a 50 naira (0.10 cent) note required to give to a child carried by his/her mother that I mentioned earlier has a causal relationship to the objective of the prayer, which is childbirth. The *sadaqa* symbolically connects what one wishes to get (a child) and the child that already exists in the material world. Moreover, it is noticeable that the pastor gave out his car as seed offering when he desired a bigger car, which was a jeep. This symbolic causal relationship is part of the function of material sacrifices, similar to a saying 'like attracts like'.

Moreover, my interlocutor Abubakar Musa told me that another function of *sadaqa* is helping the body adjust after immersion in instrumental prayers. He said some prayers have tremendous power, and they can exact immense pressure on the human body. He added that this pressure may result in pain, and it is *sadaqa* that removes the pain. He said he experienced this condition himself several times, particularly after performing powerful instrumental prayers of Surah *Ya-Sin*. This experience suggests that instrumental prayers are not merely abstract speech requests towards the Sovereign Deity. Instrumental prayers are understood to be a potent force that has a material dimension since they can interfere with the well-being of the physical human body.[19]

When a prayer failed to materialize

Abdulwahab Rahim, a thirty-six-year-old secondary schoolteacher, is an active and dedicated member of NASFAT. We became close friends during my fieldwork period in Abuja and we happened to live in the same area. Rahim is a highly dedicated Muslim who takes religious duties seriously. Contrary to many members of NASFAT that I came across, his view of prayer is somehow non-pragmatic. He has a fervent belief that prayer can replace physical action in achieving pragmatic effects. He claimed to have a vast knowledge of instrumental prayers that he could deploy to solve all his problems and achieve his desires. One day he asked me to help him write a business proposal to a wealthy businessman who has a mining company. He wanted the businessman to fund his new innovative business idea. I told him that this is going to be difficult and that the businessman may not invest his money on such a risky and costly undertaking. He said, 'No matter the difficulty I have powerful prayers which if I performed, this idea would necessarily materialize. Just help me with the proposal and I will do the rest. I have 3000 naira (6.32 euro) which I will use to buy two roosters for the *sadaqa* after the prayer.' At the end of the day I helped him in drafting the proposal and he submitted it to the businessman after he performed the prayers, but the businessman rejected the proposal outright. And Rahim never raised the issue to me again. To Rahim instrumental prayers are symbolic capital that gives him hope in achieving his goals, but on many occasions the desired results remain elusive. It is in this sense that Oberlies (2017) maintains that sometimes during prayer the aim being addressed may even recede into the background, so that the communicative aspect of praying becomes less prominent; prayer then is more an exercise in self-expression, or rather an act of relief.

Instrumental prayers have two possible outcomes: either they work and produce the aspired result, or they fail to materialize. However, people do not think of failure because prayer is directed to the supernatural world or the realm of Absolute Reality. What I observed in my interactions with my interlocutors is that they work to achieve their goals and pray about it. When they succeed, they attribute their success to the efficacy of prayer and go to the church or mosque and give testimonies and thanks to God for gratifying their prayers. I attended a service in Christ Embassy in February 2014, when a young man went to the front of the church to give his testimony. He said he applied for a South African visa, but his application was rejected. He came home and started an affirmative prayer for hours every day and kept on trying different avenues of getting the visa. But as he intensified his affirmative prayers seeing himself in South Africa, he finally got the visa through intervention by a Sudanese diplomat who has a contact in the South African embassy. The congregation began to shout Hallelujah. I also witnessed similar testimonies in NASFAT Sunday worship service. In March 2014 a member came and gave a testimony that he wanted the congregation to join him in thanking God because his prayer has been answered; he got the new job that he had been praying for a long time. These kinds of testimonies reinforce the belief about the efficacy of prayer and people often circulate success stories of others as evidence that prayer works.[20]

If the prayer fails to yield the desired result and the situation is desperate, some try other means outside the purview of the church or mosque to pursue their goals. Mary Jacobs, thirty-five years old, is a devoted member of Christ Embassy and works with a travel agency in Abuja. She came from a Roman Catholic background, but she converted to Pentecostalism and joined Christ Embassy. She told me that her greatest problem now is getting a husband because at more than thirty years old she needed the security of marriage. She said she was dating a military man, but he refused to propose to her. She stated that she had prayed tirelessly for years but without success. She became desperate about the issue because her parents and other members of her family put enormous pressure on her to marry. When she became exhausted with instrumental prayers, she decided to try another avenue. She asked her friend who is a member of an esoteric group, Eckankar, to teach her psychic or mind power techniques that she can use to solve her problem. These are para-psychological abilities which she thought all members of Eckankar possessed. But her friend told her they do not dabble in such activities and this is just an assumption by outsiders.

When I asked her whether it is proper as a Christian to go to the extent of seeking help outside the realm of Christianity, she responded that psychic powers are not magic. She said in her view what is wrong is going to the *babalawos* who conjure up demonic powers or a priest of traditional religion. She continued that the teachings of Pastor Chris made references to the power and ability of the human mind to act and effect changes in the material world. According to her, para-psychological abilities do not infringe on the doctrine of Christianity. I asked her whether she would like her Christian friends in the church to know that she sought the help of an esoteric group for her personal problem. She responded that if they knew, they would chastise her and condemn what she did even though some of them are secretly doing the same thing or, even worse, going to the *babalawos*.[21]

On many occasions no matter how hard one prayed, the intended outcome of prayer remained unanswered. Since there is a belief that God cannot fail his children or servants, an explanation must be found to rationalize why cherished goals do not materialize. Members of Christ Embassy who do not get results after praying exhaustively for a long period pause and cross-examine their prayers. If the formulation of the prayer is correct, then the problem is probably with the erroneous thought and utterances of the person praying. This is because negative thoughts and utterances can spoil prayer and result in manifesting adverse circumstances, according to the teaching of the church.[22] The responses of NASFAT members on the issue of non-materialization of prayer are based on the argument that God has answered the prayer, but withheld the result because it will not be good for the person at that time. The argument adds that God knows what is best for individuals. However, whether or not the prayer for particular desired goals is successful, people move forward with new prayers or new challenges. They dwell on the memory of the past success of prayers and ignore the failure through rationalization or downplaying it altogether.

Conclusion

This chapter has looked at three genres of prayers in Christ Embassy and NASFAT and analysed them as practices of mediation that facilitate contact with the transcendent realm. Prayers of adoration (praise and worship and melodious recitation) and aesthetic speeches (glossolalia and *zikr*) generate emotion that creates perceptions and experiences of communion with the divine. Despite the differences in forms and structures of the instrumental prayers of the two religious groups, the semiotic ideologies attributed to them share significant similarities. The similar semiotic forms of instrumental prayers in Christ Embassy and NASFAT centre on the perception of these prayers as active agents that can enact pragmatic changes in both the physical and the transcendent worlds.

Instrumental prayers are semi-magical in nature because they are conceived to possess inherent energy and spiritual potency to manipulate events, albeit with the correct application of the rules governing their performances. Furthermore, to many members of Christ Embassy and NASFAT, instrumental prayers are spiritual assets tantamount to cultural capital that give them hope and self-assurance. They cherish the awareness that they have something powerful and effective which they can resort to in times of need and crisis. Despite the fact that instrumental prayers do not always deliver results, members still sustain their faith about the efficacy of the prayers through rationalization of the failures.

Prayers address not only emotional and socio-economic distress but also problems perceived as supernatural. The fear of evil, demonic forces and spiritual attacks from perceived enemies is deep-rooted among both Christians and Muslims in Nigeria. There is no doubt that prayers in NASFAT and Christ Embassy foster confidence and a sense of immunity from these supernatural evils. Many members of the two religious groups told me that they do not feel the need to seek for protection against evil from the medicine men because they believe that they already have divine protection through their prayers.

The similarities of the forms of Christ Embassy and NASFAT prayers lie in the fact that the latter consciously organize their prayers to respond to the challenges of Pentecostals. However, it is important to note that NASFAT did not invent these prayers; the prayers already exist in the Islamic tradition. NASFAT ulama only reorganize the forms of some Islamic prayers to make them more responsive to the psychological and socio-economic needs of urban Muslims, particularly youths, working class people, and professionals. The emphasis on prayers that respond to the needs of urbanites, for instance, in the areas of finance, employment and even obtaining foreign visas reveals the influence of Pentecostals on NASFAT. In another sense, it can be argued that NASFAT has borrowed from Pentecostalism the practice of putting both devotional and instrumental prayers at the centre of their religiosity. Moreover, similarities of the forms of prayers of the two religious groups highlight that religious diversity may not always result in conflict and clash but also gives rise to mutual influence and borrowing.

Oral transmission of the sacred:
Preaching in Christ Embassy and NASFAT

Introduction

Preaching is an integral part of Islamic religion and it is one of our major activities in NASFAT. Preaching is not worship in the legal sense of Islamic *shari'ah* such as *salat* or Ramadan fasting, but it is of prime importance because it can inspire believers to be more pious and more committed in their faith. In NASFAT we place great emphasis on preaching because it reminds Muslims about their Creator and the fact that they are created to worship him alone. And preaching is one of the important means through which Islam spreads throughout the world. These are some of the reasons that we take preaching seriously and also organise preaching activities regularly in NASFAT.

These are the words of one of the assistant imams in NASFAT, Lamin Shola, during my interview with him in November 2013 after Friday prayer. He was telling me about the importance of preaching in NASFAT and Islam in general.[1] Three major tropes could be discerned in these short remarks – preaching as a reminder about the presence of God, preaching as a force for motivating people in the acts of piety and righteousness, and preaching as a medium for spreading the word of God. These three tropes could also be found in the notion of preaching in Christ Embassy.

People travel to Abuja from all corners of the country in search of economic opportunity. However, considerable numbers of these people remained unemployed or underemployed due to the city's limited resources. Poverty and deprivation are exacerbated by the poor infrastructure and lack of social services in the outskirts and satellite towns of the city. Preaching appeals to many people because it provides a coping mechanism by ascribing meaning to difficult situations and afflictions. Many urbanites find it a helpful resource for navigating the adverse conditions in Nigerian cities. Preaching also touches on the issue of personal piety and spirituality as well as the social problems of ethno-religious diversity.

Since Christians and Muslims share the same living space, it is important to compare their preaching in order to understand the religious practices that shape their everyday lives. Preaching is one of the most important activities practised by both Muslims and Christians, and plays a central role in the religious life of many believers. This chapter analyses the styles of preaching in Christ Embassy and NASFAT within the framework of performance theory. I argue that preaching is a practice of mediation that is facilitated by several factors, including the eloquence and authority of the preachers as well as aspects such as dress, background music and preaching assistants. I show that preaching is a vital instrument for empowering urban residents with the necessary mental resources for meeting the challenges of the urban environment. Preaching is one of the most regular activities in the worship services of Christ Embassy and NASFAT. It occurs at most of their religious gatherings, from congregational Sunday sermons to large-scale mass gatherings such as the Night of Bliss spectacle in Christ Embassy and the National Annual Lectures in NASFAT. In Christ Embassy, one of the purposes of preaching is a total transformation of the individual mindset and the cultivation of new norms and values. Preaching in NASFAT has the purpose of producing modern and pious Muslims who can live comfortably in pluralistic urban settings and project a positive image of Islam.

This chapter has three sections. The first section explores the major recurrent themes that occur in the preaching of Christ Embassy and NASFAT, and shows how they are anchored in the teachings and theological understandings of the two groups. The second section deals with the issue of religious authority and listening in each group. The third section analyses preaching practices in Christ Embassy and NASFAT as performances of mediation, showing that affect and emotion facilitate a sense of divine presence during preaching performance. This section also explores preaching practices as techniques of self-cultivation in Christ Embassy and NASFAT.

Preaching in Christ Embassy and NASFAT

Themes

Even though the teachings of Christ Embassy are communicated through several means, including print and digital media, the predominant mode of transmitting the teachings is preaching. Preaching in Christ Embassy is based on the command of Jesus to his disciples, 'Go ye therefore, and teach all nations, baptizing them in the name of the Father, and of the Son, and of the Holy Ghost: teaching them to observe all things whatsoever I have commanded you' (Matthew 28: 19–20). In Christ Embassy, preaching is conceived as a platform for teaching believers the precepts of Christianity and revealing hidden truths and the meaning of the Scriptures. In a nutshell, preaching serves the functions of soul-winning or evangelism, religious pedagogy and the attempt to spiritually and mentally transform the members.

One of the recurrent themes of preaching in Christ Embassy that distinguishes the church from other Pentecostals is the concept of sin. In one of his sermon broadcasts during Sunday services in the Abuja Karu branch, Pastor Chris taught that faithful Christians are free from sin because the Bible says they are justified, and the atonement death of Jesus has already conferred forgiveness on them (sermon by Pastor Chris, 1 December 2013).[2] Another radical teaching of Christ Embassy that distinguishes the church from other Pentecostal and mission churches is the view that the New Testament begins after the resurrection of Jesus in the chapter of John. The chapters of Matthew, Luke, Mark and part of John are considered part of the Old Testament (sermon by Pastor Chris, 8 December 2013).

Pastor Chris teaches his congregation that Christianity is not a religion, but it is engaging in a vital relationship with God. He argues that 'Christianity is the pulsating life and power of God in the human body' (Sunday preaching, 8 December 2013). Apart from Christ Embassy, many Pentecostals share this view of going beyond the threshold of religion. This view came as a result of an increasingly negative connotation of the term 'religion', which is associated with rigid dogma, fanaticism and stale rituals. The experiential nature of Pentecostalism and its claimed ability to receive guidance from the Holy Spirit leads some members of Christ Embassy to feel that they have transcended the rigid dogmas of religion. In many of their preaching, pastors of Christ Embassy refer to non-Pentecostal faiths within and outside of the Christian spectrum as dead religions. In one of his sermons, the senior pastor of the Karu branch in Abuja said, 'Despite the conspiracy of Muslims to take over the world; Islam cannot give life.' According to him, there is only one name that gives life, which is the name of Jesus (7 September 2014). However, despite their claim of going beyond religion, I noticed that members of Christ Embassy act and behave like other religious people with a strong sense of Christian identity. Their informal conversations involve a 'we versus them' attitude towards perceived others such as Muslims and Catholics.

The pastors of Christ Embassy rarely touch upon topics that could cause dread and anxiety in their audience, such as sin and hellfire, but instead focus on positive themes that offer delightful promises. One of the essential themes that dominate the preaching in Christ Embassy is the principle of prosperity. According to Bradley Koch, 'the prosperity gospel is a doctrine that contains the notion that God wants people to be prosperous, especially financially. Adherents to the prosperity gospel believe that wealth is a sign of God's blessing and the poor are poor because of a lack of faith' (2014: 2).

Most of the preaching I witnessed in Christ Embassy centred on the idea that God has already destined every born-again Christian to be healthy and prosperous. This principle is based on the idea of an inherent right – 'in Christ' – of the born-again person for prosperity, health and freedom from disease. One of the pastors of Christ Embassy at Nyanya branch, Abuja, Pastor Moses Arams, constantly states, 'We don't do poverty in this church.' In his preaching, he always urges members to apply the techniques given to them by Pastor Chris to make themselves rich. This technique entails focusing the entire mental resources on the state of riches or any desired goal until it is materialized. For instance, if one wants to initiate a business one should focus one's attention on the future flourishing results of the business rather than on the ways and methods of getting to that prosperous state. Moreover, one should not worry about the feasibility of the business because worry may cancel and destroy the desired outcome (sermon preached by Pastor Chris, 10 August 2015). Pastor Chris and other preachers of the church constantly encourage members to be bold, self-confident and courageous in meeting life's challenges. Members are also encouraged to apply vigorous affirmative prayers to destroy obstacles that may threaten or hinder their progress.

Another recurrent theme that distinguishes Christ Embassy's preaching from that in other churches is that spiritual warfare is to be waged against negative thoughts and speech. These are considered more deadly than demons and witchcraft because they manifest in the material world and wreck the lives of believers. Controlling thought and speech requires robust and constant vigilance that is tantamount to spiritual warfare. The preachers regularly ask members to cast out negative speech and thoughts that produce sickness and poverty. Thoughts and speech are understood to have creative potency, and their contents can take shape in the spiritual realm and eventually materialize in the natural world. This stance suggests that the spiritual realm is enmeshed and interacts with the physical reality; the entities of the spiritual world are merely invisible replicas of the physical entities. In this view the actions of people in the physical world have greater consequences beyond the ordinary course of events because people are situated in a web of invisible forces that continually influence their lives.

By contrast, other Pentecostal churches (such as the highly prominent Mountain of Fire and Miracle church) put great emphasis on the issue of deliverance from demonic forces and witchcraft attacks. Pastor Chris and his associate pastors in Christ Embassy instead focus on miraculous healing of diseases rather than placing emphasis on exorcism. Pastor Chris often emphasizes that Satan, who is the leader of demons, has already been vanquished by the risen Christ, and is incapable of ruling over true believers. This is the reason why believers do not need deliverance from demons. Pastor Chris criticizes Pentecostal preachers who practise deliverance in their preaching as being ignorant of the true meaning of Christianity. In one of his Sunday sermons he expressed this as follows:

> In Africa, there are witchcraft spirits. Most of these [deliverance] preachers are sons of native doctors, or they are former native doctors, grandsons of former native doctors, cousins of native doctors. They came from this fetish background where witchcraft is the order of the day, and they carried it into Christianity. So, all they see is demons and deliverance. No Christian needs deliverance from the devil and this is a fact. But that is not to say that a Christian could not have an attack or influence from the Satan. But the fact is if you got to know that there is a devil messing with you, all you have to do is to say, 'Devil gets out in Jesus name'.[3]

Pastor Chris pointed out that Jesus Christ authorized believers to cast out demons in his name; hence they do not need to seek deliverance elsewhere. However, even though in Christ Embassy there is a belief about the dark forces, waging spiritual warfare against them is not emphasized. In fact, the struggle against evil in Christ Embassy is viewed as a detrimental practice because dark forces can only be vanquished by shifting one's consciousness away from them. Pastor Chris and other pastors of Christ Embassy preach that fear is a negative energy that draws the objects of fear into the life of believers. Thus, fearing dark forces is indirectly inviting them and making one susceptible to their attacks. The pastors preach that at the moment one becomes a born-again person one is already immune from the attack by evil denizens of the spirit realm. Despite the fact that pastors of Christ Embassy preach that people can protect themselves from evil forces through faith and affirmative prayers, the most important means of protection are magical mental techniques of positive thinking and diligent study of the Scriptures. Christ Embassy rejects the idea of ancestral curses that run through generations of the family as preached by many Pentecostal preachers. According to Christ Embassy, when one accepts Christ one is a new creation and every past affliction is broken instantly because Satan has no legal claim over born-again persons.

Despite Pastor Chris's denunciation of deliverance, his practice of miraculous healing in his Healing School and other religious spectacles such as the Night of Bliss could also be interpreted as the performance of deliverance. Deliverance is understood by many Pentecostal pastors that I interviewed as releasing an individual from bondage of physical or psychological afflictions caused by dark agents such as witches and demons. And this may include different types of sicknesses. However, Pastor Chris differentiates himself from other Pentecostal preachers by restricting the meaning of deliverance to the public practice of exorcizing demons alone. Whether the miraculous healing crusade of Pastor Chris and his Healing School programme is deliverance or not remains a problem of definition of deliverance.

On rare occasions the preachers of Christ Embassy use Muslims as an exemplary model for Christians when they are talking about the importance of commitment to faith. During one of the Sunday services I attended in Karu branch the pastor said, 'Even though Christians have the true faith, many are not committed in their faith. Look at how Muslims are serious and devoted to their religious obligations. When a Muslim converts to Christianity you will find that he is more serious than some who were born into the Christian faith' (Wednesday preaching, 5 February 2014). Muslims sometimes appear in the preaching of Christ Embassy portrayed as either competitors to Christians or as models of inspiration regarding dedication to religion. It is noticeable that preaching is a medium through which the distinctive teachings of Christ Embassy are transmitted. At the same time, Pastor Chris uses the medium of preaching to express his peculiar understanding of biblical doctrines such as the nature of sin and the spiritual power of thought and speech mentioned earlier. It is through these particular understandings embedded in preaching practices that Christ Embassy remains distinctive among other Pentecostals in Abuja and the country in general.

In NASFAT the notion of preaching does not differ from the general conception of preaching in mainstream Islamic groups. Preaching is embedded in the series of Qur'anic verses that encourage Muslims to share the message of Islam with others. Some of the verses regularly mentioned by NASFAT preachers are: 'But teach, for teaching benefits believers' (Q 51:55), and 'Call to the way of your Lord with wisdom and fair admonition, and argue with them in the kindest way' (Q 16:125). Based on these verses, preaching is conceived by leaders of NASFAT as an act of *da'wah*. The Arabic word *da'wah* generally means a preacher or lay believer calling people towards Allah and his instructions. There are two forms of *da'wah*. One aims at proselytizing non-Muslims by conveying to them the message of Islam either through preaching or informal one-to-one dialogue. The other form of *da'wah* involves organized preaching through which Muslims are reminded of their duties and responsibilities as commanded by Allah and his messenger. It is one of the utmost virtues in Islam to guide other Muslims into the proper understanding of their faith or to convert non-Muslims to Islam (Hirschkind 2004; Račius 2004).

The recurring themes in NASFAT's preaching are based on the portrayal of the beauty of Islam and its superiority over other religions, individual piety and moral values. In fact, the stated goals of NASFAT include notions of the beauty of Islam and morality. NASFAT preachers speak about *taqwa* (fear of God), and they always exhort believers to obey Allah and his messenger and observe their religious duty. They rarely engage in inter-religious antagonistic rhetoric in their sermons, but instead preach peaceful coexistence between Muslims and Christians. The preachers always denounce the protracted ethno-religious conflicts that have become a daily occurrence in northern Nigeria. In fact, the NASFAT leaders in Abuja were some of the first major Muslim groups to categorically denounce the Boko Haram attacks on Christians and called on Muslims to protect churches. In their attempt to project a new image of Islam, they urged the media to refrain from calling Boko Haram an Islamic sect. In one of his sermons in Abuja's central branch, Ustaz Yusuf Shitu asserted, 'Every Christian is a potential Muslim; therefore, killing him or her denies them the future opportunity of converting to Islam' (Sunday preaching, 17 November 2013).

NASFAT preachers discuss social justice and the need for just and fair distribution of resources in the country. They criticize the corruption and poor governance that engender poverty and various kinds of social malaise. They encourage political leaders to be just and resist corruption. The preachers also promote quality parenting at home through proper training of children according to Islamic ideals. They encourage Muslims to keep their promises, care for orphans, give to charity, be honest and fair in their interactions and to refrain from committing adultery. It is apparent that preaching in NASFAT is overwhelmingly based on encouraging Islamic orthopraxis. While members are regularly exposed to preaching, the crux of the issue is to what extent these injunctions are put into practice by individual members. In my dealing with members over the course of my fieldwork, I noticed that many aspects of preaching remained in the realm of cherished ideals without being transmuted into practice.

NASFAT preaching differs from that of the major Islamic groups such as Izala and *Salafi* in both themes and style. The themes of Izala and *Salafi* preaching centre on the agenda of purifying Islam from innovations and returning to the fundamentals of Islam as practised by the Prophet and his immediate companions. Through ubiquitous preaching in the urban environment, Izala and *Salafi* aim to 'promote religious and social reform strictly in line with the norms set by the Qur'an and the Hadith' (Sounaye 2014: 22). While the NASFAT preaching agenda focuses on spiritual renewal, Izala preaching involves vicious attacks on other religious groups perceived as deviating from the Sunnah of the Prophet (Paden 2008). NASFAT preachers rarely attack any group; in fact, the preachers stress that NASFAT is a non-sectarian and non-ideological movement and does not engage in theological disputes with people of different religious persuasions within Islam.

Despite the fact that Christ Embassy and NASFAT are from different religious traditions – Christianity and Islam – there are similarities between the themes of their preaching. In both Christ Embassy and NASFAT, the purpose of many sermons is to connect the audience with God. The preachers in these two religious groups quote scriptural verses to make their statements authoritative. Preachers in Christ Embassy and NASFAT tell stories of the prophets and great men from the Scriptures to illustrate moral lessons. The same religious figures such as Abraham, Moses and David are occasionally mentioned in the preaching of Christ Embassy and NASFAT, since these prophets appear in both the Bible and the Qur'an. Another important theme that always appears in the preaching of Christ Embassy and NASFAT is the importance of giving money to the cause of God. Pastors in Christ Embassy encourage their congregations to pay their tithes, give seed offerings and special donations to the church. In both Christ Embassy and NASFAT members are reminded of the abundant reward awaiting those who donate money to the cause of God. Their financial support is perceived as an investment that will be returned multiple times.

However, there are substantial differences in the preaching themes of Christ Embassy and NASFAT. For instance, Christ Embassy and NASFAT preach different notions of sin. Forgiveness in NASFAT is not preordained; forgiveness still depends on God's discretion. While pastors of Christ Embassy insist that they are not a practising religion, a considerable portion of NASFAT preaching focuses on expressing the beauty of Islam as a religion. The preachers do not attempt to privatize the practice of religion and reduce it to private individual spirituality as is the case with Christ Embassy. The preachers teach their audiences the principles of Islamic dogmas, creeds and rituals. In this sense, NASFAT remains committed to Islamic tradition but at the same time negotiates how to live in a modern pluralistic society as well as a public sphere dominated by Pentecostalism. This attempt of NASFAT to negotiate challenges posed by modernity and Pentecostalism can be understood through Talal Asad's notion of Islam as a discursive tradition that is constantly being reshaped to fit with an ever-changing world (1986). NASFAT's leaders make attempts to reorient the world view and praxis of Muslims in a modern pluralistic setting within the overarching framework of Islamic tradition. Christ Embassy takes a special position within Pentecostalism, which is again a distinct movement in (Protestant) Christianity.

Religious authority, listening and styles of preaching

Effective preaching mainly depends on the acceptance and authority of the preacher. In Christ Embassy preachers believe that God calls them into the ministry. They usually enrol in a seminary to learn more about Christian theology.[4] Christ Embassy's seminary, called Loveworld Ministerial College (LMC), is not as well institutionalized as some other Pentecostal schools, such as Anagkazo Bible and Ministry Training Center in Ghana described by Bruno Reinhardt (2015). In Christ Embassy even if one studies in the Ministerial College, one has to ascend through various level of leadership in the church before assuming a full pastoral position. However, religious authority does not entirely depend on theological knowledge but above all on the fact that one is called by God to preach the gospel of Jesus Christ. Pastor Chris bases his authority on this concept of unique calling as well as the gift of miraculous healing he received from God to heal people from different kinds of afflictions such as sickness and poverty. In one of his interviews with a journalist from *Daily Champion Newspaper*, he said,

> God has something to say, and I am his mouthpiece. So he does three things. Number one is to give me the message that He wants me to communicate; number two is for Him to draw the people that He wants to hear it, and number three is to confirm the message with miraculous signs. That is the way I look at

it. It is up to him. I am not sure that I have personal control over that. I think it
is just God's grace. (2005: 2)

Here, Pastor Chris is claiming that he is a representative of God. Hence he is
not just an ordinary person but a person chosen by God to convey his message
to the world. He is implying that everything about his preaching from his
words to the size of the audience is divinely designed. Therefore, participating
in his preaching is partaking in something way beyond the ordinary mundane
affairs.

One of my interlocutors, Ustaz Saddiq Ishola, told me that the selection of
(Missioner) imams in NASFAT to lead the religious activities of the organization,
including preaching, is based on three criteria: sound Islamic knowledge,
including mastery of the Arabic language, possession of a higher institution
certificate and impeccable moral character. A missioner or imam may continue
to build his authority and gain reverence from the members by showing piety,
leadership skill and eloquence in preaching. A spiritual leader who possesses
these qualities easily excites audiences during preaching. However, NASFAT
does not have a concept of calling, even though some of its religious leaders are
treated with respect because members regard them as people who are close to
God. The absence of charismatic leadership in NASFAT may be due to the fact
that in the organization, spiritual leadership has been highly decentralized and
democratized. Adetona (2012) argues that NASFAT's success lies in its strategy
to democratize and distribute spiritual leadership among young people who
are beaming with energy and enthusiasm. In fact, the absence of centralized
authority in regard to the spiritual functionaries of the society ensures that any
member of the imam's group could officiate the Sunday service in the absence
of the chief imam.[5] Thus, the leadership is not centred on an individual but on
many spiritual leaders. The former chief national missioner of the society, Alhaji
Akingbode, is not a charismatic figure but rather a respectable Islamic scholar.
Moreover, there is an absence of the notion of preachers embodying the divine
spirit, as is found in Christ Embassy. Invoking divine presence in preaching
comes through the preachers' ability to convey God's word as eloquently as
possible.

It is noticeable that in both Christ Embassy and NASFAT, listening is an
integral part of preaching performance since preaching is ineffective without
listening. In both groups, listening is a meritorious and pious act that becomes a
medium through which religious ideals are transmitted as well as a concomitant
transformation of the individual believer. In NASFAT, members are constantly

reminded of the merit of listening to the preaching. This is because preaching serves as a reminder of one's religious obligations and duties; listening to preaching is a highly important religious duty. In one of the Sunday services I attended on 23 February 2014, the imam quoted the following Hadith of the Prophet Muhammad to show the importance of listening to sermons: 'Whoever does *ghusl* [ablution], then comes to Jumu'ah [Friday], and prays what is decreed for him, then listens attentively until the *khutba* [sermon]) is over, then prays with him [the imam], will be forgiven [his sins] between that and the next *Jumu'ah*, and three days more.' The imam elaborated that the merit and importance of listening is not restricted to Friday sermons alone but extends to all Islamic preaching in which people are reminded to fear and obey Allah and his messenger (see Hirschkind 2006).

Similarly, members of Christ Embassy stress the importance of listening to preaching; paying attention to the words coming from the man of God is held to purify the hearts of the listeners and put them in constant touch with God. The pastors of Christ Embassy encourage their congregation to buy the tapes of Pastor Chris's preaching and listen to them regularly. It is through this listening that the word of God sticks to the minds of the believers. In one of the Sunday services of Durumi branch, the senior pastor Reuben Obinna stated, 'All our materials are anointed; therefore, engaging with them is a good way of being nourished by the anointing of the Holy Spirit' (Sunday preaching, 26 September 2015). It is believed that anointing can take the form of God's abiding presence that empowers a person to function in his or her gifts of grace (Asamoah-Gyadu 2013). The pastors consistently remind their congregation to immerse themselves in listening to Pastor Chris's preaching in order to be nourished by the anointing through the voice of the man of God. Bruno Reinhardt (2014) expresses a similar idea with regard to the Anagkazo Bible and Ministry Training Center where immersive listening or soaking in tapes serves as a form of grace transmission, a pedagogical apparatus, a spiritual exercise and a method of discipleship, as well as a technology of church government. Listening to preaching in Chris Embassy incorporates all the three elements mentioned by Reinhardt; particularly the words of the pastor are believed to be divinely inspired through the power of anointing.

Style of preaching

This sub-section analyses the style of preaching in Christ Embassy and NASFAT under the framework of the concept of performance. Barbara

Kirshenblatt-Gimblett states, 'by theorizing embodiment, event and agency in relation to live (and mediated) performance, performance studies can potentially offer something of a counterweight to the emphasis in cultural studies on literature, media and text as an extended metaphor for culture' (2008: 1). It is important to recall that 'the preaching performance is repeatable weekly, it demands an expectant audience, it centers on a definitive text and requires rehearsal and preparation' (Sennett 2003: 17). Preaching in Christ Embassy and NASFAT is a regular and repeatable activity that makes it part of each group's rituals. As Herbert Sennett observes with regard to Christian preaching,

> The Christian preacher prepares for the message to be presented on Sunday (or Saturday in some traditions). Although the preparation varies with various traditions, the preacher is rehearsing for the performance on demand weekly. The message prepared is usually based upon a biblical truth or text from the Bible. That message becomes the script the performance on demand. That message is then preached (or performed) at the appointed time and place (just like a play is presented at specific times and places). (2003: 4)

In Christ Embassy, preaching is one of the most regular practices in the activities of the church. In the Abuja branches, this happens on Sunday, Wednesday and Friday. Pastor Chris is the dominant figure in the preaching of Christ Embassy of Abuja branches. In every church service, there is a session when a recorded sermon by Pastor Chris is played via big screens in front of the church. Pastor Chris is a very charismatic person in Christ Embassy with powerful oratory skills, good command of English language and skilful use of body language. He is seen not as an ordinary person but as a man ordained by God to spread the gospel of Christ. Highly respected in the church, he is always referred to as the man of God. He redefined the meaning of the term 'man of God'. In one of his addresses to the leaders of the church, he said,[6] 'There are two categories of ministers of God: a pastor and a man of God, a pastor can sin, but a man of God is carefully chosen by God to serve him, therefore, he is protected by God from temptation and sin.'

Pastor Chris is very eloquent with good command of the English language and skilful use of body language. He is not viewed as an ordinary person but as a man ordained by God to spread the gospel of Christ. Pastor Chris's preaching style is like a journey that starts slowly but increases in tempo and speed in a crescendo effect as time progresses. The preaching reaches its climax when

Pastor Chris invokes the Holy Spirit through speaking in tongues and asks the congregation to do the same. This situation causes people to fall to the ground and rub themselves on the floor. In this state, the entire structure of the preaching collapses. Afterwards many claim that they had sublime religious experiences, were healed from different kinds of ailments or acquired fresh insight into their personal problems.

Preaching in Christ Embassy is not a spontaneous act but a rather carefully crafted and organized religious performance. This can be seen in the arrangement of the platform, the dress of the pastor, his manner of speech and body language. Preaching stages in Christ Embassy are large enough to provide an enormous space for the preacher to pace back and forth, enabling him to use a variety of gestures and gaze at different sections of the audience. The stage is artistically designed and decorated with small geometrical objects coupled with a colourful arrangement of flowers. In most cases the predominant colour of the stage is blue, with other complementary colours such as gold and white. The entire stage is illuminated with different colours of light. The preaching platform is designed in such a way that the audience finds it pleasant to view. Dress and exquisite appearance are certainly crucial parts of Christ Embassy's preaching repertoires. Like most Pentecostal pastors, the most common dress of the preachers, including Pastor Chris himself, is an immaculate suit and necktie. Pastor Chris's appearance includes retouched hair (jerry curl) with a relaxer instead of a usual haircut. It is evident that dress is another medium of communication in preaching performances (see Twigg 2009). Mary Roach-Higgins (1992: 2) states, 'dress functions as an effective means of communication during the social interaction; it influences peoples' establishing identities of themselves and others, and individuals' self-identities based on assigned and achieved positions within social structures'. The flawless suits worn by the pastors of Christ Embassy communicate the spirit of the prosperity gospel and the conformity of their teachings with modernity.

One aspect of the preaching style of Christ Embassy that resonates with the concept of performance is the deployment of background music in the process of preaching. Background music amplifies the preaching performance and reinforces the tempo and the rhythm of the preacher's voice. It increases the effectiveness of preaching because music can invoke emotion and inspire the mind. This practice conforms to the rationale for the use of background music in theatrical or cinematic performance. On many occasions Pastor Chris uses the moment of his preaching to showcase his charismatic power.

Sometimes in the middle of his preaching he will stop and say God has shown him someone in the congregation who has a particular health problem. He will ask the person to come forward to the stage and receive healing. This display of charismatic power during preaching is clearly meant to show that the preacher is acting as the instrument of the divine spirit. People in the congregation thus feel they are not listening to an ordinary talk but to a message that is emanating from the anointed tongue who speaks through the inspiration of the Holy Spirit.

NASFAT preachers use preaching assistants who stand behind them. One of the assistants has the job of melodiously reciting the Qur'anic verses that the preacher intends to quote. The other assistant repeats and amplifies the critical points of the preaching, creating jokes out of them or emphasizing the sentences of the preacher that invoke fear of God. There is no doubt that preaching assistants help to make the preaching more effective and enhance its performance. Ustaz Ishaq Adepoju is one of the most celebrated preachers in the NASFAT headquarters in Abuja. He told me that since he was a student at the university, he actively engaged in the Muslim Student Society of Nigeria (MSSN) as well as in the Tijāniyya Students Association at Olabisi Onabanjo University in Ogun State. He stated that he has been engaging in preaching since that time among students. When he joined NASFAT many years ago he quickly rose to the level of missioner or imam. He combined his preaching activities with his present occupation in a financial firm in Abuja. In addition to preaching in NASFAT, he also delivers preaching on television in Abuja, including the Islamic satellite channel TV Ifriqi (Figure 5.1).

Probably because of his Sufi background, Ustaz Ishaq Adepoju's preaching usually focuses on spirituality. He regularly mentions that one can cultivate spiritual stamina through remembrance of Allah and the practice of *zikr* or chanting the names of God. This stamina moves one closer to God and offers protection against evil and spiritual attacks. Ishaq always makes his preaching more effective by melodiously reciting both Arabic and Yoruba poetry. NASFAT members admire his preaching and respond emotionally. One member told me, 'Whenever Ishaq was preaching the power of his preaching touched me, and I felt it in my spirit. Even though I am dreaming of becoming a preacher, I doubt whether it is possible for me to become like Ustaz Ishaq' (22 December 2013).

The manner of Ishaq's preaching, from his agile body language to some of the phrases used, reveals the influence of Pentecostals. On many occasions the imam begins his preaching with the phrase 'It is well with you' in a loud voice,

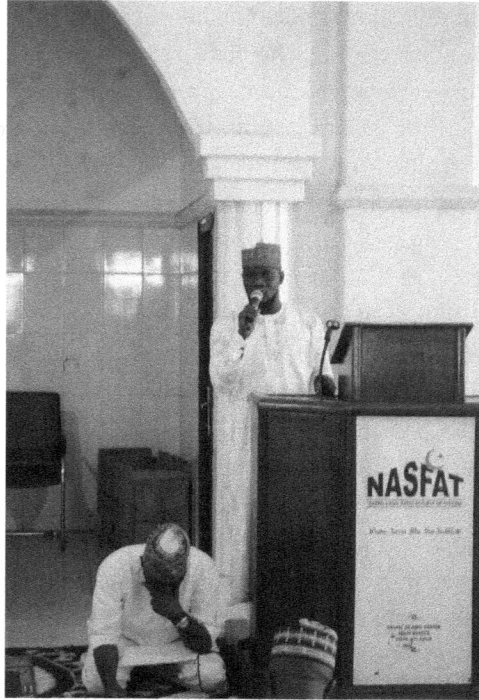

Figure 5.1 Preaching session during Asalatu. Source: Author.

pointing his hands towards the audience. I have also witnessed the utterance of this phrase both in Christ Embassy and other Pentecostal churches. On 24 November 2013 during the Sunday service preaching, the imam even used the Christian phrase 'born-again' to describe Islamic spiritual rejuvenation. He was discussing the demonic affliction and psychic attack on Muslims. He said people who are spiritually weak are more vulnerable to attack by dark forces. Muslims therefore have to be 'born-again' – meaning spiritually strong through committed acts of piety and prayers. This style of preaching differs from that of other Muslim groups such as the Izala and *Salafi* whose mode of preaching does not incorporate Pentecostal elements. In addition, the preaching of Izala and *Salafi* rarely invoke the motif of dark forces; in fact, Izala categorically denies that demons have influence on human life.

Preaching performance in both Christ Embassy and NASFAT is not a one-sided affair but involves a relationship between the preacher and the congregation. While the preacher influences the congregation with speech, gesture, movement and even appearance, the congregation also influences the preacher through paying attention, clapping of hands and loud utterances of satisfaction and approval. One may be tempted to think that the preacher has total control over the preaching performances, but this is not always the case. Peggy Phelan maintains, 'the agency of domination does not reside in the one who speaks (for it is he who is constrained), but in the one who listens and says nothing; not in the one who knows and answers, but in the one who questions and is not supposed to know' (1993: 163). When expressing approval and emotional response to preaching in NASFAT the congregation shouts '*Allahu Akbar*' while in Christ Embassy the audience screams, shouts and jumps in the church. The emotional expressions of approval by the audiences no doubt encourage and excite the preachers and sometimes lead them to exaggerate their points and gestures.

Preaching in Christ Embassy and NASFAT is a carefully configured craft that comprised of numerous factors, such as the dress and body language of the preacher, stage design and mode of amplification, which combine to achieve a profound effect. The two groups engage in different means of amplification to heighten the effect of the preaching. Christ Embassy employs background music, attractive dress and a glittering stage, while NASFAT uses preaching assistants, melodious recitation of the Qur'an and quotations of Arabic and Yoruba poetry for amplification. Another difference in the style of preaching is in the deployment of technology in Christ Embassy. The moment a pastor calls a verse, it is immediately projected on the big screen above the altar. In large branches of the church, the church services including the sermons are simultaneously projected live on the big screen.

Preaching as a performance of mediation

Preaching in both Christ Embassy and NASFAT is not restricted to communicating religious ideas and exhortations but also serves as a means of connecting people with God. Christ Embassy emphasizes the idea of anointing which means embodiment by the Holy Spirit. In one of his sermons, Pastor Chris stated that the altars of the Christ Embassy churches are permeated with the anointing of the Holy Spirit. A thirty-four-year-old junior pastor of Christ Embassy said, 'When a preacher steps on the altar he speaks under the influence of the Holy Spirit; therefore listening to preaching is an act of communion with God' (interview, 3 August 2014). In another sense, a preacher can pass the anointing of the spirit to the congregation.

All preachers in Christ Embassy are seen as carriers of the anointing of God, and they can convey that anointing to people who listen. In this vein preaching in Christ Embassy allows members to not only listen to the word of God but also to feel God in their body by becoming receptive to the anointing that is proceeding from the mouth of the preacher. An interlocutor told me, 'God is real. I heard that some philosophers denied the existence of God. But I know that he is real. This is because during worship service particularly during the preaching session I feel his presence, I feel the presence of God in my physical body' (interview, 22 June 2014). In another sense, preaching is rendered as an instrument that transmits profoundly sensuous and material ways to make the divine tangible and tactile (Butticci 2016).

NASFAT preachers invoke the presence of God in their preaching through powerful oratory that conveys the power of God and his overwhelming closeness to his servants. In one of the *Asalatu* (Sunday worship) I attended, the imam preached fervently on the importance of remembering Allah. He said,

> The greatest error a Muslim can commit is to be carried away by the glittering of this world and forget that Allah is watching him. Allah says in the Qur'an: 'I am closer to you [people] than your jugular veins.' Therefore, I urge you believers whatever you do in life always remember that you cannot escape the gaze of Allah, and you cannot escape his judgment. (10 August 2014)

The importance of remembering God and total surrender to his will consistently appear in the preaching of NASFAT. In fact, this topic is the favourite of the chief imam preaching in Abuja.

The message about the gaze of Allah on people and his judgment at the end of time touch the audience emotionally. One of the youth leaders of NASFAT related his experience during this kind of preaching: 'Sometimes this form of preaching makes me tremble and leaves me with the feeling of guilt and remorse. My heart becomes full of fear when I am reminded that Allah is with me and he is watching me' (interview, 23 July 2014). Another interlocutor said, 'It is easy for one to take for granted the presence of Allah but through preaching one can easily come to the reality of the continuous gaze of Allah' (interview, 23 July 2014).

Preaching in Christ Embassy and NASFAT goes beyond mere religious lectures; rather, it operates like a religious ritual that enables believers to experience the presence of God on a regular basis. Christ Embassy and NASFAT have different notions and ways of invoking the presence of God. For instance, there is the absence of anointing by the Holy Spirit in NASFAT and less emphasis on God's judgment in Christ Embassy. Nevertheless, despite these differences, the preaching in the two groups produces similar emotional experiences in the sense that the affect generated by the performance is interpreted as evidence of the divine presence (see Meyer 2012).

In both Christ Embassy and NASFAT, religious leaders play significant roles in the orchestration of emotions during services. Pastors of Christ Embassy regularly use suggestive statements during sensational preaching sessions, employing such phrases as 'Something is happening here,' 'God is present here, God is very close to you now.' They also employ other techniques such as excessive bodily gestures to express emotion in order to elicit the same in their congregations. It is in this vein that Riis and Woodhead (2010) posit that religious emotions happen in the realm of constructed interplay between social agent and structure. Therefore, emotion can be located between the opposite binaries of personal and relational; private and social; biological and social; active and passive. The preaching settings in both Christ Embassy and NASFAT create a suitable environment for interplay between the preacher and the audience as well as among the audience, which elicits and distributes emotions. In NASFAT, the imams quote Qur'anic verses melodiously to excite emotions by repeating a particular verse and raising up and down. The congregants follow suit by standing up, raising their voices and repeating *Allahu Akbar* with excitement and enthusiasm. In both organizations the emotion generated in the preaching practices is seen as evidence that the audience has been touched by the messages.

As mentioned earlier, the capacity of preachers to arouse powerful emotions on the congregation depends on their authority and legitimacy. Charles Hirschkind (2006) aptly elaborates this process in the role of the preacher or *Khatib* in Cairo when he argues that preachers serve as mediators that provide the listeners with a necessary bodily and mental apparatus that prepares them to receive the word of God properly. This argument can be applied as well to preaching in Christ Embassy – and other Pentecostal churches – in which preaching is regarded as the practice of delivering the word of God in a deeply experiential and embodied manner to the audience. Preaching can also be understood as a technique for energizing and vivifying the body to create a physical experience that is conducive to spiritual experience. The touching power of preaching in Christ Embassy and NASFAT affects the emotional disposition of the listener and produces emotion that is interpreted as divine presence (see Butticci 2016).

Preaching as technique of producing religious subjects

In this section I look at the preaching practices of Christ Embassy and NASFAT through the prism of Foucault's notion of governmentality. Foucault refers to governmentality as 'the broad sense of techniques and procedures for directing human behavior' (Foucault 1997: 82). The notion of governmentality extends the notion of power beyond hierarchical, top-down power of the state. Governmentality incorporates other forms of power that include systems of social control in disciplinary institutions (schools, hospitals, psychiatric institutions, etc.), as well as various forms of knowledge. Foucault's notion of governmentality and that of techniques of the self have inspired many scholars, both in the study of Muslims (Asad, Hirschkind, Mahmood) and Pentecostals (Marshall). Asad (1993) critiques Clifford Geertz's definition of religion, stressing the role of symbols, consciousness, dispositions and affirmations as the prime locus of religion. Asad instead presents an understanding of religion that pays attention to such items as disciplinary practices and systems of institutional authority that have focal importance in many (non-Protestant) religions.

Charles Hirschkind (2006) conducted an anthropological study on sermons via the medium of cassettes in Cairo, Egypt. He argues that the power of aural media is not limited to its capacity to shape and instil moral or religious ideologies but includes its effect on the human sensorium and sensibilities, cultivating ethical dispositions and forming perceptual habits of its vast audiences. Mahmood's *Politics of Piety* (2004) follows a select group of deeply pious women of a *Salafi* reformist orientation in their ritual lives in Cairo. Central to their reformist orientation is a specific notion of what being a pious and virtuous Muslim entails in terms of embodied comportment and commitment. Mahmood uses her ethnographic materials to interrogate secular feminist understandings of agency, particularly their failure to 'problematize the universality of the desire ... to be free from relations of subordination and, for women, from structures of male domination' (10). Ruth Marshall analyses how Pentecostalism, or the 'Born Again Movement', deploys techniques of the self as a form of personal transformation and as a social force of great political consequence in Nigeria. Marshall argues, 'it is this vision [of rupture, both individual and collective] and specific Born-Again program for personal and collective regeneration and renewal that have been responsible for attracting people in such great numbers' (51).

The above scholars spotlight how governmentality implicates religious practice in the sense of inducing believers into acting on themselves to cultivate or to change certain attitudes or behaviours for the purpose of reshaping the self to mirror specific religious ideals. This section adds a comparative element to the application of the notion of technology of the self in the religious domain. Informed by this notion, I suggest to understand preaching practices in Christ Embassy and NASFAT as both externalized and internalized strategies for disciplining and constructing religious subjects. The two groups developed a set of ideals and principles of how their members ought to believe, behave, think and interact with the wider society. Preaching is one of the prime tools for inculcating these ideals. In other words, preaching in Christ Embassy and NASFAT is an instrument of power with norm-setting technologies of the self that aim to shape new modern religious subjectivities.

One of the major purposes of preaching in Christ Embassy is to change the way people see themselves and the world around them or to create a new mindset and self-image. Members are required to change their way of speaking and their way of thinking. A thirty-four-year-old self-employed female and twenty-five-year-old male student stated,

> I constantly guard what I say or what I think. Ever since I learned about the creative power of thought and speech I have been making great effort to make sure that everything that comes out of me is positive. I realized that whenever I made a mistake and said I am sick within an hour I would fall ill. I am very grateful to Christ Embassy for making me understand that my destiny is in my head and mouth. (Interview, 8 January 2014)

> Through listening to preaching I totally changed my inner world. I feel happy for becoming a new creature in Christ; I feel light in my spirit because I have absolute assurance of my salvation. As a born-again person, I know that I am a special person with great power. I can change circumstances in my life through changing my attitudes. The pastor has taught us that we should never say we have a headache or any sickness because 'have' is possession, and when one utters it, it will become a reality. That is the reason why I do not joke with a negative word. I only say what I mean, because I know words and thoughts have consequences. (Interview, 28 February 2014)

As these persons point out, the preachers of Christ Embassy teach believers to see themselves in a different way because they have a new spiritual self when they become born-again. Through regular exposure to preaching, many members internalized the new teachings and adopted a new attitude towards the world around them, becoming cautious of their thoughts and speech since these two phenomena are tools of creation and destruction. Certain norms developed among the members in which proclaiming some statements such as 'I am sick' or 'I am broke' reveal the person's ignorance. If one utters a similarly negative statement about oneself or others in the circle of believers he/she feels ashamed to expose the lack of discipline in controlling speech. Members believe that they can achieve many things using the power of their mind and words. The physical struggle is secondary in realizing desired goals in life. In the view of the church one can overcome the difficulties and challenges of the urban environment such as unemployment, poverty and insecurity by applying one's mental faculties. This view is appealing to members of Christ Embassy.

Instead of the transformation of self, NASFAT preaching attempts to promote spiritual practices and values that result in both individual and collective renewal. Preachers in NASFAT intend to produce a new urban Muslim, who is an educated, tolerant, moderate, pious and morally sound person who can represent and project a new image of Islam in a multireligious urban setting. Even though this idea of a new person also exists in Christ Embassy, it is proclaimed much more explicitly in NASFAT. NASFAT leaders are of the view that the success of its preaching agenda can raise the profile of Islam in an environment that is ridden with immorality and tensile religious coexistence. Some members of NASFAT told me about their experience with preaching:

> Preaching taught me how to be a good Muslim and to be an ambassador to Islam. I learned that all my actions were also a form of preaching; they are *da'wah* in practice. To send a better message about Islam, to non-Muslims is a great meritorious act that attracts reward from Allah. (Interview, 6 July 2014)

> Listening to preaching helps me remain steadfast and committed to carry out my religious duties. Before I joined NASFAT, I was not regular in my daily prayers, but since I joined NASFAT and became exposed to preaching I never miss a prayer. I also preach to other people about the importance of observing religious duties. I respect and love my fellow Muslims and also extend my respect to Christians. It is through respect and concern that we express the beauty of Islam to others. (Interview, 7 July 2014)

Compared to Christ Embassy, NASFAT preachers take a different outlook towards internal transformation by focusing on the performance of piety through the process of self-cultivation (Mahmood 2004). Instead of struggling to transform the interiority of the self to change the outer circumstances of life, as is the case with Christ Embassy, NASFAT members are encouraged to pursue godly actions that inevitably change their interiority. This implies that strict observance of Islamic ritual prayer, fasting, almsgiving and other pious actions can transform the heart of a believer and make him/her a good servant of God as well as a good member of society.

NASFAT leadership believes that individual piety achieved through orthopraxy and cultivation of impeccable moral character is the only panacea for social malaise and corruption that are prevalent in Nigerian urban environments and Abuja in particular. While in Christ Embassy members are encouraged to apply the power of their faith and mind to transform the exterior circumstances of life, members of NASFAT are inspired to effect changes in their lives through pious and righteous activities.

Hirschkind (2006) propounds a similar idea in his analysis of recorded sermon in Egypt. He posits that listening to sermon takes the dimension of what Foucault called techniques of the self, which means a set of procedures by means of which individuals can work on their souls and bodies to achieve a distinct ethical or aesthetic form. Sermon listeners attempt to cultivate ethical dispositions that would foster a relationship with the divine. The *khatib* here serve as mediators that provide the listeners with a necessary bodily and mental apparatus that prepares them to properly receive the word of God; therefore, their role is mediatory and they have no responsibility for creating moral subjects or enforcing normative morality. The touching power of sermon is not limited to emotional dispositions of the listener; sermon audition produces bodily effects in multiple ways. The sermon can be seen as technique for energizing and vivifying the body in order to create bodily experience that is conducive to spiritual experience.

It is apparent that preaching is deployed as a potent technology of power in Christ Embassy and NASFAT, while members of the groups participate in this act of power through listening. Governmentality of preaching manifests in the process of internalizing knowledge and instructions propagated in the act of preaching that guides behaviour of the members. As mentioned earlier, the power of preachers in the two groups is predicated on their authority and the fact that they present themselves as mediators of the divine words. Through the power of their religious authorities and invocation of higher authorities (God, Scriptures), preachers of the two groups reinforce and solidify the respective norms of their organizations. As Rose indicates in his discussion on the techniques of the self, many members of Christ Embassy and NASFAT engage in constant struggle by 'working on themselves, controlling their impulses in everyday conduct and habits, and inculcating norms of conduct into their children, under the guidance of others' (1999: 73).

Conclusion

Abuja has become a cosmopolitan city in which diverse ethnic and religious groups coexist. The city's limited resources and overpopulation make living conditions difficult and competitive. Christ Embassy and NASFAT respond to these social situations through preaching. It is noticeable here that preaching is a religious practice that serves a considerable number of functions. In their study of preaching in the Gulen movement, Thijl Sunier and Mehmet Sahin demonstrate how in some sessions of preaching, 'religious knowledge production, authorization and ritual practice are inextricably linked to one another and come together' (2015: 1). In the preaching of Christ Embassy and NASFAT these three elements mentioned by Sunier and Sahin combine to make preaching an authorized and authenticated form of religious activity.

Preachers in NASFAT respond to the urban situation by encouraging Muslims to be pious, moderate, tolerant and responsible citizens so as to ensure peaceful coexistence with their Christians neighbours. They are of the view that these attitudes will improve the public image of Islam and help Muslims live a harmonious life, particularly in the pluralistic city of Abuja. Preachers of Christ Embassy promote prosperity, boldness, self-confidence, courage and new prayer techniques. Through preaching, believers are taught that as spiritual beings they are beyond the limitations of socio-economic constraints and can thus overcome all the challenges of life. Members of Christ Embassy in Abuja consider these teachings to be effective resources that help them navigate the highly precarious Nigerian urban landscape. In this sense, preaching is an important instrument for empowering urban residents with the necessary mental resources to meet the challenges posed by the urban environment.

The success of Christ Embassy and NASFAT, evidenced by their branches springing up in urban spaces across Nigeria, can be at least partly explained by the seeming effectiveness of their preaching that attracts a number of urban residents. However, the mental techniques offered by Christ Embassy encourage members to change their interiority without necessarily achieving the desired pragmatic results. Likewise, sometimes the contents of NASFAT's preaching remained as cherished ideals without being translated into practice. As I hope to have shown, the comparative approach reveals a pattern of similarities and differences between Christ Embassy and NASFAT in the performance of preaching. One of the most important similarities is that in the two religious groups preaching is organized as a performance that deploys a variety of tools such as amplifications and background music. These aspects establish preaching as an aesthetic style because of the preachers' ability to mobilize the senses of the audience, thereby making the preaching performances a highly emotional experience. It is during this moment of heightened emotionality that believers are transported beyond the limits of the ordinary and moved towards an experience of divine presence. The similarities in the preaching performance of the two groups also converge with regard to the areas of pedagogy, exhortation, spiritual rejuvenation and motivating the audience to be more committed or to change their religious perspective in certain ways.

However, preaching in the two groups differs with regard to the fact that in Christ Embassy preachers predominantly direct their preaching to individual believers and rarely to Christianity as a corporate entity, despite the emphasis on spreading the gospel. By contrast, preaching in NASFAT focuses more on addressing the Muslim *umma* and the need for collective moral reform, although individuals are also addressed. One of the important points of divergence between the two groups is that their preaching is informed by distinct theologies and world views that are grounded in Protestantism and Islam. This can be seen in NASFAT's emphasis on orthopraxis. This is more pronounced in Islam than in Protestant Christianity where the focus on meaning is stronger and ritual is rejected. Notwithstanding, it seems that Pentecostalism enters into that niche, and offers a more strongly accentuated body practice than mainline Protestantism. Arguably preaching in Christ Embassy, which is an organized and regular religious performance with the capacity to produce emotion and bodily response, is also an embodied practice. Preaching can take different forms, from private listening through electronic media, to organized collective activity in congregations or large-scale public spectacles. Through these forms preaching becomes a potent technology of the self that aims to produce and mould religious subjects, generates spiritual experience and responds to the needs of urbanites.

Mobile spirituality:
Technology-mediated religious practices
in Christ Embassy and NASFAT

Introduction

The world has changed, we now live in the digital age and we should better embrace it in our church. Technological innovations such as mobile phone and the internet have brought far reaching benefits to our lives. For instance, when I was in the boarding secondary school back in the 1970s my parents could not send money to me except through my brothers. But now I send money to my children through mobile banking who are studying far away from home in the comfort of my room and they receive the money instantly. This is the beauty of the digital technological revolution. I encourage you to use our digital materials. We have ample number of them in the digital store of our church websites.

Digital technology including mobile phone gadgets are not ideological tools that may clash with the Islamic precepts. Technology itself is neutral; but one can apply it either in a good or in a bad way. In NASFAT we have a positive view of technology. We only tell our members to use it within the framework of Islamic shari'ah. I think it is wrong for Muslims to reject the use of new technologies. Basically, technology is a practical application of wisdom and knowledge; Prophet Muhammad (peace be upon him) says, 'Wisdom is a lost property of a believer, he takes it whenever he finds it.' This Hadith of the Prophet is telling Muslims to look at new technological innovations such as mobile phones as their own properties because they are product of knowledge and wisdom that make human life easier.

The first statement is from the senior pastor of Christ Embassy Karu branch, Abuja, during the Sunday worship service. The second statement was from Ishaq Adepoju, one of the spiritual leaders of NASFAT, during my interview with him. These leaders expressed the positive view of their movements on the new digital technologies, particularly smartphones and the internet. Recently, mobile phones and related digital technologies have assumed several religious functions which Christ Embassy and NASFAT have embraced and applied in different aspects of their religious lives.

As the digital revolution gains ground in modern societies, religion is communicated, practised, represented and expressed through the medium of new digital media technology. There is increasing religious expressions through the digital space that includes religious social media sites, dating sites, software and apps, digital holy texts, internet evangelism and *da'wah* sites, online *fatwas*, online courses and online activism. The emergence of digital new media has precipitated unprecedented changes in how religious knowledge and ideas are produced and disseminated and how the new media are reshaping religious discourse and social relationship in Nigeria. Many cyber groups provide spaces for religious discourse, theological arguments, sharing news and information, circulating Islamic videos, images as well as the appearance of religious digital culture. The new media also facilitate the emergence of new cyber pastors and imams who acquire online followers and build their authority online, which result in shifting the nature of traditional religious authority and interpretive rights. This development spawns a new online cyber religious public that mirrored and empowered the offline public.

The ways in which mobile phone technology has been appropriated as a religious medium among both Christians and Muslims are rapidly expanding.[1] Mobile network operators, in their attempt to expand their sources of revenue, have profiled mobile phones as items in a massive digital spiritual market by creating and distributing religious services for subscription.[2] These companies offer religious services to their subscribers in highly creative and competitive ways. The services include gospel music, Qur'anic recitation and sensational words of famous preachers as caller tunes and ringtones. They also include devotional prayers, daily quotes from Scriptures, religious text messages and special religious packages during religious seasons such as Eid, Ramadan, Christmas and Easter.

Most Nigerians use their mobile phones to access the internet. The use of a notebook computer is rare due to its high cost and the lack of stable power supply. Wi-Fi internet connectivity is almost non-existent in the country. Internet data services provided by mobile service operators are the main source of internet connection. Access to religious websites and other forms of technologically mediated religious practices and participations happens via the medium of the mobile phone. The intersection of religious practices and digital technologies is what Bell (2006: 142) called 'emergent techno-spiritual practices'. These emergent practices are increasingly becoming accepted and routinized among religious groups in Nigeria.

Digital religion is defined by Heidi Campbell (2012: 1) as a concept 'which does not simply refer to religion as it is performed and articulated online, but points to how digital media and spaces are shaping and being shaped by religious practice'. Christopher Helland (2005: 1) proposes a theoretical distinction between 'religion online and online religion'. Online religion describes websites where people could act with a high level of interactivity. Religion online refers to religious websites which seemed to provide only religious information and no possibility to interact. Both online religion and religion online services are provided by religious organizations in Nigeria.

The availability of mobile phones and the appearance of Bluetooth that makes file sharing straightforward rapidly ushered in the dawn of digital religious practices. The new digital technology increases the mobility of spiritual resources (sounds, texts, images) and enhances their accessibility. For instance, sermon now is no longer limited to a fixed indoor or outdoor space but can be accessed by people on the move with an earpiece anywhere, anytime in public or in private spaces. Many people in Nigerian urban environments maintain intimacy with the religious sounds, texts and images through listening, reading or viewing on their mobile phones while driving or walking in the street. In this sense the mobile phone has made private religious practices (listening, reading or viewing) part of the structure of urban life and woven these practices seamlessly into day-to-day living. Digital mobile technology has conferred on individual believers a great deal of control over which kind of religious material to access and offered the possibility for users to immerse themselves by choosing among a myriad of religious resources on the phones, thereby creating their own religious experience.

In the footsteps of the previous chapters, this chapter also takes the view of religion as a practice of mediation that necessarily required media (Meyer 2009; de Witte 2009). De Witte (2009: 186) states, 'Religion always needs media. Ranging from the bible to the body, from prophets to television, and from compact disc to cowry shells, such media enable people to conceive of and establish, maintain, and renew ties with the presence of spirit beings.' In the same manner, this chapter argues that mobile phone technology in Christ Embassy and NASFAT is used as a religious medium that mediates religious experience. The chapter looks into how digital technology, particularly smartphones, facilitates religious mediation through hosting varieties of religious resources such as sermons, Qur'anic recitation, religious music, text, online religious performances and images among members of NASFAT and Christ Embassy.

Both Christ Embassy and NASFAT make use of the same technologies and negotiate them in the light of their religious world views. In addition, the appropriation of this technology in the two religious groups also involves borrowing which is however not mutual, as NASFAT copies more from Christ Embassy as the new successful format than vice versa. The fact of using the same technologies and borrowing in Christ Embassy and NASFAT generates similarities in some of their techno-religious practices and experiences. Moreover, the technology-mediated religious practices in Christ Embassy and NASFAT also involve several differences since the two groups negotiate the practices through their distinct theologies.

The chapter is divided into four sections. The first section examines digital religious practices in Christ Embassy and NASFAT. The remaining sections dwell on the digital religious practices related to sound, text, virtual participation and images in Christ Embassy and NASFAT.

Digital religiosity in Christ Embassy and NASFAT

Christ Embassy and NASFAT are some of the most technologically savvy religious groups in the country. Unlike some religious groups such as the Deeper Life and some Sufi groups that express scepticism of new technology, Christ Embassy and NASFAT embraced the new development and perceived it as a potent means to extend their outreach. The two religious groups have quickly appropriated the new digital technology and applied it in various ways that include cyber evangelism/*da'wah*, pedagogy and online social activities.[3]

Christ Embassy has developed one of the most modern internet marketing strategies, with varieties of programmes on its website.[4] One of the cells in Christ Embassy is called 'professional cell' and it comprises experts and students from information and communication technologies (ICTs). Members of this cell organize workshops for the general congregation on how to use the new digital resources of the church. They are also assigned responsibility to develop apps for the use of the church members. There is an annual award which is equivalent to one thousand euro given to the IT expert or student who develops the best app for the church. The Christ Embassy Online Store is a rich online market for Christian materials, offering a wide variety of topical messages from Chris

Oyakhilome in the formats of e-books, DVDs, mp4s and mp3s. The messages in digital formats include numerous teachings on Christian living, faith, health and wealth, love, success and prosperity, confessions, evangelism and Christian character. One can subscribe to these materials using online payment such as PayPal, debit or credit card.

For the purpose of wider outreach and desire to go with the trendy technology, Christ Embassy entered into the digital religious market through cooperating with MTN, which is the largest mobile network operator in the country, to sell its devotional prayers. The messages are written by Pastor Chris.[5] I subscribed to this service during my fieldwork in Abuja at the cost of 50 naira per month (0.10 cent). Examples of the text messages I received every morning are as follows:

1. *Noon or night the blessings of God will rest upon you. You are protected from every wind of evil, sickness, destruction and violence in the Name of Jesus.*
2. *You shall not be hindered today & every hindering force that steps in your path shall be crushed into pieces by the power of the Holy Spirit in Jesus Name.*
3. *Circumstances, men and materials will fall into place for your good. Doors of opportunities are opening for you now in the name of Jesus.*

These messages remind the reader that there is a higher power that is concerned about his/her welfare. They can elevate the spirit and hope of the person in going through the rigour of life in the highly precarious Nigerian urban environment. A member of the church in Abuja told me, 'These messages come to me at the right time, when I was in a state of distress and things become dark and doors of opportunities seem to be locked. The moment I received these text messages or open and read the existing ones, I immediately experienced light and hope in my life' (interview, 20 July 2014). When the messages come at the time of material and psychological difficulties, people ideally interpret them as if they are messages from heaven to raise their faith. This kind of experience has been confirmed to me by many members of the church. Apparently subscribing to these messages is tantamount to buying hope that reminds people that God is in control of their lives. The messages also echo daily horoscopes that appear on daily newspapers that serve the same purpose of rendering hope to the readers who believe in them.[6]

NASFAT leaders also promote the use of new technologies and view it positively.[7] The former president of NASFAT, Alhaji Bolarinwa, is an expert on information technology. NASFAT is far ahead of many Muslims organizations in the use of ICT materials. It has a very rich website with varieties of textual and sound resources, which members download and use in their smartphones. Similar to Christ Embassy, NASFAT has launched an initiative through liaising with MTN to distribute short Islamic text messages to the public. The SMSs include daily verses from the Qur'an, its meaning and underlying spiritual messages. The SMS is called the NASFAT Daily Ayaat. The aim of the initiative, according to NASFAT officials, is to develop an enlightened Muslim society nurtured by a true understanding of Islam for the spiritual and moral development of the community. Olakunle Hassan, the executive secretary of NASFAT, is quoted as follows by Balancing Act Magazine (2005: 10) during the launching of the initiative:

> Apart from the Friday and Sunday services which allow our Muslim brothers to gather and worship on the ground, we believe this will be an avenue for them to stay connected to the teachings of the Qur'an. Text messages are received everyday in the morning for 6 days, so if you wake up in the morning either before or after the morning prayers, you receive a word from the teachings of the great Prophet Mohammed (SAW). We believe this is a good innovation [through] which our members and other Muslims will gain encouragement and motivation for facing a hectic day.

The Daily Ayaat service, which is available to all MTN subscribers, allows individuals to receive the teachings of the Prophet Mohammed on their mobile phones every morning. MTN mobile phone users need to dial 300 161 from their mobile phones and they will receive inspirational messages from the Hadith or Qur'an every morning for a period of six days for a cost of N100, which pays for the cost of text messages being sent and for management of the service.[8] The subscribers to the Daily Ayaat allow the messages of Islam to come to them around 8 o'clock in the morning every day. From my interactions with the subscribers I understood that many of them take these messages as daily ritual, which they reflect on and carry on their conscience during their daily routines. In this way, the messages serve the purpose of connecting subscribers to the words of God.

The mobile phone here has become a medium that transmits religious inspiration and teachings on a daily basis. The medium of the mobile phone transforms Qur'anic verses and Hadiths into portable resources. Individuals move around the city with these materials in their pockets. An interlocutor stated, 'Islam encourages sharing the word of Allah as reminder. This is because the human mind has a strong propensity to deviate and fall into temptation, this makes the Daily Ayaat SMS particularly important in setting the minds of

Muslims straight' (interview, 11 September 2015, Abuja). The sudden appearance of Qur'anic verses or words of the Prophet out of the air may create the feeling in the recipients that these words descend from the spiritual world right away – a pure message from God. This is captured by an interlocutor who stated, 'The Qur'anic verses and Hadith from the Daily Ayaat sometimes speak to my problems or what I am thinking perfectly at the right time. In this situation I feel as if God send his words to me' (interview, 19 September 2015, Abuja). In this sense the mobile phone has become a medium of religious mediation.

Moreover, the adoption of the Daily Ayaat by NASFAT reveals another important trend of borrowing and mutual influences among religious groups in Nigeria. Brian Larkin (2014a: 67) observes, 'Religious movements are heteroglossic assemblages rather than homogeneous blocs contained in self-enclosed silos, mutually opposed to each other. They are dynamic, continually responsive to other movements, and quick to incorporate elements from other movements that are useful to their own.' Pentecostal digital practices in this regard apparently influenced NASFAT's decision to initiate the Daily Ayaat SMS with MTN.[9] It is a typical example of NASFAT copying religious form of Pentecostalism.

Digital sound practices

The mobile phone has replaced cassettes and VCDs as the main source of accessing and listening to religious auditory materials such as sermons, melodious recitation of the Quran, praise and worship music.[10] Many of my interlocutors across Christ Embassy and NASFAT told me that they frequently use their mobile phones for listening to varieties of religious sounds. Martin Nass (1971: 303) argues that 'the quality of the auditory cognitive experience is of a different order [than visual cognition] in terms of its intensity and its ability to "hold" its receiver. It narrows object distance and is more closely related developmentally to experiences of holding and experiences of touch'. It is arguable that the qualities of sound Nass describes, such as intensity, holding attention and creating haptic experiences of touch, make the mobile phone a potent medium for religious mediation.

Moreover, the practice of private listening to religious sounds via mobile phone can be seen in the framework of 'acousmatic sound'. As pointed out by Brian Kane (2014), the concept of acousmatic sound was used by Pierre Schaeffer to describe sound one hears without seeing the original source or cause. Any sound is acousmatic if the source of the sound is unseen. Kane highlights that, in Schaeffer's view, acousmatic listening is an experience that reduces sounds to the field of hearing alone. This experience takes away the attention of the listeners from the physical object responsible for aural perception and towards the content of this perception. Schaeffer maintains that the acousmatic reduction is immediately produced when one listens to a playback of a sound recording. Kane (2014) maintains that *akousmatikoi* is an ancient Greek term associated with disciples of Pythagoras who were allegedly demanded to listen to their master behind a veil in order to concentrate on his words and avoid visual distractions caused by his physical presence. There is a parallel between this situation and the technologically mediated experience of listening to sounds through a figurative 'veil' of loudspeakers.

Religious acousmatic listening is a spiritual participation without engaging with physical repertoires associated with religious performance. For religious believers, listening to sound through an earpiece or headset allows digital technology to transmit vocal and sonic presence. Acousmatic listening helps listeners to concentrate their entire attention on the sound perception and creates what Judith Becker (2004) calls 'deep listening'. Becker sees the deep listener as one whose experiences of music appear to have cosmic import or convey a sense of something that transcends the self. Becker's ideas about deep listening to music can fruitfully be applied to the listening habits of many believers who engage with sounds, such as devotional music or melodious recitation of the Qur'an, via mobile phones. In this process the physical object of media technology dissolves and the listening is reduced to pure aural mediation.

Music in the form of worship songs plays a significant role in the spiritual lives of the members of Christ Embassy. The church has one of the largest music recording studios in Nigeria, with state-of-the-art facilities called the LoveWorld Music. Sinachi Kālu, who is one of the greatest gospel artists in the country with over three hundred written songs, is a member of Christ Embassy (Sean 2015: 1). Christ Embassy offers a considerable number of digital music artists for subscription from its online digital store. The music can be downloaded on any operating system of a mobile phone. The digital store also provides music apps that make the access to music simpler. In the online digital store of the church, the music app is introduced as follows:

> Get unlimited and instant access to the best Christian music collection from your LoveWorld All Star Artists. This is the official LoveWorld Music Ministry app, designed with easy access to all your favourite music albums. It's a digital

music app that notifies you of the newest and hottest albums from your LoveWorld music artists. You can listen to a preview of any track of your choice before purchase. It's a must have application!

As a result of this app, members of Christ Embassy do not need to go to the music shop to buy or see music albums of the church. Access to the digital music becomes widespread among the members because a majority of them possess Android phones. The availability of the digital gospel music in Christ Embassy increases the possibility of deep and acousmatic listening to the gospel music among the members of the church. A member of the church told me that listening to the worship songs via his mobile phone is the secret of his spiritual growth. He further remarks, 'Listening to worship songs completely transformed my spiritual life. Constant listening to worship songs impressed the word of God in my heart and allowed me to feel his presence continually' (interview, 19 March 2014, Abuja).

Listening to gospel music is seen as a spiritual activity in Christ Embassy; it is in fact a silent form of worship. This silent worship is performed by mental faculties through contemplating and enjoying praises to God. Members of Christ Embassy believe that regular and deep listening to gospel music helps them in focusing their minds on God and purifying their hearts. In addition, regular contemplation on God, which is induced by listening to the praise songs, is believed to uplift the mind spiritually and to sanctify the personality. Deep and acousmatic listening to gospel music also generates feelings of joy and pleasure. One interlocutor stated, 'Sometimes I become so engrossed in listening to the gospel music to the extent that I become enwrapped in a state of bliss and I feel warm sensation enveloped my entire body' (interview, 29 February 2014, Abuja). Many of my interlocutors related similar experiences to me. And they usually interpret sensational affects as the evidence of the presence of the Holy Spirit. In this sense, mobile phone technology mediates the presence of God for believers.

Most of the members of NASFAT have melodious Qur'anic recitations in their mobile phones and many of them are regular listeners. Some of the reciters people listen to include Abdul Basit Abdul Samad, Saddiq al Manshawi and Abdul Rahman Sudais. I visited the house of Nasir Musa, who scheduled an interview for me. Immediately as I approached his room I heard the sound of melodious Qur'anic recitation arising from the room. After he welcomed me and asked me to sit down, he turned off the recitation. I asked him why he turned off the player, because I enjoyed the voice of the reciter (Abdul Basit Abdul Samad).

He replied that it is wrong for people to be talking while Qur'anic recitation was playing. He quoted the verse of the Qur'an that says, 'So, when the Qur'an is recited, listen to it, and be silent that you may receive mercy' (Q 7:204). He continued that it is important to listen to the Qur'an attentively to receive the blessings that emanate from the word of Allah.

One university student of mass communication stated, 'Listening to music makes me think of worldly things, but listening to Qur'anic recitation, which I downloaded into my mobile phone from Google Play online store, makes me completely forget about mundane affairs. I feel very close to God and my faith greatly increases' (interview, 23 March 2014, Abuja). Another member of NASFAT, whose work involves a lot of travelling, told me that what he enjoys much is listening to melodious recitation of the NASFAT prayer book on his mobile phone as he is travelling from one part of the country to another. He said, 'I can traverse long distances completely immersed in the melodious sound of the recitation. The sound touches my heart and elevates my spirit' (interview, 22 March 2014). Another member who studied health technology and was working in a hospital in Abuja told me that he feels overwhelmed by the NASFAT prayer book whenever he immerses himself in listening to it via his mobile phone. He quoted a section of the book which, he said, delves him into spiritual ecstasy. He recited the Arabic version of that particular passage; an English translation of the passage is as follows:

> Oh Lord! I am your servant, son of your male servant, the son of your female servant, my forelock is in Your hand, Your order concerning me would be executed and just is Your judgment upon me. I ask You with all of Your names that You named Yourself, or revealed in Your Book, or taught any of Your creatures from Your hidden knowledge, to make the Holy Quran a soothing for my heart, the light for my chest, make it to overwhelm my grief, remove my agony and replace my sorrow with joy. (NASFAT Prayer Book, 78)

These experiences have shown that the role of mobile phone technology as a religious medium facilitates an experience of immediacy. Deep and acousmatic listening enables the listeners to absorb themselves into the emotionally touching melody of the religious sounds and their often strong language or lyrics. Pure aural mediation facilitated by mobile phone technology enables religious believers to inhabit both material and spiritual worlds at will by deciding to focus their attention on either religious melody or mundane affairs.[11] Some members of Christ Embassy and NASFAT indicate that listening to religious tunes particularly with a headset helps them control or shut down inner noise and thereby focus on the spiritual dimension of life. They contend that the inner noise or runaway thoughts that hinder concentration are more distracting in a person's attempt to focus on God than sound from the environment. Wrightson (2000: 10) quotes Schaeffer describing this process as 'an audio-analgesic'. If community and environmental noise is the enemy without, the noise of unwanted thoughts and feelings represents the enemy within. The use of sound as an 'audio-analgesic' sound wall to block the unceasing inner dialogue and the uncomfortable emotions the dialogue evinces provide the illusion of mastery over emotion. Some of the NASFAT members listen to Qur'an and other religious sounds for the purpose of concentrating the mind on the divine. Musa Yusuf related to me his experience:

> Immediately I retire to bed at night and turn off the light it is like opening a big screen in my mind. A stream of bewildering images play endlessly in my mind that stimulates the unpleasant memories of shame, humiliation, guilt, and disappointment that I experienced in the past. I used to find it difficult to sleep because of these countless images and thoughts that invade and overpower my mind. The only thing that saves me is listening to the Qur'anic recitations, preaching, and Islamic music that I stored on my mobile phone. Listening to these materials transports my mind into the presence of Allah my creator. This usually cools me down and helps me relax and feel peace and tranquillity and eventually sleep. (Interview, 28 December 2013)

In this instance, listening to melodious Qur'anic recitation is used as a form of therapy for both relieving insomnia and holding in check runaway thoughts. Members of NASFAT believe that deep and acousmatic listening to the Qur'an concentrates the mind and focuses it on the word of Allah. This is similar to how in Christ Embassy focusing on God is understood as a spiritual act that purifies the mind. One person remarked, 'There are many verses of the Holy Qur'an that emphasise the importance of remembering Allah. To me listening to *qira'a* or recitation of the Holy Qur'an from my mobile phone directs my attention toward remembrance of Allah' (interview, 23 March 2014). Through the lens of the notion of sensational form, it can be asserted that the aesthetic of deep listening to the melodious recitation of the Qur'an affects both the thinking faculty and sensation of the listener. As this member stated, listening to the Qur'an stimulates remembrance of God and reflection on his words.

Moreover, deep and acousmatic listening to the Qur'anic recitation generates special semiotic qualities. The first step to understanding the semiotic of the Qur'anic recitation is to recognize that the voice of the reciter mediates the voice of God. In the case of listening to a recorded recitation, the body of the reciter is not present and hence cannot disturb or distract the listener. As a result, it is the voice that mediates the divine. However, even the voice could disappear as the mediator because Muslims believe that the Qur'an is the literal word of God. In deep listening one is listening to God through listening to his word. To borrow the idea of Jeremy Wallach (2003) on the indexicality of sound, it can be argued that the semiotic of deep listening to the recorded Qur'an could be described in the framework of indexical qualisign of Peircean semiotics. Wallach (2003: 36) states, 'As a succession of vibrations in air molecules emanating from a source, sound possesses the capacity to be used as an index of that source due to the ability of sound waves to collapse physical distance between objects and create an experience of co-presence.' Thus, sound waves of the melodious recitation can index God by transmitting his words. Thus, it can be suggested that listening to the Qur'anic recitation announces the presence of God via the sound of his words. These practices substantiate the notion that 'media is intrinsic to religion' (Meyer 2009: 1). And 'what look as media from an outsider's perspective may be fully embedded in religious practice' (Meyer 2009: 12).

Sacred liquid texts in the digital space

Apart from auditory spiritual resources there are numerous digital textual contents on mobile phone devices, ranging from the digital Bible, Quran, Hadith, religious quotations and varieties of texts that encourage piety and religious pedagogy. Members of Christ Embassy and NASFAT use mobile devices to study their Holy Scriptures and other religious texts. Traditionally, Christians go to church with their Bible and when the pastor quotes from the Scripture, people flip through its pages to find the chapter and verse. Now this practice is changing with the advent of smartphones. Many people in Christ Embassy use the Bible app on their mobile phones in the church. There are different types of digital Bible apps available for download. Most of the print versions of the Bible have their free digital counterpart on Android, iOS, Windows and other platforms. According to Hutchings (2014b: 1), the developers of YouVersion Bible app state, 'We believe we could see half a billion people or even a billion engaging with Scripture through the Bible App. What the printing press did for Bible engagement more than 400 years ago, YouVersion has the potential to do for Bible engagement in this digital age.' The developers of YouVersion expect that the digital Bible might create more engagement with Scripture than the printed copy. In one of his sermons played during a Sunday worship service in Abuja central branch, Pastor Chris had this to say:

> Do you have a Bible on your phones? Any phone which does not have a Bible is not a phone but a stone. It is not a phone and does not worth taken along with. Nowadays phones have become so personal that one goes anywhere with them. And nothing supposes to follow you anywhere than your Bible. (18 October 2015)

Many members of the audience responded to these remarks by shouting and raising up their phones to show that they have a digital copy of the Bible. This situation shows how mobile phones have become an integral part of people's religious life. In his remarks, Pastor Chris has authenticated the practice of studying the Bible through mobile phones and even delegitimized the phones which did not contain the word of God. Meyer (2009: 12) writes, 'The media intrinsic to religious mediation are exempted from the sphere of "mere" technology. In so doing, media are authenticated as being part and parcel of the very transcendental that is the target of – and from a more sceptical perspective: invoked by – mediation.' In many branches of Christ Embassy that I visited, many members and the pastors themselves use their mobile phones to quote and read from the Bible. The question here is, what are the consequences of this gradual digital revolution on the printed copy of the Holy Scripture? Clare Clivaz (2014: 1) expresses this concern when she states, 'The New Testament is becoming a very small booklet lost in the World Wide Web, losing more and more of its covers and becoming potentially a "liquid book".' Quoting Rachel Wagner, Hutchings (2014b: 2) points out, 'The Bible itself becomes fluid as a digital text, "its fixed covers dissolving into a host of linked sites that describe competing biblical histories" available for the individual to select and combine as they wish.' This apprehension is based on the fear that the digital Bible might give an excessive autonomy to individual Christians and thereby undermines religious authority.

Reading Scripture in both print and digital form is an important aspect of spiritual practices in Christ Embassy. In fact, Christ Embassy calls itself a 'word based church' to express its commitment to the letters of the Bible. It is in this vein that Thomas Kirsch (2008) illustrates how letters of the Bible animated the spirit world of African Christianity through preparing an encounter with the Holy Spirit. In Christ Embassy members believe that Scripture is invested with potent divine power; therefore, reading it is understood to be an interaction with the Holy Spirit. As more members of Christ Embassy begin to use digital

Bibles, this encounter with the Holy Spirit and interacting with it may well happen via the medium of the smartphone. Apart from the digital Bible, Chris Embassy has numerous digital textual apps which members can pay to subscribe to and download into their smartphone on all the major operating systems. These apps include numerous Pastor Chris books, booklets and other written materials. There are also apps for Healing School programmes and Christ Embassy's international satellite channel LoveWorld Plus. Interaction with these religious materials creates certain subjective experiences which members see as a relationship with the Holy Spirit.

Moreover, Pastor Chris launched a social networking website called Yookos in 2011 for the use of members of Christ Embassy. Recently, the site has been opened to the general public and the number of subscribers has risen significantly. The subscribers have the ability to develop and post profiles, status updates and blogs; upload a document or a picture or a video; start a discussion; or generate a poll. They can also connect with friends and loved ones through private or group messages. Subscribers can access Yookos on their mobile phone and computers, which are available on Android, BlackBerry and iOS. The site can be accessed by visiting m.yookos.com on mobile phones. Most of Chris Embassy's online activities on Yookos revolve around commentaries on Pastor Chris's blogging. Unlike NASFAT religious leaders, Pastor Chris asserts his religious authority on Yookos. He constantly posts micro-blogs (short discourses) which his followers perceive as sacred texts because the messages are inspired by the Holy Spirit. With this site Pastor Chris reaches a large audience that cuts across regional boundaries. Here is an example of Pastor Chris's micro sacred texts posted on 9 September 2015:

> Grace is the beauty of God in your spirit, expressed in your life. It is the fullness of God in your spirit that brings favour, righteousness and all the glorious blessings of God in Christ. Every day, take advantage of the grace of God in your life, and live to your full potentials in Christ.

This is a typical message of Pastor Chris, which does not command people to do something but tells them about blessings that, he claims, God has already bestowed on them. Members of Christ Embassy find these messages appealing and inspiring. Many members become captivated by the short messages and develop a habit of studying them as daily rituals. 'I read the micro blogging of the man of God everyday because his words enrich my spirit. I am convinced that the words are inspired by the Holy Spirit' (interview, 30 June 2014, Abuja). This is how many members perceive these messages as divinely inspired. Since members believed the messages are inspired by the Holy Spirit, reading them is conceived as being as spiritually uplifting as studying the Scriptures. Members also post comments after reading the messages to show gratitude to Pastor Chris and express how the applications of the messages transformed their lives. Some examples are, 'Thank you DADDY LORD[12] for the entrance of your word brings understanding to the wise, Amen'; 'Amen! Thank you Lord I worship you Lord Jesus, Glory to God'; and 'Amen, thank you Lord for touching me.' This interactivity, in which believers respond to the message of their pastor, is one of the important features of online religiosity.

During the Sunday worship in NASFAT service, there is a session for Qur'anic recitation that is led by the imam. In one of the Sunday services the imam talked briefly about the merit of reciting the Qur'an. He said the recitation is the most important activity in the Sunday service. He quoted a verse of the Qur'an and Hadith of the Prophet to buttress his point. 'Had We sent down this Qur'an on a mountain, you would surely have seen it humbling itself and rending asunder by the fear of Allah. Such are the parables which We put forward to mankind that they may reflect' (Q 59:21). During the recitation people bring out their copy of the Qur'an and recite after the imam. I noticed that, as in Christ Embassy, some members used their smartphones to recite the Qur'an. This digital Qur'an is mobile and handy and it seems to be easier to navigate through than the printed version.

NASFAT youths in Abuja and other cities initiated a Facebook forum for posting religious lessons, insights and religious experiences, verses of the Qur'an, and Hadiths and their commentaries. One can also ask questions pertaining to Islamic theology or ritual performance and get an answer instantly from other members of the online community.[13] Most of the members, particularly youths, use this forum through their smartphones and find it more convenient to express themselves in the online community than in the offline religious congregation. A male member asked the following question in the online forum: 'Shall I marry a Christian lady?'[14] He received the following answer:

As salaam, even though Islam permits interfaith marriage between a Muslim man and a chaste woman from the people of the book (Jews and Christians) according to Qur'an Chapter 5 verse 5, Scholars have however discouraged it due to the following reasons among others: (1) Implication on raising Islamically oriented children (Children are naturally closer to their mothers and are likely to be influenced in their choice of religion by her). (2) Confusion as to which way of life should be adopted by the couple/family. What is prohibited in one religion in terms of food, drink, values, attitudes etc. may not be prohibited in another religion, so there will always be conflict of religious ideals, values, culture etc. For example, if a marriage does not work out in Islam, the couple has an option of separating, but in another religion, it is not allowed. 'To the married I give this charge (not I, but the Lord): the wife should not separate from her husband (but if she does, she should remain unmarried or else be reconciled to her husband), and the husband should not divorce his wife (1 Corinthians 7:10–16)'. (3) Research has shown that the rate of divorce and marital breakdown is higher in interfaith marriage than in intra faith marriages. (4) What will be the faith of our numerous Muslim ladies who don't have the equal opportunity of marrying from people of other faiths? Any Christian who believes in his religious scripture will never marry a non-Christian (2 Corinthians 6:14). Conclusively, I advise the questioner to be more prayerful. There are so many virtuous, Islam-conscious and well bred Muslim ladies. May Allah provide for him, Allah knows best.

Sharing this type of religious knowledge in NASFAT's social media is an act of informal Islamic pedagogy. This question about interfaith marriage portrays the problems facing youths in the increasingly diverse urban environments. Religious diversity has brought people of different faiths together as neighbours and increases the level of inter-religious dating and relationships. The answer also reveals the influence of religious coexistence in Nigerian urban spaces as the person who wrote the answer quoted biblical verses to buttress his points. He is showing his awareness of Christian teaching and denying the interfaith marriage through reasoning with the questioner and articulating his disagreement in a logical, point-by-point manner. Both the question and the answer indicate that people who engage with NASFAT social media are urban educated youths who are attempting to face urban challenges within the framework of Islamic precepts. Other postings relate to the issue of piety and Islamic exhortations. One post titled *Encounter with God* reads as follows:

'Did you think that We have created you in vain and that you would never be recalled to Us? (Q23:115)' God Almighty is fair towards all men. He has equally blessed all human beings with the gift of life and given them senses and perception and intellectual faculties to distinguish between good and bad, right and wrong. God has made promises and sent warnings; He has given some people good health and inflicted others with ailments; He made life a mixture of happiness and suffering; all of this in order to enrich the human experience and make people recognize the reality and value of God. People can choose either to be vigilant and prepare for their encounter with God, and invest for life in the hereafter, or they can choose to reject God and dismiss any accountability to Him. God will judge both with fairness and justice; but when it is too late, excuses will avail no one. (Muhammad al-Ghazali, 'A Thematic Commentary on the Quran,' 373)

This message portrays the imagery of the power of God to the reader. It is clearly an attempt to inculcate consciousness of the divine in the mind of the readers. These religious sites, which many members access through their mobile phones, are new spiritual social spaces that give believers alternative modes of religious participation. The issue of authority arises here. Does online sharing of religious knowledge erode religious authority in NASFAT by making members less dependent on the religious leaders? Campbell (2007: 145) states, 'The question of authority is often raised in relation to the internet, as authority is seen as a key area to be challenged by network communications.' Bryan Turner (2007: 1) maintains that a 'networked religious community poses considerable challenges to traditional authority by rapidly increasing the flow of religious knowledge and products. This situation means that control cannot be sustained for long and knowledge is democratically produced.' This situation is less relevant to NASFAT because there is no single charismatic leader whose religious authority can be challenged. In fact, NASFAT democratized religious leadership (Adetona 2012).

However, online activity in Christ Embassy is one of the means through which Pastor Chris reasserts his authority and legitimacy. It can be argued that the advent of the mobile phone, through which most digital and online activities of Christ Embassy occur, increased the religious authority of Pastor Chris. In this respect, the question of authority interconnects with the issue of power. This concern with power is probably the reason why Christ Embassy initiates its own social media (Yookos) and instant messenger (Kingschat) instead of using Facebook or WhatsApp. Hutchings (2014b: 155) argues, 'In a network, power is located with those who own, structure and restricts the system of communication. This includes those who control the underlying technology, but also those users who can form the most valuable connections and encourage others to listen to and communicate their message.' By creating its own social media platforms with their independent server and technical crew, Christ Embassy ensures control over the technology and sharing of knowledge and excluding negative criticisms of the church's teachings and practices.[15] In addition, Pastor Chris has dominated the dissemination of information through his micro-blogging in order to protect and consolidate his power and authority in the online religious community. Christ Embassy employs the expertise of members who specialize in ICTs to develop its programmes and tailor them according to the needs of the church. Heidi Campbell (2010: 61) called this process of negotiating technology into the logic of religion the 'religious shaping of technology'. Christ Embassy has achieved mastery in this regard and now the church is at the forefront in techno-spiritual practices.

While in Christ Embassy online religious knowledge sharing is highly focused on the postings of Pastor Chris, NASFAT online postings are decentralized, in the sense that individuals freely post and share religious insights without relying on a single religious figure. This free sharing of digital religious resources in NASFAT creates spaces of religious engagement and knowledge sharing with horizontal participation. Moreover, NASFAT did not establish its own social media. As I mentioned earlier, members of NASFAT use the common social media such as Facebook and Twitter, and therefore do not have total control and power over the shaping of technology, as is the case with the Christ Embassy. In both Christ Embassy and NASFAT online religious interactions can be regarded as emerging online religious communities that are mediated by digital technology.

Religious performance and participation in virtual sacred space

Since the 1990s virtual online churches have emerged throughout the world (MacDonald 2008). Some of them combine both offline and online services at the same time, while others, such as iChurch, St. Pixels and the Cathedral of Second Life, are completely online (Hutchings 2014a: 2).[16] Christ Embassy has introduced what it called a virtual church service in the sense that people can participate in the service online.[17] The app for virtual church service is available at the website of the church and it can be downloaded on Android, iOS and Windows operating systems. To access the service one has to register online and the information and reminder about the service are sent via email. The service is a live streaming of the Sunday worship of the church. There is a window where one can send comments to the administrators of the site.[18] The purpose of the virtual church is to provide opportunity for those who could not be present at the church service offline to benefit from the service by participating online. What is believed to make the participation effective is the registration. One can register and log in and send comments about the benefit he/she derives from the online participation. As Marleen de Witte (2009: 193) affirms, 'Watching a religious TV broadcast with an international body, "in mimetic sympathy" with the attentive audience onscreen and off-screen, may trigger the viewer's embodied sensory memory of live church events and thereby evoke an experience of spirit presence.' From what I observed, live internet streaming via digital device also generates the feeling of live participation with the concomitant spiritual experiences.

During important events, such as New Year celebration and Holy Communion service, all branches of the church worldwide are expected to suspend their programmes and connect with the virtual church service via a big screen in front of their church. All the international branches participate in the event at the same time following the instruction of Pastor Chris. There is underlying belief that performing the service under the leadership and guidance of the charismatic Pastor Chris and the sheer number of participants that cut across transcontinental regions increased the efficacy of the service. Members of Christ Embassy believed that the anointing power of Pastor Chris could transcend time and space and become mediated by new digital technologies.

During the Holy Communion period, two assistants of Pastor Chris receive and announce messages from people around the world who got healing as they participated in the online service. As people are throwing away their crutches and wheelchairs to express their new state of health during the Holy Communion service of 2015, Pastor Ray announced that a 'brother from Zimbabwe sent a message that he was healed from spinal cord injury'. He announced again that 'there is another miracle from The Philippines: a brother was healed from mysterious illness in his neck'. Pastor Ray kept on announcing varieties of healing from different parts of the world. This virtual church service is what Bell (2006) refers to as technologizing of sacred spaces. It can be argued here that technology mediates the presence of sacred space. This is because the real space of the church has been virtually extended across time and space, enabling others in distant places to participate in spiritual services.

Furthermore, Pastor Chris has initiated online global prayers in which all interested members are expected to log in to the prayer site on their social media site Yookos at exactly noon and 10.00 pm (GMT) every Monday and Wednesday everywhere in the world for fifteen minutes of prayer. Pastor Chris posted the following remarks for the preparation of one of the prayer sessions:

> In both 15 minute sessions at 12noon and 10pm (GMT), we will pray mostly and fervidly in tongues, while also worshiping the Lord and thanking Him for more doors of opportunity granted us for the preaching of the gospel of Christ everywhere, with signs and wonders and great harvests of souls. Prayer

especially for our brethren, pastors and leaders who are ministering in villages, towns, cities and nations under siege of terrorists, criminals or wicked and unreasonable men and women. 'Pray the Lord' grants them protection and delivers them from evil work and fills them with boldness to fulfil His will. The Word declares in 2Th. 3:3 '... the Lord is faithful, who shall establish you, and keep you from evil.' Halleluiah, God bless you.

All the participants are expected to pray in tongues, putting their request at the back of their minds. The coordinators of this programme claimed that millions of people log in to this global prayer all over the world. They encourage more members to join this prayer because of its efficacy and power to transform the individual. The reason for the effectiveness of this prayer is held to be the power of technology to harness the individual flow of the spirit through speaking in tongues and make it into a united powerful global force that is much more powerful and effective than mere atomized individual prayer. This practice implies that a technological device can serve as a conduit through which charismatic power flows to effect changes across long spatial distance.

This perspective is similar to the incident of claimed healing through watching or touching the screen when Pastor Chris is praying. A forty-year-old woman in Christ Embassy told me that she was having a mysterious pain in her waist. She said she prayed several times for two weeks, but to no avail. She even went to the pharmacy and was prescribed some medications but still the pain persisted. As she was watching a programme called 'Atmosphere of Miracle' on her mobile phone, seeing Pastor Chris performing a miracle, she claimed to have instantly received healing and the pain completely disappeared. There are numerous similar cases of people who claimed to receive healing by watching Pastor Chris performing a miracle that was transmitted via their technological device.

Mediating spiritual power that effects healing from physical illness illustrates how the mobile phone not only becomes a medium that connects people but also serves as a religious media that connects people with the spiritual realm. Members of Christ Embassy appropriate the potential of the material properties of this technology and reconstitute its functionality for the purpose of connecting with the transcendental world. The material media of technology in this sense certainly 'disappear' when practitioners immerse themselves in virtual religious participation or global prayer service. This is highlighted by Patrick Eisenlohr (2011: 46) when he observes that in some practices the process of mediating something media 'is capable of drawing attention away from their own materiality and technicality in order to redirect attention to what is being mediated'. Moreover, a mobile device is a technological gadget with highly mundane functions; in this case it becomes a temporarily enchanted object when it is involved in the practice of divine mediation.[19] This is certainly not a new experience among Nigerians, because there is already a trend of enchanting new technological devices in the country. There have been rumours of demons calling people through mobile phones in order to kill or enrich them as well as informal conversation about some astrological formulas or secret name of God which manufacturers inserted into the phones to make them work and perform wonderful functions.[20]

Christ Embassy has introduced the practice of online conversion. To receive Christ and become a born-again believer in Christ Embassy requires a ritual of sitting close to the pastor who can facilitate the impartation of the Holy Spirit to the would-be born-again believer. The pastor recites a prayer and confession and the aspirant repeats the prayer after him. Immediately after the aspirant finishes reciting the prayer and confession, he/she has become a born-again person and becomes a new creature in the sight of God. Recently, this ritual also occurs in the cyberspace. Pastor Chris has personally written the prayer in the website of the church. The site contains the following questions:

> Do you know Jesus? Do you want to rededicate your life to God? Do you want to experience peace in your life? You too can begin a NEW LIFE with JESUS CHRIST Today. We invite you to make Jesus Christ the Lord of your life by praying this prayer.

If one is ready to receive Christ, he/she can recite the following prayer:

> O Lord God, I come to You in the Name of Jesus Christ. Your Word says, '... whosoever shall call on the name of the Lord shall be saved' (Acts 2:21). I ask Jesus to come into my heart to be the Lord of my life. I receive eternal life into my spirit and according to Romans 10:9, 'That if thou shalt confess with thy mouth the Lord Jesus, and shalt believe in thine heart that God hath raised Him from the dead, thou shalt be saved', I declare that I am saved; I am born-again; I am a child of God! I now have Christ dwelling in me, and greater is He that is in me than he that is in the world! (1 John 4:4). I now walk in the consciousness of my new life in Christ Jesus. Hallelujah!

To conclude the process the website contains this information:

> Congratulations! You are now a child of God. Kindly Fill The Form Below If You Said The Salvation Prayer And Also To Download A Free E-Copy book By

Pastor Chris, Thank you. An email containing the book 'Now that you are born again' has been sent to your email address. God bless you.

A final year university student told me about his experience with online conversion:

> I was raised a nominal Christian because my parents are not religious at all. We hardly go to Church and I am not regular in prayer. Through the influence of school friends I began to attend the services of Christ Embassy in the campus. I have become captivated with the teachings of Pastor Christ and his personality. When I decided to finally become a born again in the church I desire to receive Christ from the great man of God Pastor Chris. When I come to know that Pastor Chris personally administers the online prayer for becoming born again I rushed to my smart phone, accessed the website, took the prayer and signed up my name. When I finished the process I became very happy that I received Christ from Pastor Chris. Thank God with the new technology since I have no opportunity to meet the pastor in real life now I met him online.

This online service is believed to be as effective as offline personal contact with the pastor, because the prayer carries the anointing of the man of God Pastor Chris. Members believed that the online conversion is authentic and special since it comes directly from the man of God. Modern technology is believed to allow the impartation of anointing from the man of God to touch people who agree to receive Jesus Christ online.

NASFAT has introduced similar but more limited virtual participation in its religious services with online streaming of the national *Lailatul Qadr* prayer in Lagos. If one registers and logs in to the live streaming of the prayer, one can partake in the spiritual benefit of the prayer. However, it is not allowed for members to join the prayer online. They can only participate through watching alone. This is because there is a long-standing *fatwa* by many Islamic scholars in Nigeria that prohibits joining and participating in *salat* ritual prayer through live television broadcasting. This *fatwa* is based on the ruling of Islamic jurists that limit the distance between the imam and the worshipper who follow the imam outside the mosque.[21] In both Christ Embassy and NASFAT the purpose of the service is the same: to extend the reach of the services and sacred grounds beyond the limitations of time and space. Moreover, new technology is also believed to extend the spiritual effect of these religious services in the sense that people believed that they can access spiritual blessings online.

While the previous section of sharing religious knowledge raised the issue of authority, this section brings to the fore the question of authenticity. Some pastors of ECWA Church and other Izala ulama criticized internet-mediated religious participation based on the perceived inauthenticity of the services due to its disembodied nature. The critiques usually point out that the lack of presence of worshippers in the congregation undermines the spiritual effect of the religious performances. However, apparently the novelty of digital technology and its mundane nature do not render ritual performed through it inauthentic in Christ Embassy. Christ Embassy embraces digital technology as a welcome development that opens up a myriad of doors of opportunity to them. By developing and controlling their own digital platforms (Yookos, Kingschat), Christ Embassy holds the medium in check and ensures that members do not turn away from Pastor Chris, so that he remains the authority necessary to authenticate digitally mediated experiences. Since engagement of NASFAT with technology-mediated religious participation is limited, the leadership has not yet articulated a comprehensive view about religious performances mediated by technology.

Digital religious images and the experience of haptic vision

There is widespread circulation of religious images through mobile phones among NASFAT and Christ Embassy members. The mobile phone recently has become a pervasive medium that contains varieties of images, sounds and texts. People download and share images particularly through Bluetooth and messaging apps such as WhatsApp Messenger. This section has adopted a broad view of images that include digital Islamic calligraphy and pictures. Calligraphy is defined by Claude Mediavilla (1996: 17) as 'the art of giving form to signs in an expressive, harmonious, and skillful manner'. Islamic calligraphy or Arabic calligraphy, according to Titus Burckhardt (1987), is the artistic practice of handwriting based upon the Arabic language and alphabet in the lands sharing a common Islamic cultural heritage. It is known in Arabic as *khatt* which was derived from the word 'line', 'design' or 'construction'. The calligraphic images used are mostly the word 'Allah' and 'Muhammad'. Nowadays Islamic calligraphy has been increasingly rendered in digital forms through graphics software.

These electronic calligraphies come with exquisite design and appear in conspicuous colours and sometimes adorned with intricate arrangements of flowers and illuminated with light. The meaning of light in the images is apparently due to its symbolic significance in religious traditions. The ceremonial use of lights is found in the practice of many religions across the globe. Candles are extremely common and other forms of light, whether fire or other, are utilized to convey the sense of holiness. Therefore, light that adorns the names of Allah and the Prophet Muhammad signifies their sacredness or holiness similar to the halo that accompanies medieval Catholic saints. Apart from beautifying the images, flowers are the symbols of love. Therefore, they create the impression that Allah and his Prophet are objects of love. In combining design, colours, light and flowers, the creators of these images tend to portray the visual aesthetic that expresses the perceived beauty and eternal qualities of God and lasting significance of his Prophet.

The use of calligraphic images among NASFAT members is not seen as contrary to Islamic injunctions. In Islam, prohibition on the use of images is restricted to the creation of images of sentient living beings. Protestant Christianity has a similar attitude towards images. This is the reason why Joseph Koerner (2003: 151–2) argues that iconoclastic Protestants radically 'linguistified' the sacred, which was 'formerly manifested objectively'. Koerner's argument can well be extended into the domain of Islam. This is understandable if we look at the importance of verbal and poetic renderings of the Qur'an and names of God in Islamic tradition. However, I would argue that the written language in Islam has taken form and become an image via calligraphy. Calligraphy is an image because of its artistic elements and the special way it is handled, which is based on calling attention in order to be seen and to be appreciated. Its artistic forms are designed to appeal to the human senses. Calligraphic rendering of the word Allah and Muhammad has gone deep into many Islamic cultures through a long period of repetition and circulation. Therefore the two words now take the forms of images that create a flash of recognition among members of that culture, whether literate or non-literate. Members of NASFAT implicitly agree that the calligraphic names of Allah and Muhammad are images or pictorial forms. One of my respondents, a forty-nine-year-old teacher in Abuja, stated,

I know that Islamic calligraphies are supposed to be respected and handle[d] with care but still I regard them as precious objects for decorating my sitting room, my computer screen and my handset. Instead of hanging pictures of people on the wall of my sitting room or place them on the screen of my mobile phone, I preferred to use the calligraphic name of Allah or Prophet Muhammad. Pictures of people could remind me worldly events but calligraphic name of

Allah and his Prophet or some verses of the Qur'an could remind me spiritual side of life. (Interview, 12 February 2014)

I have witnessed similar remarks among members of NASFAT, indicating that they have taken Islamic calligraphies as images even though they are not ready to go into complex academic discourse of what is an image and what is not. The view of my respondent grounded both soft and hard versions of Islamic calligraphies in the realm of images by seeing them as decorative objects that could be used in place of human pictures, not as written signs that convey linguistic meaning. In my interview with him, one of the youth leaders in NASFAT said, 'I always like and revere these images. Whenever I see the name of Allah beautifully rendered in design I feel overwhelmed with his presence and love' (interview, 21 December 2013). Another member who is a thirty-nine-year-old banker in Abuja stated the following:

I think there is something mysterious about the calligraphic names of Allah and Muhammad because coming into contact with them change[s] my feeling and mood. Whenever I feel the propensity to commit sin, the moment I look unto the screen of my phone and see the names of Allah and Muhammad I instantly feel guilty and withdraw from my bad intention. I am also feeling that I cannot be able to do something bad in a house where calligraphic name of Allah and Muhammad are displayed on the wall. It makes me feel as if they are watching me. I know there are people who do not feel this way, people who forget Allah and even commit sin when they have name of Allah in their houses or cell phones to remind them his presence. But my feeling is very different from such people. I see Islamic calligraphy as powerful reminder of the presence of Allah.

These assertions confirm David Morgan's (2010) observation that enacting the presence of the sacred is one of the functions of a religious image. Morgan maintains that images can mediate and provide access through gazing, kissing, touching, veneration or even worship. Moreover, Alison Ross (2016: 22) argues, 'What is distinctive about the image is that it possesses a communicative force that is surplus to its perceptible form. It is this force that differentiates the image from other kinds of perceptible form.' So, it is arguable here that in this respect the Islamic calligraphies are images or religious media that bring the transcendent closer to the believers and connect them with its presence, since the act of seeing them is accompanied with a feeling of divine presence coupled with reverence and veneration. Thielemans (2015: 1) maintains that the experience of looking at artworks is multisensory and affective. He states that 'the emotional impact of this experience becomes part of the process of interpretation, the viewer an embodied spectator rather than a disembodied eye'. The pre-verbal sensation of affect generated by the experience of looking at the calligraphic rendering of the names of Allah and Muhammad is always subsequently interpreted by members of NASFAT as divine touch on the heart of believers. In another sense, coming into contact with the pictorial name of God induces divine remembrance that is felt as a special calmness in the mind. In light of the work of W. T. J. Mitchell (2005) the calligraphic rendering of the name of God can be regarded as an active agent that sets in motion processes in both the body and mind of the beholder. Furthermore, another function of these images has to do with the affirmation and expression of Muslim identity. Using these images as a screen wallpaper or hanging the printed frame of the image on the wall in houses or offices announces the religious identity of the owner.

Mobility of the mobile phone and its consequent instability

As mentioned above, mobile technology harboured religious contents. Mitchell (2005: 198) remarks, 'If images are life-forms, and objects are the bodies they animate, then media are the habitats or ecosystems in which pictures come alive'. To paraphrase Mitchell it can be stated that the mobile phone has become a habitat where varieties of images reside and come to life. Since calligraphic renderings of the names of Allah and the Prophet are regarded as holy symbols, they create certain restrictions on the use of the material media they now inhabit. This is because this medium, which provides efficient and convenient access to the digital religious resources, creates instability because of its very mobility. The mobile nature of the gadget creates the possibility of taking the gadget to environments some regard as polluted or profane. The instability caused by this problem has engendered hot arguments among Muslim scholars in the country. Some argue that it is completely wrong to put religious symbols such as the word of God into the highly mundane piece of technology.[22] This is where the issue of contestation of technology as religious media comes into play. While others argue that it is permissible for Muslims to upload religious texts, sound and images on the mobile phone, the caveat is that the phone should not be taken to the profane environment, for instance, a toilet. When I asked the NASFAT leaders about this problem their response was that it is permissible to go to places such as toilet with the phone. However, it should remain off and it is not permissible to use it there. There are few people among NASFAT members who expressed different views regarding this controversial issue. Ali Muyideen, a twenty-seven-year-old secondary school teacher in Abuja, stated,

> In my view the calligraphic name of Allah and Muhammad and Qur'anic verses that come in frames are better than the digital copies which people upload on their mobile phones. This is because the copies are fixed in one location and there is no tendency to take them to inappropriate places. However, I have mixed feelings about uploading names of Allah on the mobile phone. Personally, I could not go to toilet with my phone if it contains name of Allah or recitation of the Holy Qur'an. Even if the phone is turned off I still feel it carries the weight of the name of Allah and Prophet Muhammad. Despite the fact that some Islamic scholars allow people to upload Islamic arts and other related things, still I am not comfortable with that. (Interview, 11 February 2014, Abuja)

This comment has raised an important issue that the name of Allah, once it is created in whatever form, has weight or presence that can never be erased. The invisibility of the image through turning off the phone or switching to another file cannot collapse the holy presence until the name is deleted entirely from the phone. The comment also suggests that there is a contrast between the soft and hard versions of images (screen and paper images). As the comment implies, some people contest the use of electronic pictorial name of God because the digital screen images are not stable; they appear and disappear at the flip of an eye when the screen is turned on or turned off. As a result, the images do not provide a fixed and stable presence of God as is the case with the calligraphic frames hung on the wall.

Another issue that is perceived as problematic is the tendency by some young people to put religious materials such as the digital name of Allah on their cell phone and at the same time download profane materials such as pornography into the phone. This raises the question whether it is acceptable in the Islamic *shari'ah* to place religious and profane files in one digital device. Ulama in NASFAT and the broader Muslim community condemn this practice and ask youths to desist from it. They state that it is an act of sacrilege to place religious materials such as the verses of the Qur'an or name of Allah side by side with pornography. Despite this prohibition many youths do not find a contradiction in using both religious and profane contents on their phones. They can engage with any content as if the other does not exist. However, some handle their mobile phones with extra care if they contain religious materials.

Questions such as the following arise here: Does what is considered as sacred, such as the text of the Qur'an, sacralize its material container? When the text of the Qur'an or name of Allah is open on the phone, does the phone instantly become a religious object like the printed copy of the Qur'an? The view of Islamic scholars that prohibits the use of the religious materials on the phone and the one that forbids taking the phone to defiled spaces imply that the sacred contents create surplus value that permeates its container and thereby transforms the material component of the container into a religious object. The view of NASFAT's ulama, which holds that the phone which contains names of Allah should be turned off at unclean spaces, implies that religious materials in non-active digital form such as when the phone is off cannot be regarded as a sacred object until it is activated and becomes perceptible to the human senses. In this view, to paraphrase Mitchell again, the images would only come to life and animate the phone with their spiritual aura when it is turned on. However, the images die with the phone as it is turned off.

Images in Christ Embassy

The use of religious images is highly restricted in Christ Embassy. In line with the general Protestant suspicion of images, the leadership of the church does not approve the use of images of Jesus or crucifixes.[23] Aversion towards the use of images among the members of both Christ Embassy and NASFAT is rooted in the fear of digression to idolatry. 'The pictures of Jesus popularised by the media are fakes because no one knows exactly how Jesus looked like since there was no camera when he walked upon this earth' (interview, 12 January 2014).

However, despite the outright rejection of images in Christ Embassy, the pictures of Pastor Chris are displayed in the church and members use the pictures on their mobile phones. Members also circulate these images on their Yookos and Kingschat account profiles. I asked one of my interlocutors about the reasons for using the images and his response was that 'we do not revere the image of Pastor Chris the way Roman Catholics revere the picture of Jesus'. It appears that members of Christ Embassy use the image of Pastor Chris out of love and admiration, similar to the ways fans of celebrities use the images of their stars. Mass usage of images of Pastor Chris transformed them into icons of the church. The pictures symbolized Christ Embassy to members of the church and the Nigerian public.

Furthermore, the ubiquity of Pastor Chris's images in the digital devices of members of Christ Embassy resembles the use of Islamic images among members of NASFAT. The difference is that in NASFAT images of the calligraphic rendering of the names of Allah and the Prophet Muhammad are venerated and handled with care. Even though the picture of Pastor Chris in Christ Embassy is given special respect, it does not command profound veneration. Other images used by members of Christ Embassy in their mobile devices are pictures of church buildings, church choirs in practice or the church logo. These images serve a similar purpose of reaffirming religious identity or expression of loyalty to Pastor Chris by putting his picture on mobile phone wallpaper.

Conclusion

This chapter explored how mobile phone technology was appropriated by members of Christ Embassy and NASFAT and transformed into a potent religious medium that facilitates a link with the divine. The acceptance of digital technology by Christ Embassy and NASFAT as highlighted by the two quotations of their leaders in the opening remarks of the chapter precipitates technologically mediated religious practices among the members of the two religious groups. Comparing these practices as related to the religious digital sounds, texts and images reveals similarities and differences between the two groups. Some practices of NASFAT, such as Daily Ayaat, are apparently an imitation of Christ Embassy. This suggests that coexistence across religious difference may engender not only mutual influences and borrowing but also affirmations of difference. Moreover, the chapter has demonstrated that the impact of new digital technology on religious practices has raised issues regarding religious authority, authenticity and contestations.[24] These issues affect Christ Embassy and NASFAT in different ways. Techno-spiritual practices in Christ Embassy and NASFAT are an example of how religious practices shape, and are being shaped by, the use of new digital media. There is no indication that the rapid technologizing of religious practices and resources among Christian and Muslim groups, such as those found among members of Christ Embassy and NASFAT, would radically change the face of Christianity and Islam beyond recognition. However, the emergent techno-spiritual practices in Christ Embassy and NASFAT have redefined some religious practices in both organizations. Indeed, as Meyer (2009: 2) argues, 'the rearticulation of religion necessarily implies some kind of transformation, which entails shifts of its position in relation to the state and the market, as well as the shape of the religious message, structures of authority, and mode and moods of binding and belonging'.

Through technology spiritual practices spawn the development of a new religious community that is mediated through cyberspace with concomitant new ways of sharing religious experiences and insights, and of establishing networking among the faithful. It is noteworthy that the portability of digital technology has made religious resources highly mobile and more accessible. Despite the differences in the digital religious practices between the members of Christ Embassy and NASFAT, the common point of convergence is based on the fact that in both movements digital religious engagement generates similar religious experiences. On many occasions in Christ Embassy and NASFAT, religious sounds, texts and images mediated by digital technology generate affect and emotion that members interpret as the presence of (or closeness with) the divine. Even though Christ Embassy is a pacesetter in engaging with the new media, there is strong indication that NASFAT will continue to engage with new media technologies and even initiate their own similar to Christ Embassy. As both Christ Embassy and NASFAT embrace modernity, they perceive appropriation of new media technology as an aspect of being modern. Moreover, NASFAT's leadership sees open-mindedness as another way of expression of modernity; this openness certainly would pave the way for new experiments and innovative practices with the ever-evolving new media.

Conclusion

In the introduction, I stated that a growing number of scholars call for an anthropology of religion that studies Islam and Christianity under a single framework. This book has attempted to do that by treating Christ Embassy and NASFAT within a single comparative parameter of analysis. It would have been possible to take the study of each of these organizations into a different trajectory of research, for instance, embedding it into the anthropology of Christianity or Islam respectively. However, opting for a single anthropology that focuses on comparing two distinct religious groups that share the same habitat but differ in theology and religious practice reveals some unique religious dynamics. The important question here is: what does the comparative approach show?

Chapter 1 explored religious coexistence and its implications in the city of Abuja. Religious pluralism in Abuja results in diverse confessional groups sharing the same neighbourhood and becoming exposed to each other's practices. This engenders intrusion on each other's privacy and space through amplification of sound and blockage of public roads. The chapter showed how various kinds of public religious manifestations – from buildings, to sounds and images – transform Abuja's cityscape. The comparison noted that elements of soft or non-aggressive intra- and inter-religious competitions underlie the inscription of religion in public spaces of the city. Furthermore, the comparative approach shows that despite the seemingly opposed world views and divergences between Muslims and Christians in the urban environment, they face similar challenges and apply similar techniques for meeting the challenges of precarious Nigerian urban environments.

Chapters 2 and 3 introduced Christ Embassy and NASFAT and showed how they stand in critique to mainline Christianity and Islam. I also demonstrated how in certain respects they resemble each other more than Christ Embassy would resemble organizations in mainline Christianity and NASFAT in mainline Islam. In addition, the comparative approach noted similar ways of doing or living religion in Christ Embassy and NASFAT. The chapters suggested that the success of Christ Embassy may be embedded in the empowerment of the individual members with the mental resources to handle quotidian existence. And the popularity of NASFAT underscores its provision of sensational religious practices and socio-economic services that are borrowed from Pentecostalism.

Chapter 4 started the process of comparing selected practices of Christ Embassy and NASFAT in order to determine convergences and divergences as well as mutual influences between the two groups. The chapter examined three genres of prayers as a starting point for comparison. The genres of prayers compared in the chapter were prayers of adoration, prayers of aesthetic speech and prayers of instrumentality. The comparative approach indicated that in the two movements, prayers of adoration and prayers of aesthetic speech generate a sense of contact with the divine by orchestrating bodily experiences of affect and emotion which members interpret as evidence of the presence of God. The comparative approach also revealed that instrumental prayers in both groups initiate communication with the Divine and gratify the desired goals through the performative power and semiotic systems ascribed to the language of the prayers. The different genres of prayers disclosed some similarities in practices, semiotic systems and emotions produced by different religious performances. It has been shown in this chapter that NASFAT consciously reshaped the structure of Islamic prayers in order to respond to the challenges of Pentecostalism and meet the special needs of urban Muslims.

Chapter 5 compared preaching practices in Christ Embassy and NASFAT. The comparative approach demonstrated that there are in the two groups some similarities in different aspects of preaching such as themes, styles, religious authority and ethics of listening to preaching. The comparison also suggested that preaching in Christ Embassy and NASFAT is a practice of mediation that is enhanced by several factors such as the eloquence and authority of the preachers as well as preaching accoutrements such as dress, background music and preaching assistants. These factors established preaching as an aesthetic style based on their ability to mobilize human senses and thereby make preaching performances a highly emotional experience.

Chapter 6 compared technologically mediated practices and showed the importance of material media in Christ Embassy and NASFAT. The comparison pointed out how the mobile phone became a multivalent religious object (while also being an ordinary device people use to contact other people). As a result of the multilayered applications of the mobile phone in the religious sphere, the leadership of both groups authenticated its use and accommodated it in their religious performances. Authenticating the use of mobile phones in a religious setting defined the role of new media as an integral part of religious practice. For instance, private listening to the sacred sonic materials via the mobile phone – particularly by earpiece – generates a sense of aural mediation. Engaging with the sacred digital text revolutionizes the textual practices in the two groups and challenges the traditional engagement with the print version of religious texts. Circulating religious text messages has become a new digital religious culture of exchanging symbolic value. And religious performances and participation through the phone have transformed it (the phone) into a potent conduit that transmits charismatic power. In addition, distribution of digital religious images and interactions with them via the medium of the mobile phone serve as a reminder of the perpetual Divine presence as well as an expression of religious identity in Christ Embassy and NASFAT.

In Chapter 1, I stated that Meyer and Larkin (2006) stress similarities between Pentecostals and Islamic reformists. Their main argument is 'that Pentecostalism and reformist Islam actually share a great deal of common ground and, while disagreeing on doctrine, overlap in several of the religious practices on which they depend and the social processes they set in motion' (2006: 286). Conversely, Peel (2015) takes a different view and criticizes Meyer and Larkin for over-emphasizing similarities between Islamic reformists and Pentecostals. Peel maintains that there is a fundamental divergence between the two movements in the sense that Pentecostalism emphasizes prosperity, healing, deliverance from evil spirits and individual empowerment, while Islamic reformists discourage traditional Islamic healing practices and stress the importance of frugality instead of prosperity. In her response to Peel in a special section of *Africa*, Meyer (2015b) argues that a comparative study of Islam and Christianity should take lived religion and practices as a starting point rather than insisting on intrinsic differences between the two traditions. According to Meyer, actual similarities between Muslims and Christians come into view through a focus on religious practices. Similarly, in his response Larkin (2014a: 22) situates comparison between Pentecostalism and reformist Islam at the level of shared religious form, which he refers to as 'stylistic elements that emerge within a particular tradition but are then severed from those origins and move into other domains'.

This book agrees with the call of Meyer and Larkin to adopt a comparative approach that looks for similarities between Christianity and Islam. This thesis established many similarities in the forms and practices of Christ Embassy and NASFAT. For instance, there is conspicuous similarity in the structures of Sunday worship services in the two groups. It is also telling how even the form of the individual activities of the Sunday service in the two groups, such as prayers, preaching, testimony, prayer request, announcing job vacancies and welcoming new comers, have many things in common. Furthermore, NASFAT and Christ Embassy use the same new media technology that serves to mediate religious practices. Applying the same technology as a medium in religious practices generates similar listening and reading habits as well as similar interactions with digital religious materials among the members of the two religious groups. Through borrowing form of practices from Pentecostalism, NASFAT offers a new way of doing Islam, which is still true to Islam as tradition (at least for the NASFAT members), despite copying some elements from outside Islam.

However, even though I agree with Meyer and Larkin's responses to Peel's critique, it is important to realize that borrowing takes place under unequal power relations. The comparative approach adopted in this thesis showed that the dynamic of borrowing is not balanced since NASFAT usually follows the trail set by Pentecostalism. In addition, the unbalanced inter-religious borrowing is not a random imitation of Pentecostals by NASFAT but rather a negotiated form of borrowing contextualized within Islamic religious tradition. This can be seen in the ways NASFAT appropriated different genres of prayers from Islamic sources and restructured them in the form similar to Pentecostal prayers. Furthermore, it should be noted that in addition to certain similarities, certain differences also remain. For example, the themes of preaching in the two groups are significantly different from each other. NASFAT emphasizes Islamic orthopraxis, piety, and individual and collective moral reforms. Christ Embassy stresses personal faith and puts overwhelming importance on the power of faith in confronting and solving challenges of life. The two groups also differ in the sense that NASFAT is not dominated by a powerful charismatic figure, as is the case with Pastor Chris in Christ Embassy. Pastor Chris uses his charismatic power to initiate some practices claimed to be based on inspiration from the Holy Spirit, such as the 'spiritual significance of time', discussed in Chapter 2. One of the marked differences in this regard is that there is an absence of such divinely inspired messages through a charismatic leader in NASFAT. Finally, this thesis affirmed that comparing different religious traditions that share the same habitat through practices is effective in revealing similarities, mutual influences and inter-religious borrowing, as well as difference.

The contribution of this book lies in combining the paradigm of material turn and the anthropological comparative framework. This approach is fruitful as it is easier and more accessible to compare concrete material engagement or embodied practice than immaterial belief systems or creeds. Combining materiality and comparison has multiple advantages, since diverse religious groups can use the same or similar material component as a platform for religious practice or expression. As indicated in the use of mobile phones, deploying similar material platforms generates similar religious practices. This similarity may be a result of mutual influence or arise due to the logical constraint of certain material things. Another promise of material comparison is that material things and embodied practices lend themselves more easily to being copied by others, whether from within or outside the original practitioners' religious orientation. It is very apparent that certain material practices could easily be borrowed and adapted by other religious groups, rather than belief systems or dogmas. As I highlighted in the introduction, religious encounter happens within the domain of materiality and practice. This book has attempted to show that anthropological comparison through juxtaposition with a focus on materiality enhances our understanding of various forms of religious engagement because, on many occasions, it reveals the origin, adaptation and innovative dimension of forms of religious practices. I also advocated in the introduction and demonstrated in the body of the book that opting for and applying different approaches to material turn such as symbols, material disciplines and phenomenology is more promising since religion is constituted by various elements with a multiplicity of expressions. The results of this monograph indicate that anthropological comparison centred on materiality is a crucial investigative tool for understanding the entangled religious pluralism that defines contemporary African urban centres. As a result, this monograph pleads for this kind of research that conflates anthropological comparison with the paradigm of materiality in African urban settings. These urban centres are dynamic sites of religious pluriform with increasing innovative practices fostered by a rapidly changing environment due to the complex interaction between global and local forces.

Notes

Introduction

1 In order to protect the identity of the interlocutors all the names that appeared in this text are pseudonyms.

2 See Nolte (2015).

3 Prophetic medicine shops or *sunnah* pharmacies established by *Salafi* scholars are spreading rapidly in all corners of Nigerian urban spaces.

4 Nolte (2015) discusses the role of the customary in relation to an encounter between Islam and Christianity in Yorubaland. Nolte sketches the historical development of the institutions of Obas in Yoruba towns from the late eighteenth century through colonial and post-colonial periods and highlights their struggle with conversion to monotheistic religions. The problem of being a monotheist and the imperative of being faithful to tradition is explained by Nolte as the politics of customary, which emerged during the colonial era, even though it has strong links with the pre-colonial past. Customary, according to Nolte, is 'associated with local and historical practices of the community' (2005: 1). According to Nolte, the customary sphere flourished around the office of Obas who act as custodians of the institutions. Nolte argues that even when Obas converted to Islam, they resisted the Islamization of the institutions; traditional practices still remain paramount in the palaces. Nolte highlights the disquiet experienced by Yoruba Muslims as a result of the dominance of the public sphere by Pentecostalism. With the failure of Islamic reformists to take root in Yorubaland, some movements emerged to resist the threat of growing Pentecostalism. Nolte notes that the most popular among these was the NASFAT.

Chapter 1

1 See Iwuchukwu, Marinus and Stiltner (2013) for a comprehensive exploration of religious conflict in northern Nigeria and dialogues initiated by government as well as religious leaders.

2 Abuja is a city that differs from other major urban centres in Nigeria in the sense that it was built recently and has loose social ties and high costs of residential properties. As a result, many people decide to leave their families in their

hometowns when taking up employment in the city. In the course of my fieldwork, I noticed high religious participation and affective community bonding among all the religious groups I interacted with, including the members of Christ Embassy and NASFAT. Religious involvement and the sense of communal bonding is very strong in the city. For example, among all the branches in the country, it is the Abuja branch that adopted a Pentecostal practice of dividing its members into smaller units for fellowship and extra religious activities. Consequently, it can be argued that there is a link between active religious participation and the need for a sense of belonging in the city of Abuja. Many people claimed to have found personal fulfilment through bonding with their religious brethren and active participation in religious activities. This personal fulfilment complements their disrupted sense of identity, engendered by the severing of their ties with their immediate family and original places of origin.

3 See Dilger (2014) for a comparative study of revivalist Muslims and a neo-Pentecostal attempt at place-making through establishing health intervention institutions in Tanzania.

4 In the early 2000s some mountaineers from Germany came to Abuja and conquered Zuma for the first time.

5 Land in Abuja is very expensive and as a result only churches that have huge financial clout can afford to buy land to build religious space within the city. Smaller churches have to go to the outskirts of the city where land is cheap.

6 See Dilger (2014) for an analysis of a similar phenomenon in urban Tanzania.

7 Eckankar is one of the largest New Religious Movements in Abuja with branches in most of the main districts of the city, and they are more visible in public space and airwaves. Eckankar holds an annual seminar in Abuja, which is a big spectacle event with people coming from all over the country. These minor religions are relatively tolerated in the sense that they are free to establish their places of worship and organize proselytizing activities. Nevertheless, they still experience slight social discrimination as on the issue of political appointment or rejection by some employers. They are also called with derogatory names such as cult or secret societies.

8 Christian groups and individuals initiated many faith-based organizations that engage in relief activities. Some of the most influential organizations are the Christian Association of Nigeria, Christian Aid in Nigeria, Christian Aid Mission, Aglow International, Bill Glass Ministry, Christian Financial Concept, Christians in Recovery, Christian Stewardship Ministries, Christian Business Man Committee, Gateway to Joy, Prison Fellowship Ministries and Rest Ministries.

9 See Philip Ostien (2009) for a detailed study of how indigene and settler problems transformed into protracted religious conflicts in Jos.

10 This council has legal status similar to all the federal government's institutions.

11 In northern Nigerian cities, including Abuja, ATRs are almost entirely invisible. As a result they become irrelevant in urban religious discourse. Indigenous religions are often found in remote villages in the north. However, practitioners of ATR are protected by law since Nigerian Constitution affirmed the freedom of religion.

12 See Enyinna S. Nwauche (2008) for a detailed study of the relationship between law, religion and human rights in Nigeria and how Islam and Christianity almost became unacknowledged de facto state religions, and the resulting neglect of other religions.

13 Read more at https://www.nigeriarights.gov.ng/focus-areas/freedom-of-religion-or-belief-and-peaceful-assembly.html.

14 A Roman Catholic reverend father told me that some Pentecostals disapproved of their religious dialogue with Muslims. He said on many occasions Pentecostals accuse Roman Catholics of sitting and talking with the enemies.

15 The first time I encountered the name 'NASFAT' was from a sticker pasted on a handbag of a lady in Jos around 2006. From that time I began to notice the stickers in different places, particularly bumper stickers on cars in Jos.

Chapter 2

1 Probably due to the financial and marital scandals around Pastor Chris, the church goes the extra mile to protect him from outside scrutiny. So despite all my efforts I was not able to get details of his historical background.

2 Members of Christ Embassy are hostile to interviews and even if they agreed to be interviewed, they are highly economical in their words. They do not seem to know details about the life of Pastor Chris. This is the limited information that I gathered from some interlocutors piece by piece.

3 Oyakhilome received honorary doctorates from Ambrose Alli University and Benson Idahosa University in 2015.

4 With a gigantic empire, Pastor Chris Oyakhilome of Christ Embassy is arguably among the top five richest clergy in Nigeria. According to the Encomium Magazine, Pastor Chris is worth over N300 billion.

5 At that time Anita was the only female among the members of CEC.

6 Partners here are people who sponsor some major programmes of the church.

7 It is important to note that there is a bank in Nigeria with the name Zenith Bank. This bank has no connection with Zenith Cell.

8 Even though these people know that I am a researcher, they want me to participate in all their activities so that I may appreciate them and convert to Christianity.

9 Christ Embassy members and leadership do not want to talk about money and business ventures of their church. Most of the information in this section comes

from outside observers and Encomium Magazine. According to the Encomium (2014), businesses from Christ Embassy span from publishing to broadcasting, entertainment, hospitality, as well as banking. Other significant enterprises are Superscreen TV and National Standard magazine. The church also has a free-to-air channel in South Africa which produces and airs Christian movies and TV series. The satellite televisions have an average of 1 million subscribers across the world.

    According to Encomium (2014), one of the most significant business ventures of the church is the digital printing press called GlobalPlus, located on Ikosi Road, Oregun, Lagos. The printing press makes a profit of more than 2 billion naira per annum (4,216,740 euro). This is the company that publishes the Rhapsody of Reality devotional booklet using state-of-the-art machines that churn out hundreds of thousands of copies per day. This daily devotional that is published monthly and in many languages generates a lot of money for the church and Pastor Chris and his former wife, Anita. Rhapsody of Reality is now one of the famous devotional booklets in Nigeria, and it can be seen in many places such as hotels, hospitals, offices and even prison yards. The book is distributed to most of the African countries, Europe, Asia, North and South America. When Rhapsody was first published in 2005, it cost 300 naira (0.63 cents), but due to mass printing the price is down to 150 naira (0.31 cents). Members are encouraged to buy it and other products of the church in bulk and distribute them freely to friends and family members and organizations. Another vital enterprise is LoveWorld Records Limited, which was incorporated in 2008 as a private limited liability company to carry on with the business of music, entertainment and gospel merchandise. It is credited with producing many artists, who are mainly members of the church. It is the only label in Nigeria that focuses primarily on publishing, producing, marketing and distributing gospel music and the promotion of artists. Their music videos and CDs are in the UK, Canada, the United States, South Africa and Ghana. The studio holds the franchise of record labels of Believers LoveWorld Incorporated (Encomium 2014). However, due to the sensitivity of the issue of money in the church, information regarding how the businesses are run, decision-making processes, sharing of profit and ownership of the businesses in a legal sense all remain secret. The church does not share this information with outsiders.

10 There is no transparency on where the money is going and how it is being spent. Members of Christ Embassy are not allowed to discuss issues of money with outsiders. However, amidst this secrecy Pastor Christ has emerged as one of the richest pastors in Nigeria.

11 The practice of testimony is one of the most important religious activities of Christ Embassy. Testimony is an account given by members of the congregation to portray the intervention of God in their lives. There is a special session close to the end of the service where people are called to come forward and recount their testimonies.

A member who is interested in giving the testimony would inform the pastor before the service begins and submit his/her name. The stories usually involve elements of surprise, inexplicable incidents that required supernatural explanation and other forms of extraordinary events. Testimonies bring the reality of the supernatural to the congregation and validate the existence of the supernatural and illustrate how it interacts with the material. Plüss (1988: 55) writes, 'Testimony is understood as a discourse in which means of symbolic tradition fuses event and meaning. This symbolic tradition mediates a relation between meaning and event, and thus manifests an interpretation. Testimony is a mediator between secular and the sacred, between the meaning of life and the events that shape it.' The worldview of the church is used as an instrument for assigning meaning into the significant life experience that is interpreted as testimony. As highlighted by Pluss, testimonies provide vivid imageries of how supernatural forces encounter the ordinary in the lives of believers. Predominant numbers of testimonies involve supernatural intervention in the area of healing and financial reward. Torr (2013: 206) describes testimonies as 'accounts of powerful'. Peacock (1984: 41) states that 'the testimony brings the private experience to the public rite a transition crucial for those who seek to be healed by faith. To be healed, one must "claim" it. Telling a story assists individuals to engage in sense-making about their experiences, to order events in a coherent fashion, relate an event to other events and attribute causality' (Singleton 2001: 121–2).

12 2 Corinthians 13:14.
13 See Caroline W. Bynum (2012) where she argues that the most important material manifestation of the holy in the western European Middle Ages was the Eucharist.
14 The Healing School service is also broadcast on various media of Christ Embassy under different titles such as 'Enter the Healing School with Pastor Chris', 'Healing to the Nations' and 'Healing School Live'. There is also a highly interactive and user-friendly Healing School website, where one can access the activities of the Healing School and testimonies of people who received healing at any time. The website contains videos of several miracles and podcasts with the title the 'Divine Health Realities'.
15 Pastor Oyakhilome being suspicious of biomedicine is further revealed in his recent approaches to the Covid-19 pandemic. Pastor Chris Oyakhilome subscribes to a conspiracy theory that unites misapprehensions about 5G technology and the coronavirus. In one of his online sermons published on YouTube on 8 April 2020, Oyakhilome stated that both the coronavirus and 5G technology are the products of satanic secret agent illuminati, with the aim of transforming mankind into a hybrid of human and machine. According to Oyakhilome, these satanic agents will soon introduce a Covid-19 vaccine which will actually be a serum filled with nano-microchips that will be introduced into the human body. These microchips, which

will be controlled via 5G technology, are designed to read and influence human thought, undermine human agency and free will, and force people to worship Satan instead of God. He has further stated that the federal government lockdown of Abuja and Lagos is in fact intended to allow the secret installation of 5G antennas and other equipment. Pastor Oyakhilome has maintained that the microchips that will be injected into human bodies are the 'mark of the beast', as foretold in the book of Revelation of the New Testament.

16 Extended discussion about the unique teachings of Christ Embassy will appear in Chapter 6.

Chapter 3

1 I got the contact of the chief imam through Mustapha Bello, the deputy national secretary of NASFAT, whom I got to know through Marloes Jansen.

2 Not his real name.

3 Among the Yoruba Muslims in the southwest, Islamic organizations and movements have a long history. The influential Islamic groups such as Ansar-Ud-Deen Society, Nurudeen Society and Nawaruddeen Society were established in the early decades of the twentieth century, and they arose partly in reaction to the activities and challenges of Christian missionaries.

4 Adetona (2012) also traces the origin of prayer groups in Yoruba land to the precolonial period, showing that modern prayer groups had their origin in many Sufi orders such as Tijjaniya and Quadirriya. The offshoot of these orders is the *Asalatu* prayer group. Mainly, these groups were part of the *ratibi* mosques in Lagos and in some divisions; they all came together on Friday for special *Asalatu* prayers at Jumat mosques. A few of these groups operated beyond these two levels. Examples of such included the *Asalatu* of Jama'at-ul-Suadai, with headquarters at Kuti Mosque, Lagos. Muqaddam Adeniyi, a student of Shaykh Ahmad Tijani Awelenje Shaki, was the founder. All through the 1970s and until the death of the Muqaddam, Lagos Muslims believed so much in the efficacy of prayers that were offered at this *Asalatu* group. The prayer used to be held between 8.00 pm and 10.00 pm every Friday at the Kuti Mosque. The mosque was always filled to capacity.

5 The new executive members are Barr S. O. Q. Giwa (chairman), Dr Nasir Raji (vice-chairman), Alh Ishaq Ajao (secretary), Shakir Quadir-Adu (asst. sec.), Kamarudeen Ogundele (publicity sec.) and Abdurasaq Sulaiman (empowerment sec.). Others include Alhaja Habeebat Babata-Sulaiman (women's leader), Kazeem D. Gbolagade (business sec.), Alhaja Simbiat Onize Lawal (children affairs), Munkaila Abdul-Raheem (welfare), Suraju Abdulmumeen (youth sec.), and Akeem Aderogba (finance sec.), among others.

6 Accepting NASFAT to conduct Sunday worship service in the central mosque is an indication of recognition of NASFAT in the north. In addition, northern Muslims also attend NASFAT mosques for Friday prayers in Abuja. Even though NASFAT does not attract membership from Hausa Muslim background, this has more to do with the language barrier than lack of recognition.

7 By spiritual NASFAT is referring to the religious duties.

8 International membership of the organization is mostly restricted to the Nigerian diasporas, particularly Yoruba Muslims.

9 According to Mustapha Bello, NASFAT's membership is open to all Muslim families, with the core of present membership comprising young professionals: engineers, doctors, lawyers, bankers, accountants, architects, academicians, educators, Islamic scholars, civil servants, journalists, company directors, business executives, computer experts, members of police and armed forces, members of the judiciary, politicians, state commissioners, legislators, traders, artisans and students.

10 See Johnson Mbillah (2004) on the issue of Muslim preachers of the Bible. 'Interfaith Relations and the Quest for Peace in Africa', in C. Hock (ed.), *The Interface between Research and Dialogue: Christian-Muslim Relations in Africa* (Münster: Litt Verlag, 2004), 69 (66–79).

11 According to Nolte (2015) there is growing criticism of customary practices by Pentecostals and also by Muslims in recent times. These criticisms occur through redefining the customary as vestiges of traditional religion. According to Nolte, the critiques see traditional festivals, Obaship and traditional chieftaincy as more based on traditional religion than as an aspect of culture, marking them as potentially idolatrous practices (12). As the criticism is ongoing, there is increasing influence of monotheistic religions on the institutions of Obas. This influence is ostensibly on the gradual demise of some practices that are perceived to be contrary to the teachings of Islam and Christianity. According to Nolte, the important transformation that is taking place and the increasing openness towards both Islam and Christianity suggest that the customary has retained many aspects of its function as a place of religious diversity and encounter (13).

12 The name *caliphate* is strange and I asked many people why NASFAT chose the name to refer to smaller units, but they said that it was the chief imam who used the name. And I was unable to visit him again to find the reason for choosing that name.

13 Roman Loimeier (1997) depicts a clear picture of the rise of Islamic reformism vis-à-vis a long history of political and social developments in northern Nigeria. He traces the history of the Sufi brotherhoods of *Tijjaniyya* and *Qadiriyya* from the precolonial period and their changing relationship with the political powers in the region. The social dominance of the two brotherhoods was challenged by late Sheikh Abubakar Gumi, who opposes their ideologies as evil innovation that

contradicts the teaching of authentic Islam. The brotherhoods unite and put to rest their own differences and conflicts in order to face the common enemy. According to Loimeier, supporters of Gumi formed the Izala movement in order to challenge the perceived un-Islamic practices of Sufi brotherhoods and replace them with *sunna* of the prophet. Loimeier asserts that the vicious criticism of Izala by the Sufis has caused the former to lose many members, and many people became emancipated from hitherto traditional and spiritual bondage that prescribed obligation on them towards certain strata of society.

Chapter 4

1 The Children's Room is a big room where Sunday school takes place for the children. Some of the newcomers take their lessons in that room if there is no space in the foundation classrooms.

2 The concept of prosperity gospel will be discussed in the next chapter.

3 Even though the practices and meaning of prayer in Christ Embassy are remarkably similar to those of other Pentecostals, slight differences still exist. For instance, the Lord's Prayer ('Our Father who art in heaven, Hallowed be thy name. Thy kingdom come …'), recited by most Christians, is not recognized by Christ Embassy. According to the teaching of Pastor Chris, this prayer belongs to the people of the Old Testament. Therefore it would not work today since the old contract has ended. According to Pastor Chris, at the time Jesus taught his disciples to pray this prayer the Kingdom had not yet come. So he prayed, 'Thy Kingdom come.' Oyakhilome continued that when Jesus taught his disciples this prayer before his death, his name was never used. But in the New Testament, Christians are commanded to pray in his name (Oyakhilome 2012: 7).

4 Because of the intra-religious diversity it cannot be said that these similarities can be applied to all Muslim and Christian groups in the country. Pentecostals engage much more in hyper-emotional practices than the historical churches. Among the Muslim groups in urban Nigeria, emotional prayers are spearheaded by prayer groups which Ebenezer Obadare (2016) called Charismatic Muslims. You should refer to his work already in Chapter 1.

5 Most of the mainline churches in Nigeria disapprove of speaking in tongues as practised by Pentecostals. Pastor Clement Haruna of ECWA Church Abuja criticizes speaking in tongues particularly as practised in Christ Embassy. He said that most churches tell members to arise and begin to pray. But in Christ Embassy, the person ministering said, 'Arise and begin to speak in tongues.' This doctrinal issue or interpretation is quite different from other Pentecostal or Orthodox doctrines. Most Pentecostal churches believe that speaking in tongues is a gift. The Bible, however,

states that the gifts of the Holy Spirit are a promise including the gift of speaking in tongues to those who repent and receive Christ in faith. God had given some gifts of healing, teaching tongues and so on; not all have the gift of tongues, not all have the gift of healing. The doctrine that all should rise and speak in tongues is a 'church' doctrine peculiar to Christ Embassy and not a biblical doctrine. Pastor Clement affirmed that it is a false doctrine to claim that everybody has a right to speak in tongues as evidence of the baptism of the Holy Spirit. Similarly, it is a wrong teaching to attempt to inspire people to speak in tongues or to make those who cannot speak to feel unworthy. It is the discretion of God to confer the gift of tongues to people he has chosen. Clement continued that in the ECWA Church they do not ask people to speak in tongues or teach that baptism of the Holy Spirit must be followed by speaking in tongues. If an individual is given such a gift, it is his personal experience and he does not need to share it with the congregation.

6 Weiss (1989: 119) illustrates how the absence of subject and object and the absence of temporal reference lend themselves to a different mode of signification in Pentecostal circle. He frames his argument in the following way:

> All ordinary language entails the determination of the speaking subject, by means of deictic (sth missing?), as a central feature of discourse (i.e. by using by using the linguistic shifters whose reference changes with every change of speaking subject; e.g. I, here, there, now, etc.). Glossolalic utterances, to the contrary, permit no differentiation between the subject of the utterance and the subject of the statement, no real determination of the subject. It is for this very reason such speech acts may be deemed of divine inspiration: if the subject cannot be located as a function of the enunciation, then the origin of the enunciation cannot be linguistically determined. The speaker escapes the 'circuit of discourse' by giving voice to an absolute statement.

7 Performances of zikr in NASFAT are slightly different with the Sufis.

8 Csordas (1994) sees embodiment as a perceptual experience and as a mode of presence and engagement in the world. Religious performances of glossolalia and *zikr* incorporate the three elements of embodiment.

9 See Asamoah-Gyadu (2015) for detailed explanation about the power of the spoken words in contemporary Pentecostalism.

10 Many mainstream Christians contest this view that human speech has the power of creation. Over the years I have heard many pastors criticizing Pentecostals for elevating themselves into little gods by investing on themselves the power of creation. American Pastor Christopher Gregory aptly summarized this criticism in the website *The Prophetic News* as follows:

There is a simple fact that every believer must acknowledge in their walk with Christ, and that is this, you and I, are not God. Nor are we little gods. Nor do we have the same power or ability to think and act and create like God. Even more so, neither do our words have the same power as Gods words. The simple fact is, man is a creation of God, made a little above the angels itself, without the ability nor power to imitate God in action or in deeds, or in this case – words. The truth is, our words are not on the same level as God almighty and have virtually no power within themselves. In other words, when we speak nothing happens, but when God speaks everything happens, because he's God and we're not. Yet there is a teaching which has gained prominence within the Charismatic/Pentecostal circles by suggesting that not only are we little gods, not only can we duplicate what God can do, we can equally speak things as a god and see those words literally transform nothing into something. It is called Positive Affirmation, or what is generally referred to by some as *the power within the tongue*. The belief is very simple, and very dangerous, but it goes something like this; a believer has a special need (money, health, career change, relationship, etc.) and they desire this with great fervor, but they don't know how to bring it to pass. The answer? Simply speak it into existence. Sounds farfetched right? Yet if the truth be told, there are millions of Christians within the Charismatic/Pentecostal circles who have bought into this lie that says if one desires to change their circumstances in life, all one has to do is simply speak it into being and it will come. The problem is that it never works.

11 According to the website biblestudy.org, the word 'Rhema' is Greek in origin and is defined as an utterance. In the Bible, Rhema is many times translated as 'word'. It can be used to refer to Jesus Himself, the messages he gave or the message about him. Its first appearance in the New Testament comes as part of Jesus' response to the devil's temptation that he turn stones into bread (Matthew 4:4). The second place it is found is in Jesus' response in Matthew 12 to some self-righteous religious leaders who stated he cast out demons by the power of Satan himself.

12 In Christ Embassy, due to the power attributed to human speech to manifest in the material world, negative words are not to be uttered by believers. But even when one said something negative mistakenly, one can use a formula 'greater is he who is in me than he who is in the world' to erase the negative spiritual effect of the uttered word. I discuss this issue in more detail in the next chapter on preaching.

13 Surah Yasin is the thirty-sixth surah of the Quran. It has eighty-three verses. The theme of the surah dwells mainly on the sovereignty and the unlimited power of God.

14 See Asamoah-Gyadu (2013).

15 During my fieldwork period in Abuja I heard my landlady engaging in a serious imprecatory prayer against her business rivals who conspired for her downfall. She

spent hours in the middle of the night calling for the death of her rivals. She was invoking the wrath and fire of God upon them.

16 There are about five deputy imams in each branch of NASFAT who are called missioners. NASFAT is influenced by churches which have the tradition of having several junior pastors in their branches.

17 However, in Islam there are specialists whose words carry power to manifest things, particularly negative things. If such people cast a curse on somebody, that person's life would seriously be affected. There are prayers provided specifically for protection against the tongues of such people.

18 This practice invokes Marcel Mauss's theory of gift exchange. But the cases of seed offering and *sadaqa* serve as a kind of gift exchange between believer and the deity.

19 Nevertheless, the toll on the human body is understandable if one looks at how some spent hours repeating certain words or phrases or a complete surah of the Qur'an hundreds or thousands of times. Bodily exhaustion will surely follow these extreme practices.

20 Media contents of Christ Embassy are full of testimonies of success stories about the efficacy of prayer. The media of the church never portray instances of failure of prayer. Surely in Christ Embassy media has played a key role in reinforcing a fervent belief on the efficacy of prayer. However, NASFAT's use of media is highly restricted, hence its limited deployment of media techniques to circulate prayer testimonies.

21 In September 2015, I was in the Sunday worship service in NASFAT when the imam made a big announcement. He said that he was angry about what was going on in the circle of some women members. He stated that he was told that some women bring magical charms into the mosque. He said this was a great transgression which cannot be tolerated. Any woman involved in these activities must repent and immediately desist from it. Among both Christ Embassy and NASFAT members, it is likely that some secretly resorted to other means such as modern esoteric or magical techniques in search of a solution to desperate situations in their lives.

22 Detailed discussion of the effect of negative thought and speech on human life follows in Chapter 6.

Chapter 5

1 NASFAT does not allow women to preach. In northern Nigeria there is a growing number of female preachers who are even preaching on the media in a situation very similar to what Dorothea Schulz (2012) describes in Mali.

2 These are preaching of Pastor Chris broadcast on the screen during Sunday services at which I took notes and recordings on my phone. I did the same at NASFAT's preaching sessions I visited.

3 Sunday worship service broadcast live in Abuja central branch, 26 January 2014.

4 Apart from Pastor Anita I have never come across a woman preaching in Christ Embassy. There are female deacons but their role is largely administrative services, not preaching. It can be argued that with the exception of Anita, Christ Embassy does not give women freedom to preach in the church. And she is out now. (See Chapter 3.)

5 There are no females among the NASFAT Mission Board, the body that produces imams. The deputy national secretary told me Islam does not allow women to lead prayers or spiritual leadership.

6 This was a short video broadcast in the branches of Christ Embassy. The video showed Pastor Chris addressing leaders of Christ Embassy, apparently trying to extricate himself against the accusation of sexual misconduct when his wife filed a suit of divorce against him.

Chapter 6

1 The advent of ICTs has spurred dramatic changes in Nigerian society. These revolutionary changes have been felt in all aspects of life from economy, politics, health, culture and so on. The number of mobile internet users in Nigeria exceeded 101.7 million (Ceci 2021).

2 Globacom is another mobile operator network that introduces varieties of religious services such as Glo Faith Portal and Globacom Christianity Portal. The Glo Faith Portal is an exciting service offered for both Islamic and Christian faithful to be enjoyed on a daily basis and providing an avenue for a more intimate relationship with the creator. There are needs in our individual lives that only oneness with the Almighty can provide, and this need is catered for with the Glo Faith Portal. Globacom Christianity Portal is an intelligent interactive voice response (IVR)-based portal which not only satisfies user's religious needs but also tracks their behaviour and responds accordingly. It offers users Bible readings, inspirational gospels and uplifting sermons. The Portal also allows users to download or dedicate their favourite gospels and/or set them as their ringtone back. Daily Islamic Digest (Ramadan and beyond) is an SMS alert subscription service that provides customers with daily alerts on Prayers for success in the world and hereafter, verses of daily meditation and Quran/Hadith quotation on their phone.

3 For extensive discussion on Islamic online evangelism, see Hew WaiWeng, 'Dakwah 2.0: Digital Dakwah, Street Dakwah and Cyber-Urban Activism among Chinese Muslims in Malaysia and Indonesia.'

4 Christ Embassy website contains numerous apps for download. Below are samples of the apps that can be downloaded in all formats. LoveWorld SAT Mobile App, LoveWorld Cyber Suite App, LoveWorld Music Store App, LoveWorld Books

App, LoveWorld TV 2.0 App, LoveWorld News App, The Pastor Chris Online App, Healing School App, The Pastor Chris Digital Library App, Ministry Apps, Rhapsody of Realities App, LoveWorld Internet Radio App, LoveWorld Cloud Storage App, CeFlix Live TV App.

5 According to the online news agency Pulse.ng, the Nigeria Communication Commission (NCC) released data, as of May 2015, which is that MTN market share accounts for 43 percent of the mobile subscription market in Nigeria, which is about 62,747 million subscribers.

6 Even though these messages have similarity with astrological horoscope, Christ Embassy and most Pentecostals in Nigeria reject it and see it as occult practices. In Christ Embassy the legitimate way of foreseeing the future is through the inspiration of the Holy Spirit that occurs usually in dreams and vision. However, one has to be careful to differentiate between Holy Spirit–inspired dreams and visions from those that are inspired by the Devil and his agents.

7 Bart A. Barendregt (2015) in his article titled 'Mobile Religiosity in Indonesia: Mobilized Islam, Islamized Mobility and the Potential of Islamic Techno Nationalism' reads the appropriation of ICT in the Islamic religious domain by youth as a new way of being modern. He argues young Southeast Asian Muslims 'make themselves modern' in creatively adapting and appropriating mobile communication tools and practices in their everyday lives.

8 I was unable to determine precisely why NASFAT Daily Ayaat is more expensive than the daily subscription of Christ Embassy. But probably it is that Christ Embassy has its own ICT volunteer team that offer services free of charge to the church, while NASFAT has to pay for the same services.

9 However, not all NASFAT digital religious practices were due to the Pentecostal influence; certainly many of the practices proceeded from the logic of the new digital technologies.

10 The increasing shift from the old media towards the new media, particularly mobile phones, is not restricted to the religious sphere alone. It includes many other activities in the secular domain.

11 The link between sound and the spiritual world has been recognized by Hackett (2012) and she cited many scholars who explore this link in various religious traditions, from shamanic practices to aboriginal societies.

12 Reference to God.

13 Recently many *Salafi* scholars in the north initiate Facebook preaching and some of them, such as Aminu Daurawa and Isa Pantami, have gathered many followers. Some have gone to the extent of creating android apps for their recorded preaching and Islamic pedagogy.

14 This situation is similar to counselling services of Pentecostal organizations in Botswana described by Rijk van Dijk. According to van Dijk this counselling

emphasizes the refashioning of relationships by mediating moral imperatives and by engaging with psychological knowledge on personal behaviour and on techniques of counselling in a changing context of sexuality. However, even though the questions and answers in NASFAT social media are similar to Pentecostal counselling it is different in the sense that it is attempting at refashioning of the life of an individual member according to the Islamic ideals. Another difference is that counselling is a private affair while online questions and answers are public; the information provided is meant to be shared by all the members of the online group.

15 Christ Embassy's Yookos and Kingschat are not dependent on the larger social media platforms such as Facebook or Twitter. They are independently developed and monitored by Christ Embassy's own IT experts.

16 These are strictly online religious services build around the idea of the Second Life. People participate in the congregation using the avatar in a virtual church building. Recently a number of related online religious communities have flourished around the world, particularly in North America.

17 Christ Embassy called this online participation 'Virtual Church Service'.

18 In computer terminology which is defined by *Encarta Encyclopedia* as a rectangular frame on a computer screen in which images output by application programs can be displayed, moved around or resized.

19 Enchantment of mobile phone technology is widespread in Nigeria. From time to time, rumours about demonic and witch invasion of the technology erupt. The rumours are usually about a demonic phone number that calls people and whoever picks the phone would die instantly. Sometimes young ladies are warned not to pick any number because some men use sorcery to hypnotize them into falling in love with them if they pick the magical number the men used to call them. One example of this trend is the following message circulated via WhatsApp Messenger:

> There is a number starting with +233 on WhatsApp, with the picture of a young guy with his friend in a partially dark place. Please do not respond to his msg but! block the number Asap. He is a satanic agent looking for blood through internet. His name is Nat Some people are dead already so don't be a victim. Share with everyone u know and' save souls +233 544971115: the number is taking over now, 11 people died this morning in Swedru after receiving a call from this number. +233 544971115 and please I beg you, send this number to all your family members leave then to all people you love or people you don't want to lose and tell them not to answer any call from this number. It's URGENT: Tell all contacts from your list. Beware it is very dangerous. They announced it today on the radio. Pass on to as many as you can.

20 During the announcement session in one of the Sunday services I attended in NASFAT, the announcer stated,

> I am asked to warn about what is happening now in the city. If any one of you sees black laptop or black berry phone on the corner of streets in the city he/she should not take it. These things belong to the secret cult society which they use as a bait to trap innocent people into their fold. They moment one takes these devices he/she would be instantly initiated into the cult with terrible consequences.

21 In the Shafie and Maliki school, it is stated that if there is a worshipper following the imam leading salah from outside the masjid, there should not be a gap of more than three hundred *dhiraa'a* (arm's length distance), nor a closed door between them.

22 See Larkin (2008) for a detailed explanation of northern Nigerian Muslims' early apprehension of broadcasting religious programmes on the then new media of radio and television.

23 See Birgit Meyer's (2010a) detailed analysis of mass-produced pictures of Jesus in Ghana. Meyer highlights how Pentecostals express an ambivalent attitude towards the picture of Jesus where it is regarded as both a site for prayer and contemplation as well as a potential object where the devil can take over and cast an evil spell through a haptic gaze on the onlookers.

24 See Cheong et al. (2010) for an in-depth analysis on how core religious understandings of identity, community and authority shape and be (re)shaped by the possibilities of communicative aspects of the digital technologies.

References

Adebanwi, Wale. 2011. 'Abuja'. In *Capital Cities in Sub-Saharan Africa*, edited by Goran Therborn and Simon Bekker, 84–102. Pretoria and Dakar: HSRC & CODESRIA.

Adeboye, Olufunke. 2006. 'Pentecostal Challenges in Africa and Latin America: A Comparative Focus on Nigeria and Brazil'. *Afrika Zamani*, 11 and 12: 136–59.

Adeniyi, O. Musa. 2013. 'Dynamics of Islamic Religious Movements in Nigeria: A Case Study of Nasru-Lahil-Fatih Society of Nigeria'. In *Religion on the Move: New Dynamics of Religious Expansion in a Globalizing World*, edited by Afe Adogame and Shobana Shankar, 323–40. Leiden: Brill.

Adetona, L. Mobolaji. 2012. 'NASFAT: A Modern Prayer Group and Its Contributions to the Propagation of Islam in Lagos'. *World Journal of Islamic History and Civilization*, 2(2): 102–7.

Adeyeri, Aderonke. 2016. 'Women Are Bridge Building – Bolarinwa'. *Vanguard*. www.vanguardngr.com. Accessed 11 June 2017.

Adeyimi, Adisa. 2011. 'National Ecumenical Center Abuja'. http://www.cometonigeria.com/wheretogo/national-ecumenical-centre-abuja/. Accessed 11 June 2017.

Adogame, Afe. 2011. *Who Is Afraid of the Holy Ghost? Pentecostalism and Globalization in Africa and Beyond*. Trenton, NJ: Africa World Press.

Ajileye, Muddasir. 2011. *Ash-Shifa'u (Healing and Deliverance) Muslim Prayer*. Ikirun: Al Halal Publication.

Alofetekun, Akin. 2008. 'All Eyes on Zuma Rock'. *Daily Sun*. Archived from the original on 23 March 2010.

Anderson, Allan Bergunder, Michael and Droogers, Andre. 2010. *Studying Global Pentecostalism Theories and Methods*. Berkeley: University of California Press.

ArchNet. 2002. 'Abuja Central Mosque'. *Massachusetts Institute of Technology*. https://archnet.org/sites/703/media_contents/18822. Accessed 6 November 2017.

Asad, Talal. 1986. *The Idea of an Anthropology of Islam*. Washington, DC: Georgetown University Center for Contemporary Arab Studies.

Asad, Talal. 1993. *Genealogies of Religion: Discipline and Reasons of Power Islam*. Baltimore, MD: Johns Hopkins University Press.

Asamoah-Gyadu, J. Kwabena. 2004. *African Charismatics: Current Developments within Independent Indigenous Pentecostalism in Ghana*. Leiden: Brill.

Asamoah-Gyadu, J. Kwabena. 2013. *Contemporary Pentecostal Christianity: Interpretations from an African Context*. Oxford: Regnum Books International.

Asamoah-Gyadu, J. Kwabena. 2015. *Sighs and Signs of the Spirit: Ghanaian Perspectives on Pentecostalism and Renewal in Africa*. Oxford: Regnum Africa.

Austin, L. John. 1962. *How to Do Things with Words*. Oxford: Oxford University Press.

Balancing Act Magazine. 2005. 'Nasfat Partners with Mtech to Launch Daily Ayaat Service on MTN Network'. Issue 259. http://www.balancingact-africa.com/news/telecoms-en/7470/nasfat-partners-with-mtech-to-launch-daily-ayaat-service-on-mtn-network. Accessed 11 June 2017.

Barendregt, Bart. 2009. 'Mobile Religiosity in Indonesia: Mobilized Islam, Islamized Mobility and the Potential of Islamic Techno Nationalism'. In *Living the Information Society in Asia*, edited by E. Alampay, 73–93. ISEAS-Yusof Ishak Institute. Cambridge: Cambridge University Press.

Barker, Isabelle V. 2007. 'Charismatic Economies: Pentecostalism, Economic Restructuring, and Social Reproduction'. *New Political Science*, 29(4): 407–427.

Becker, Judith. 2004. *Deep Listeners: Music, Emotion, and Trancing*. Bloomington: Indiana University Press.

Beekers, Daan. 2020. 'Toward a Comparative Anthropology of Muslim and Christian Lived Religion'. *Social Analysis*, 64(1): 102–10. doi:10.3167/sa.640106.

Bekker, Simon, and Therborn, Göran. 2012. *Capital Cities in Africa: Power and Powerless*. Cape Town: HRCS Press.

Bell, Genevieve. 2006. 'No More SMS from Jesus: Ubicomp, Religion and Techno-spiritual Practices'. In *Ubicomp, Lecture Notes in Computer Science*, vol. 4206, edited by P. Dourish and A. Friday, 141–58. Berlin, Heidelberg: Springer-Verlag.

Bello, A. Mustapha. 2013. 'The Dynamics of Managing Modern Islamic Organisation: A Case Study of NASFAT' (Paper presented at the International Conference of the Global Prayers Congress under the auspices of *Haus der Kulturen der Welt*, Berlin, Germany, between 13 and 16 November 2013).

Bennett, Jane. 2010. *Vibrant Matter: A Political Ecology of Things*. Durham, NC: Duke University Press.

Bolarinwa, Kamil. 2016. 'Muslims Leaders Should Unite against Terrorism'. *Nigerian Tribune*. http://tribuneonlineng.com. Accessed 18 March 2016.

Bonsu, K. Samuel, and Russell W. Belk. 2010. 'Marketing a New African God: Pentecostalism and Material Salvation in Ghana'. *International Journal of Non-profit and Voluntary Sector Marketing (Special Issue: Marketing and Religion)*, 15(4): 305–23.

Bourdieu, Pierre, and Wacquant, J. D. Loic. 1992. *An Invitation to Reflexive Sociology*. Chicago: University of Chicago Press.

Brigaglia, Andrea. 2014. 'Sufi Revival and Islamic Literacy: Tijani Writings in Twentieth-Century Nigeria'. *Annual Review of Islam in Africa*, 12(1): 2013–14.

Burckhardt, Titus. 1987. *Mirror of the Intellect: Essays on Traditional Science & Sacred Art*. New York: SUNY Press.

Butticci, Annalisa. 2010. 'Lagos Spiritual Warfare and Travelling Spirits: A Transnational Multi-Sense Journey from Lagos to the Diaspora'. *Global Prayers: Redemption and Liberation in the City*. First Workshop, Haus der Kulturen der Welt, 11–17 July 2010.

Butticci, Annalisa. 2016. *African Pentecostals in Catholic Europe: The Politics of Presence in the Twenty-First Century*. Cambridge, MA: Harvard University Press.

Bynum, W. Caroline. 2012. 'The Sacrality of Things: An Inquiry into Divine Materiality in the Christian Middle Ages'. *Irish Theological Quarterly*, 78(1): 3–18. DOI:10.1177/0021140012465035. Accessed 11 June 2017.

Campbell, Heidi. 2007. 'Who's Got the Power? Religious Authority and the Internet'. *Journal of Computer-Mediated Communication*, 12(3): 1043–62. DOI:10.1111/j.1083-6101.2007.00362.x. Accessed 11 June 2017.

Campbell, Heidi. 2010. *When Religion Meets New Media*. London: Routledge.

Campbell, Heidi. 2012. *Digital Religions: Understanding Religious Practice in New Media World*. New York: Routledge.

Ceci, L. 2021. 'Nigeria: mobile internet user penetration', Statista 2016-2026. 24 August 2021. https://www.statista.com/statistics/972900/internet-user-reach-nigeria/.

Cheong, Pauline Hope, Fischer-Nielsen, Peter, Gelfgren, Stefan, and Ess, Charles. 2021. *Digital Religion, Social Media and Culture*. New York: Peter Lang Verlag.

Clivaz, Clare. 2014. 'New Testament in a Digital Culture: A Biblaridion (Little Book) Lost in the World Wide Web?' *Journal of Religion Media and Digital Culture*, 3(3): 20–38.

Corrigan, John. 2004. *Emotion and Religion: Approaches and Interpretation*. Oxford: Oxford University Press.

Csordas, Thomas J. 1988. 'Elements of Charismatic Persuasion and Healing'. *Medical Anthropology Quarterly*, 2: 121–42.

Csordas, Thomas J. 1994. *The Sacred Self: A Cultural Phenomenology of Charismatic Healing*. Berkeley: University of California Press.

Csordas, Thomas J. 2002. 'The Rhetoric of Transformation in Ritual Healing'. In *Body, Meaning, Healing*, edited by T. J. Csordas, 11–87. New York: Palgrave Macmillan.

Daily Champion Newspapers. 17 January 2005. 'His Eyes on the World: Pastor Chris Oyakhilome'. Interview in Daily Champion Newspapers, Nigeria. http://www.dossiers.tk/pastor-chris-oyakhilome20050117-interview.htm. Accessed 11 June 2017.

Daily Post. 5 February 2015. 'Jonathan dumps Oritsejafor for Oyedepo, Enenche others – Report'. http://dailypost.ng/2015/02/05/jonathan-dumps-oritsejafor-oyedepo-enenche- others-report/. Accessed 11 June 2017.

De Witte, Marleen. 2008. *Spirit Media: Charismatic, Traditionalists, and Mediation Practices in Ghana*. PhD Dissertation, University of Amsterdam.

De Witte, Marleen. 2009. 'Modes of Binding, Moments of Bonding. Mediating Divine Touch in Ghanaian Pentecostalism and Traditionalism'. In *Aesthetic Formations: Media, Religion and the Senses*, edited by Birgit Meyer, 1–30. New York: Palgrave Macmillan.

Dilger, Hansjörg. 2014. 'Claiming Territory: Medical Mission, Interreligious Revivalism, and the Spatialization of Health Interventions in Urban Tanzania'. *Medical*

Anthropology, 33(1): 52–67. DOI:10.1080/01459740.2013.821987. Accessed 11 June 2017.

Dow, James. 1986. 'Universal Aspects of Symbolic Healing: A Theoretical Synthesis'. *American Anthropologist*, New Series, 88: 56–69.

Eisenlohr, Patrick. 2011. 'The Anthropology of Media and the Question of Ethnic and Religious Pluralism'. *Social Anthropology/Anthropologie Sociale*, 19(1): 40–55. DOI:10.1111/j.1469-8676.2010.00136.x. Accessed 11 June 2017.

Elleh, Nnamdi. 2001. *Abuja: The Single Most Ambitious Urban Design Project of the 20th Century*. Weimar: VDG.

Encomium. 9 September 2014. 'Oyakhilome's Divorce Mess'. http://encomium.ng/oyakhilomes-divorce-mess-1-all-the-messy-details-about-the-23-year-old-crashed-marriage-of-rev-chrisoyakhilome/. Accessed 11 June 2017.

Fainstein, Susan. 1994. *The City Builders: Property, Politics, and Planning in London and New York*. Cambridge, MA: Blackwell.

Folarin, O. George. 2010. 'The Prosperity Gospel in Nigeria: A Re-examination of the Concept, Its Impact, and an Evaluation'. *Cyber Journal for Pentecostal Charismatic Research*, 16. http://www.pctii.org/cyberj/cyberj16/folarin.html. Accessed 11 June 2017.

Folarin, Samson. 2021. '70% of Noise Pollution in Lagos State Caused by Churches, Mosques'. *Punch*, 8 January 2021. https://punchng.com/70-of-noise-pollution-in-lagos-state-caused-by-churches-mosques-lasepa-gm-fasawe/

Foucault, Michel. 1997. 'Essential Works of Foucault, 1954–1984, vol. 1.' In *Ethics: Subjectivity and Truth*, edited by Paul Rabinow, 82. New York: New Press.

Frederiks, Martha. 2010. 'Let Us Understand Our Differences: Current Trends in Christian-Muslim Relations in Sub-Saharan Africa'. *Transformation*, 27(4): 261–74. DOI:10.1177/0265378810378562. Accessed 11 June 2017.

Geertz, Clifford. 1973. *The Interpretation of Cultures*. New York: Basic Books.

Gifford, Paul. 2004. *Ghana's New Christianity*. Bloomington: Indiana University Press.

Gifford, Paul. 2015. *Christianity, Development and Modernity in Africa*. London: Hurst.

Gilloch, Graeme. 2002. *Walter Benjamin: Critical Constellations*. Oxford: Blackwell.

Goss, Jon. 1993. 'The "Magic of the Mall": An Analysis of Form, Function, and Meaning in the Contemporary Retail Built Environment'. *Annals of the Association of American Geographers*, 83(1): 18–47.

Gottschall, Marilyn. 2004. 'Introducing Islam through Qur'anic Recitation'. *Academic Exchange Quarterly*, 8: 35–9.

The Guardian. 2016. 'Why NASFAT Is Celebrating 21st Anniversary'. https://guardian.ng/features/why-nasfat-is-celebrating-21st-anniversary/. Accessed 11 June 2017.

Hackett, Rosalind. 2012. 'Sound, Music, and the Study of Religion'. *Temenos*, 48(1): 11–27.

Hassan, H. Ibrahim. 2015. 'An Introduction to Islamic Movements and Modes of Thought in Nigeria'. PAS/ISITA Working Papers vol. 1.

Hazard, Sonia. 2013. 'The Material Turn in the Study of Religion'. *Religion and Society: Advances in Research*, 4: 58–78.

Helland, Christopher. 2005. 'Online Religion as Lived Religion: Methodological Issues in the Study of Religious Participation on the Internet'. *Online – Heidelberg Journal of Religions on the Internet*, 1(1). DOI:10.11588/heidok.00005823. Accessed 11 June 2017.

Hirschkind, Charles. 2004. 'Civic Virtue and Religious Reason: An Islamic Counter-Public'. In *Aural Cultures*, edited by Jim Drobnick, 189–207. Toronto: YYZ Books.

Hirschkind, Charles. 2006. *The Ethical Soundscape: Cassette Sermons and Islamic Counter Publics*. New York: Columbia University Press.

Houtman, D., and Meyer, B. (eds). 2012. *Things: Religion and the Question of Materiality*. New York: Fordham University Press. http://dx.doi.org/10.5422/ fordha m/9780823239450.001.000i.

Hunt, Stephen. 2000. 'Winning Ways: Globalisation and the Impact of the Health and Wealth Gospel'. *Journal of Contemporary Religion*, 15(3): 331–47.

Hutchings, Tim. 2014a. 'The Dis/Embodied Church: Worship, New Media and the Body'. In *Christianity in the Modern World*, edited by Giselle Vincett and Elijah Obinna, 37–58. Farnham: Ashgate.

Hutchings, Tim. 2014b. 'Now the Bible Is an App: Digital Media and Changing Patterns of Religious Authority'. In *Religion, Media and Social Change*, edited by Kennet Granholm, Marcus Moberg, and Sofia Sjö, 143–61. Abingdon: Routledge. DOI:10.1080/17432200.2016.1192149. Accessed 11 June 2017.

Iwuchukwu, C. Marinus, and Stiltner, Brian. 2013. *Can Muslims and Christians Resolve Their Religious and Social Conflicts?: Cases from Africa and the United States*. Lewiston, NY: Edwin Mellen Press.

James, Paul. 2013. 'Managing Metropolises by Negotiating Mega-Urban Growth'. In *Institution and Social Innovation for Sustainable Urban Development*, edited by Herald Mieg and Klaus Töpfer, 217–32. Abingdon: Routledge.

Janson, Marloes. 2014. *Islam, Youth, and Modernity in the Gambia: The Tablighi Jama'at*. Cambridge: Cambridge University Press.

Janson, Marloes, and Akinleye, Akintunde. 2015. 'The Spiritual Highway: Religious World Making in Megacity Lagos (Nigeria)'. *Material Religion*, 11(4): 550–62. DOI:10.1080/17432200.2015.1103484. Accessed 15 May 2017.

Jones, Tamsin. 2016. 'Introduction'. In *Religious Experience and New Materialism. Radical Theologies*, edited by J. Rieger and E. Waggoner. New York: Palgrave Macmillan. https://doi.org/10.1007/978-1-137-56844-1_1.

Kalu, Ogbu. 2008. *African Pentecostalism: An Introduction*. Oxford: Oxford University Press.

Kane, Brian. 2014. *Sound Unseen: Acousmatic Sound in Theory and Practice*. Oxford: Oxford University Press.

Katrin, B. Anacker. 2009. *Gated Communities: International Perspectives*. Edited by
　Rowland Atkinson and Sarah Blandy. *Journal of Urban Affairs*, 31(4): 511–12.
　DOI:10.1111/j.1467-9906.2009.00469.x.

Kayode-Adedeji, Dimeji. 2015. 'Dasukigate: We Rejected Jonathan's $3 Million – Islamic
　Groups'. *Premium Times*. http://www.premiumtimesng.com/news/headlines/195
　797-dasukigate-we-rejected-jonathans-3-million-islamic-groups.html. Accessed 11
　June 2017.

Keane, Webb. 2003. 'Semiotics and the Social Analysis of Material Things'. *Language &
　Communication*, 23: 409–25.

Keane, Webb. 2008. 'The Evidence of the Senses and the Materiality of Religion'. *Journal
　of the Royal Anthropological Institute (N.S.)*, S110–S127.

Kirsch, G. Thomas. 2008. *Spirit and Letters: Reading, Writing and Charisma in African
　Christianity*. New York: Berghahn.

Kirshenblatt-Gimblett, Barbara. 2008. *Performance Studies*. Oxford: Oxford
　University Press.

Klomp, Mirella. 2020. *Playing on: Re-staging the Passion after the Death of God*.
　Leiden, Netherlands: Brill.

Knudsen, T. Britta, and Carsten, Stage. 2014. *Global Media, Biopolitics, and Affect:
　Bodily Vulnerability*. New York: Routledge.

Koch, A. Bradley. 2014. 'Who Are the Prosperity Gospel Adherents?' *Journal of
　Ideology*, 36: 1–46.

Koerner, Joseph. 2003. *The Reformation of the Image*. Chicago: University of
　Chicago Press.

Koic, Elvira, Pavo Filaković, Sanea Nađ, and Ivan Ćelić. 2005. 'Glossolalia'. *Collegium
　Antropologicum*, 29(1): 307–13.

Kuusela, Hanna. 2016. 'The Forms and Uses of Contemporary
　Books: Studying the Book as a Mass Produced Commodity and an Intimate Object'.
　TRANSFORMATIONS. Issue No. 27 – Thing Theory, Material Culture, and Object-
　Oriented Ontology.

Lado, Ludovic. 2009. *Catholic Pentecostalism and the Paradoxes of Africanization:
　Processes of Localization in a Catholic Charismatic Movement in Cameroon*.
　Leiden: Brill.

Larkin, Brian. 2008. *Signal and Noise: Media, Infrastructure, and Urban Culture in
　Nigeria*. Durham, NC: Duke University Press.

Larkin, Brian. 2014a. 'Binary Islam: Media and Religious Movements in Nigeria'. In
　New Media and Religious Transformation in Africa, edited by Rosalind Hackett and
　Benjamin Soares, 63–81. Bloomington: Indiana University Press.

Larkin, Brian. 2014b. 'Techniques of Inattention: The Mediality of Loudspeakers in
　Nigeria'. *Anthropological Quarterly*, 87(4): 989–1015. DOI:10.1353/anq.2014.0067.
　Accessed 11 June 2017.

Laurent, Pierre-Joseph. 2001. 'The Faith-Healers of the Assemblies of God in Burkina Faso: Taking Responsibility for Diseases Related to "Living Together"'. *Social Compass*, 48: 333–51.

Lesnard, Laurent. 2014. 'Using Optimal Matching Analysis in Sociology: Cost Setting and Sociology of Time'. *Advance in Sequence Analysis: Theory, Method, Applications*, 2: 39–50.

Lin, Nan. 1991. 'Building a Network Theory of Social Capital'. *Connections*, 22(1): 28–51.

Loimeier, Roman. 1997. *Islamic Reform and Political Change in Northern Nigeria*. Evanston, IL: Northwestern University Press.

Low, M. Setha. 2001. 'The Edge and the Center: Gated Communities and the Discourse of Urban Fear'. *American Anthropologist*, New Series, 103(1): 45–58.

MacDonald, Gordon. 2008. *Who Stole My Church? What to Do When the Church You Love Tries to Enter the 21st Century*. Nashville, TN: Thomas Nelson.

Macrotrends. 2022. 'Abuja, Nigeria Metro Area Population 1950–2022'. https://www.macrotrends.net/cities/21976/abuja/population.

Mahmood, Sabah. 2004. *Politics of Piety: The Islamic Revival and the Feminist Subject*. Princeton, NJ: Princeton University Press.

Marshall, Ruth. 2009. *Political Spiritualities: The Pentecostal Revolution in Nigeria*. Chicago: University of Chicago Press.

Marshall, Ruth. 2015. "Dealing with the Prince over Lagos": Pentecostal Arts of Citizenship'. Paper presented at the Political Science EDGS Speaker Series on 22 January 2015.

Martin, B. Dale. 1995. *The Corinthian Body*. New Haven, CT: Yale University Press.

Marx, Karl. 1990. *Capital*. London: Penguin Classics.

Mauss, Marcel. [1922] 1990. *The Gift: Forms and Functions of Exchange in Archaic Societies*. London: Routledge.

Mauss, Marcel. 2003. *On Prayer* (translated by Susan Leslie, and edited and introduced by W. S. F. Pickering). New York: Berghahn.

Meyer, Birgit. 1998. 'Commodities and the Power of Prayer: Pentecostalist Attitudes towards Consumption in Contemporary Ghana'. In *Globalization and Identity: Dialectics of Flow and Closure, Development and Change*, edited by Birgit Meyer and Peter Geschiere, 151–76. Oxford: Blackwell.

Meyer, Birgit. 2009. 'Introduction: From Imagined Communities to Aesthetic Formations: Religious Mediations, Sensational Forms, and Styles of Binding'. In *Aesthetic Formations: Media, Religion and the Senses*, edited by Birgit Meyer, 1–30. New York: Palgrave Macmillan.

Meyer, Birgit. 2010a. 'Aesthetics of Persuasion: Global Christianity and Pentecostalism's Sensational Forms'. *South Atlantic Quarterly*, 109(4): 741–63.

Meyer, Birgit. 2010b. *Aesthetic Formations: Media, Religion and Senses*. Basingstoke: Palgrave Macmillan.

Meyer, Birgit. 2011. 'Mediation and Immediacy: Sensational Forms, Semiotic Ideologies and the Question of the Medium'. *Social Anthropology*, 19(1): 23–39. DOI:10.1111/j.1469-8676.2010.00137.x. Accessed 11 June 2017.

Meyer, Birgit. 2012. *Mediation and the Genesis of Presence: Towards a Material Approach to Religion*. Inaugural Lecture, University of Utrecht.

Meyer, Birgit. 2015a. *Sensational Movies: Video, Vision, and Christianity in Ghana*. Oakland: University of California Press.

Meyer, Birgit. 2015b. 'How to Capture the "Wow." R.R. Marett's Notion of Awe and the Study of Religion'. *Journal of the Royal Anthropological Institute*, 22(1): 7–26.

Meyer, Birgit, and Larkin, Brian. 2006. 'Pentecostalism, Islam and Culture: New Religious Movements in West Africa'. In *Themes in West Africa's History*, edited by Emmanuel Akyeampong, 286–313. Athens, OH: Ohio University Press.

Mitchell, W. J. T. 2005. *What Do Pictures Want? The Lives and Loves of Images*. Chicago: University of Chicago Press.

Morgan, David. 2010. *Religion and Material Culture: The Matter of Belief*. London: Routledge.

Mwakimako, Hassan. 2010. 'Christian–Muslim Relations in Kenya: A Catalogue of Events and Meanings'. *Islam and Christian–Muslim Relations*, 18(2): 287–307. DOI: 10.1080/09596410701214266. Accessed 12 May 2017.

NASFAT Constitution. 2007. https://nasfatwoolwich.webs.com/documents/NASFAT%20Constitution%20_New_%20-With%20Article%2042_Restriction-1.pdf.

Nass, Martin. 1971. 'Some Considerations of a Psychoanalytic Interpretation of Music'. *Psychoanalytic Quarterly*, 40(2): 303–16. 10.1080/21674086.1971.11926562.

Nolte, Insa. 2015. 'Transformations of the Customary: Traditional Rulers and Religious Tolerance in Yorubaland, Nigeria'. In *Chiefship and the Customary in Contemporary Africa*, edited by Comaroff J. Chicago: University of Chicago Press.

Nolte, Insa, and Jones, Rebecca. 2015. 'Who Is Most Likely to Be in Favour of Inter-Religious Marriages in Southwestern Nigeria'. *Knowing Each Other*. www.knowingeachother.com. Accessed 17 March 2015.

Nwauche, S. Enyinna. 2008. 'Law, Religion and Human Rights in Nigeria'. *African Human Rights Law Journal*, 8(2): 568–95.

Obadare, Ebenezer. 2006. 'Pentecostal Presidency? The Lagos-Ibadan "Theocratic Class" & the Muslim "Other"'. *Review of African Political Economy*, 110: 665–78.

Oberlies, Thomas. 2017. 'Prayer'. In *Vocabulary for the Study of Religion*, edited by Robert A. Segal. http://dx.doi.org.proxy.library.uu.nl/10.1163/9789004249707_vsr_COM_00000418. Accessed 11 June 2017.

Ojo, A. Matthews. 2006. *The End-Time Army: Charismatic Movements in Modern Nigeria*. Trenton, NJ: Africa World Press.

Onaiyekan, O. John. 'A Discussion with Archbishop John Onaiyekan of Abuja'. Interview by Christopher O'Connor. *Berkeley Center for Religion, Peace and World*

Affairs. https://berkleycenter.georgetown.edu/interviews/a-discussion-with-archbis hop-john-onaiyekan-of-abuja-nigeria. Accessed 1 July 2010.

Orikeye, Olukayode. 14 June 2009. 'Why NASFAT Is Growing'. *Islamic Perspective*. http://nuru-deen.blogspot.nl/2009/06/why-nasfat-is-growing.html. Accessed 11 June 2017.

Osinulu, Adedamola. 2013. *The Miraculous City: Pentecostal Appropriations of Lagos's Urbanism*. http://ssrn.com/abstract=2253736. Accessed 11 June 2017.

Oyakhilome, Chris. 2001. *None of These Diseases*. Lagos: LoveWorld.

Oyakhilome, Chris. 2004. *Praying the Right Way*. Lagos: LoveWorld.

Oyakhilome, Chris. 2012. *How to Pray Effectively*. Lagos: LoveWorld.

Oyakhilome, Chris, and Oyakhilome, Anita. 2008. *Rhapsody of Realities*. Lagos: LoveWorld.

Paden, N. John. 2008. *Faith and Politics in Nigeria: Nigeria as a Pivotal State in the Muslim World*. Washington, DC: US Institute of Peace Press.

Peacock, James. 1984. 'Symbolic and Psychological Anthropology: The Case of Pentecostal Healing'. *Ethos*, 12(1): 37–53.

Peel, D. Y. John. 2011. 'Islam, Christianity and the Unfinished Making of the Yoruba' (Mellon Foundation Sawyer Seminar. University of Michigan, 1–2 April 2011).

Peel, D. Y. John. 2015. *Christianity, Islam, and Orisa Religion: Three Traditions in Comparison and Interaction*. Oakland: University of California Press. DOI: http://dx.doi.org/10.1525/luminos.8. Accessed 13 May 2017.

Pew Research Forum. 2006. 'Spirit and Power: A Ten Country Survey of Pentecostals'. https://www.pewforum.org/2006/10/05/spirit-and-power-a-10-country-survey-of-pentecostals3/.

Phelan, Peggy. 1993. *Unmarked: The Politics of Performance*. London: Routledge.

Pile, Steve. 2005. *Real Cities: Modernity, Space and the Phantasmagoria of City Life*. London: Sage.

Plüss, Jean-Daniel. 1988. *Therapeutic and Prophetic Narratives in Worship: A Hermeneutic Study of Testimonies and Visions – Their Potential Significance for Christian Worship and Secular Society*. Frankfurt am Main: Peter Lang GmbH.

Policy and Legal Advocacy Center. 2006. 'Legal Notice on Publication of Census Final Result'. Accessed 22 March 2015.

Postill, John. 2002. 'Clock and Calendar Time: A Missing Anthropological Problem'. *Time and Society*, 11(2/3): 251–70.

Račius, Egdunas. 2004. 'The Multiple Nature of the Islamic Da'wa'. PhD Dissertation, University of Helsinki, Faculty of Arts, Institute of Asian and African Studies, Arabic and Islamic Studies and Vilnius University, Institute of International Relations and Political Science, 2014.

Reckwitz, Andreas. 2012. 'Affective Spaces: A Praxeological Outlook'. *Rethinking History*, 16(2): 241–58.

Reichard, Gladys. 1988. *Prayer: The Compulsive Word*. New York: AMS Press.

Reinhardt, Bruno. 2014. 'Soaking in Tapes: The Haptic Voice of Global Pentecostal Pedagogy in Ghana'. *Journal of the Royal Anthropological Institute*, 20(2): 315–36. DOI: 10.1111/1467-9655.12106. Accessed 11 June 2017.

Reinhardt, Bruno. 2015. 'Flowing and Framing: Language Ideology, Circulation, and Authority in a Pentecostal Bible School'. *Pragmatics and Society*, 6(2): 261–87.

Riis, Ole, and Woodhead, Linda. 2010. *A Sociology of Religious Emotion*. Oxford: Oxford University Press.

Roach-Higgins, Mary Ellen, and Joanne B. Eicher. 1992. 'Dress and Identity'. *Clothing and Textiles Research Journal*, 10(4) (June): 1–8.

Rose, N. 1999. *Powers of Freedom: Reframing Political Thought*. Cambridge: Cambridge University Press.

Ross, Alison. 2016. 'What Is an Image? Form as a Category of Meaning in Philosophical Anthropology'. *Parrhesia*, 26: 20–39.

Samarin, J. William. 1972. *Tongue of Men and Angels: The Religious Language of Pentecostalism*. New York: Macmillan.

Sander, H. Thomas, and Lowney, Kathleen. 2006. 'Social Capital Building Toolkit'. Saguaro Seminar: Civic Engagement in America, John F. Kennedy School of Government, Harvard University. https://ascend.aspeninstitute.org/wp-content/uploads/2017/10/skbuildingtoolkitversion1.2.pdf.

Sanni, O. Amidu. 2006. 'Challenges and Realities in the Healing and Power – Accession Custom of the Yoruba Muslims of Nigeria'. *Journal of Oriental and African Studies*, 15: 145–56.

Scheer, Monique. 2012. 'Are Emotions a Kind of Practice (and Is That What Makes Them Have a History)? A Bourdieuian Approach to Understanding Emotion'. *History and Theory*, 51(2):191–220.

Schulz, Dorothea. 2012. 'Dis/Embodying Authority: Female Radio "Preachers" and the Ambivalences of Mass-Mediated Speech in Mali'. *International Journal of Middle East Studies*, 44(1): 23–43.

Sean. 2015. 'Biography of Gospel Award Winning Songwriter, Vocalist and Singer Sinach'. https://sinachmusic.com/biography/.

Sennett, Herbert. 2003. 'Preaching as Performance Art: A Preliminary Model'. *Journal of Religion and Theatre*, 2(1).

Shouse, Eric. 2005. 'Feeling, Emotion, Affect'. *M/C Journal*, 8(6). https://doi.org/10.5204/mcj.2443.

Singleton, Andrew. 2001. '"Your Faith Has Made You Well": The Role of Storytelling in the Experience of Miraculous Healing'. *Review of Religious Research*, 43(2): 121–38.

Soares, F. Benjamin. 2006. *Muslim-Christian Encounters in Africa*. Leiden: Brill.

Soares, F. Benjamin. 2009. 'An Islamic Social Movement in Contemporary West Africa: NASFAT of Nigeria'. In *Movers and Shakers: Social Movements in Africa*, edited by Stephen Ellis and Ineke Kessel, 178–96. Leiden: Brill.

Sounaye, Abdoulaye. 2014. 'Mobile Sunna: Islam, Small Media and Community in Niger'. *Social Compass*, 61(1): 21–29.

Stocker, Michael. 2013. *Hear Where We Are: Sound, Ecology, and Sense of Place*. New York: Springer.

Stolz, Jörg. 2011. '"All Things Are Possible": Towards a Sociological Explanation of Pentecostal Miracles and Healing'. *Sociology of Religion*, 72(4): 456–82.

Sunier, Thijl, and Şahin, Mehmet. 2015. 'The Weeping Sermon: Persuasion, Binding and Authority within the Gülen-Movement'. *Culture and Religion*, 16(2): 228–41.

Suvakovic, Miodrag. 2014. 'General Theory of Ideology and Architecture'. In *Architecture and Ideology*, edited by Vladimir Mako, Mirjana Roter Blagojevic and Marta Vukotic Lazar, 2–12. Cambridge: Cambridge Scholars.

Thielemans, Veerle. 2015. 'Beyond Visuality: Review on Materiality and Affect'. *Perspective. Actualité en Histoire de l'Art*, 2: 1–8.

Thrift, Nigel. 2008. *Non-representational Theory: Space, Politics, Affect*. New York: Routledge.

Torr, C. Stephen. 2013. *A Dramatic Pentecostal/Charismatic Anti-Theodicy: Improvising On a Divine Performance of Lament*. Eugene, OR: Pickwick.

Turner, S. Bryan. 2007. 'Religious Authority and the New Media'. *Theory, Culture & Society*, 24(2): 117–34.

Twigg, Julia. 2009. 'Clothing, Identity and the Embodiment of Age'. In *Aging and Identity: A Postmodern Dialogue*, edited by Jason Powell and Tony Gilbert, 93–104. New York: Nova Science.

Tylor, B. Edward. 1873. *Primitive Culture*. London: John Murray.

Ukah, Asonzeh. 2007. 'African Christianities: Features, Promises, and Problems'. Working paper, Department of Anthropology and African Studies, Gutenberg Universität, Mainz.

Van de Kamp, Linda. 2010. 'Burying Life: Pentecostal Religion and Development in Urban Mozambique'. In *Development and Politics from Below: Exploring Religious Space in the African State*, edited by Barbara Bompani and Maria Frahm-Arp, 152–71. London: Palgrave Macmillan.

Van der Veer, Peter. 2016. *The Value of Comparison*. Durham, NC: Duke University Press.

Vásquez, A. Manuel. 2011. *More Than Belief: A Materialist Theory of Religion*. Oxford: Oxford University Press.

Wallach, Jeremy. 2003. 'The Poetics of Electrosonic Presence: Recorded Music and the Materiality of Sound'. *Journal of Popular Music Studies*, 15(1): 34–64.

Watson, Vanessa. 2013. 'African Urban Fantasies: Dreams or Nightmares?' *Environment & Urbanization*, 26(1): 215–231. DOI: 10.1177/0956247813513705.

Weiner, Isaac. 2014. *Religion Out Loud: Religious Sound, Public Space, and American Pluralism*. New York: New York University Press.

Weiss, S. Allen. 1989. *The Aesthetics of Excess*. Albany: State University of New York Press.

Wilson, J. Matthew. 2007. *From Pews to Polling Places: Faith and Politics in the American Religious Mosaic*. Washington, DC: Georgetown University Press.

Woodward, Ian. 2007. *Understanding Material Culture*. London: Sage.

Wrightson, Kendall. 2000. 'An Introduction to Acoustic Ecology Soundscape'. *Journal of Acoustic Ecology*, 1: 10–13.

Zukin, Sharon. 1990. 'Socio-spatial Prototypes of a New Organization of Consumption: The Role of Real Cultural Capital'. *Sociology*, 24(1): 37–56.

Index

www.ingramcontent.com/pod-product-compliance
Lightning Source LLC
Chambersburg PA
CBHW050426280326
41932CB00013BA/2011